T0328841

The UCLA Anderson Business and Information Technologies (BIT) Project

A Global Study of Technology and Business Practice (2016)

The UCLA Anderson Business and Information Technologies (BIT) Project

A Global Study of Technology and Business Practice (2016)

editors

Vandana Mangal
University of California, Los Angeles, USA

Andreina Mandelli
SDA Bocconi School of Management, Italy

Uday Karmarkar
University of California, Los Angeles, USA

Antonella La Rocca
Università della Svizzera Italiana, Switzerland

World Scientific

NEW JERSEY · LONDON · SINGAPORE · BEIJING · SHANGHAI · HONG KONG · TAIPEI · CHENNAI · TOKYO

Published by

World Scientific Publishing Co. Pte. Ltd.

5 Toh Tuck Link, Singapore 596224

USA office: 27 Warren Street, Suite 401-402, Hackensack, NJ 07601

UK office: 57 Shelton Street, Covent Garden, London WC2H 9HE

Library of Congress Cataloging-in-Publication Data
Names: Mangal, Vandana, editor. | UCLA Anderson Business and Information Technologies (BIT) Project.
Title: The UCLA Anderson Business and Information Technologies (BIT) project : a global study of technology
    and business practice (2016) / Vandana Mangal (UCLA), Uday Karmarkar (UCLA),
    Andreina Mandelli (SDA Bocconi School of Management, Italy), Antonella La Rocca
    (Universitá della Svizzera Italiana, Switzerland).
Description: New Jersey : World Scientific, [2016]
Identifiers: LCCN 2015040675 | ISBN 9789814713986 (alk. paper)
Subjects: LCSH: Information technology--Management. | Industrial management.
Classification: LCC HD30.2 .U36 2016 | DDC 658.8/72--dc23
LC record available at http://lccn.loc.gov/2015040675

British Library Cataloguing-in-Publication Data
A catalogue record for this book is available from the British Library.

Desk Editors: Suraj Kumar/Pui Yee

Typeset by Stallion Press
Email: enquiries@stallionpress.com

Printed in Singapore

CONTENTS

ACKNOWLEDGMENT

The authors would like to acknowledge the tremendous help provided by Jaymie Jinkyung Park for this book. They would also like to acknowledge the Center for Global Management at UCLA Anderson School of Management for their support of the BIT project.

ABOUT THE EDITORS

Vandana Mangal

Dr. Mangal is Executive Director for the Easton Technology Management Center and the Research Director for Business and Information Technologies at the UCLA Anderson School of Management. She is on the Executive Board of the IS Associates at UCLA and an Inaugural Member of the LA Media Lab. Dr. Mangal has published several papers and articles in journals and magazines, many in collaboration with global researchers. She has published three books. She has given talks at several domestic and global conferences, participated in panels and chaired conference sessions. Vandana has served as the guest editor of a special issue of the Journal of Engineering Management and Economics titled 'Technology, Operations and Strategy in Innovation and Entrepreneurship'. Her areas of interest include Big Data, Internet of Things, Technology Impacts, and Business Practices.

Before joining UCLA, Dr. Mangal worked at Intel and AE Business Solutions Consulting and taught at the University of Wisconsin, Madison's School of Business and at the University of Wisconsin, Platteville's Computer Science department. She completed her PhD from the Heinz School at Carnegie Mellon University; her undergraduate degree is in Electrical Engineering from PEC University of Technology.

Andreina Mandelli

Andreina Mandelli obtained her PhD in Mass Communication from Indiana University, Bloomington (USA), after completing MBA from Università Bocconi. She is presently working as an SDA professor at the Faculty of Marketing &

Communication since 1995. She is also adjunct professor at USI, Lugano, and IE, Madrid since 2010 and faculty at Bocconi Global Business School, MISB Bocconi in Mumbai, India from 2013. She had previously worked as Senior research fellow at 'Center for Digital Future', Annenberg School for Communication, USC, Los Angeles (USA). She has been one of the Founding partners of World Internet Project (WIP) and Business Information Technology study (BIT) international research networks, coordinated at Annenberg School for Communication, University of Southern California, e UCLA Los Angeles. Her research interests include digital innovation in communication, marketing, consumer behavior and services.

Uday Karmarkar

Uday Karmarkar is a UCLA Distinguished Professor, and the LA Times Chair Professor of Technology and Strategy at the UCLA School of Management. He previously taught at the Graduate School of Business at the University of Chicago (1975–1979) and the Simon School at the University of Rochester (1979–1994), where he held the Xerox Chair in Operations. Professor Karmarkar has published over 100 research papers and articles, has founded two academic journals, and serves on several editorial boards. His research interests include the information economy, service industrialization, technology management, and competitive strategy. He has undertaken projects in technology management, industrial marketing, manufacturing systems, supply chain management, and service strategy with over 50 firms in the U.S., Europe, and Asia. Professor Karmarkar holds a B.Tech. from IIT Bombay and a PhD in Management Science from M.I.T. He served on the Advisory Board of IIT Bombay until 2007, the Advisory Board of the SJM School of Management, IITB till 2011, and is on the board of directors of the IITB Heritage Fund (USA). He has received the Distinguished Alumnus and Distinguished Service awards from IITB and the Distinguished Service Award from M&SOM (Informs). He received an IBM faculty award in 2004. He was elected an Honorary Institute Fellow of IITB in 2008, and a Distinguished Fellow of MSOM in 2014. Professor Karmarkar was on the International Council (Ministry of the Economy) reviewing the Digital Strategy for Chile 2008–2010. He has been an advisor to or director of several companies in both traditional and new technology sectors.

Antonella La Rocca

Dr. Antonella La Rocca received her PhD from the University of Lugano — USI (Switzerland), Faculty of Communication Sciences, with a dissertation on Interaction and Actors' Identities in Business Relationships. Her current research interests are in innovation and entrepreneurship in B2B businesses and in particular the interplay between intra- and inter-organizational processes. She has been post-doc research fellow at University of Lugano and consultant for the University start-up promotion center. She was visiting research fellow at University of Graz (Austria) and at BI Norwegian Business School. She published in IMP Journal, Industrial Marketing Management, Journal of Business, and Industrial Marketing and Management Decision. Currently, she is in staff of the Research Centre at Akershus University Hospital (Oslo Area, Norway), where she is working on a research project funded by the Research Council of Norway on organizing of technological innovation within the health care sector.

PREFACE

The digital revolution is continuing to show its disruption effects on businesses and economies.

Consumers around the world increase their move toward adopting new media of communication, and change their social and shopping activities online, with profound consequences for business making and the structure of industries and economies.

The use of social media has changed the behavior of people, increasingly activating consumers in the relationships with companies and brands, but it has also started to change the fabric of the industries, in the direction of what we call today "collaborative economy". Resource sharing is affecting the competition in industries like hospitality (after platforms like AirBnB have revolutionized the service offering), but also personal transportation and even banking. It is also changing the relationships between companies, since digital makes collaboration and network-based supply chain more effective.

Companies need to understand what are the success factors in the new digital age. Products are increasingly designed and consumed as services; consumption is increasingly designed and lived as an experience process. Products and brands are social, meaning that their meanings and value are co-created through collaboration among the different stakeholders of the company. In this scenario, companies need to understand the (new) way to make the difference in the markets.

If competition in the market is customer centric, the increasingly precise capability to learn what matters in each context of the company-customer relationship (the customer journey) becomes crucial. The new digital today brings this to the table: the learning power of big data. A continuous flow of data in real time is telling the decision-maker what is relevant in the dynamic contexts of the relationships (real-time customer service or contextual advertising like in the case of programmatic advertising and retargeting). According to IDC study "Worldwide Big Data Technology and Services, 2012–2015 Forecast" big data technology and services are expected to grow worldwide at a compound annual growth rate of 40% — about seven times that of the ICT market overall. This gives an idea of how fast is the new data-driven wave of digital disruption. In the age of mobile communications, Internet of things and augmented reality, this also gives an idea of how pervasive is the possibility to augment the value creation processes.

In this context the BIT project at the UCLA Anderson School of Management (Karmarkar and Mangal, 2004) has been conducting studies and disseminating its research results, with the collaboration of several international academic partners from around the world. The project was started in 2003, and has researched the changes in business making and industries connected with the digital impact since then. In this time horizon several studies were conducted, by the international research affiliates, with different specific research questions and methodological frameworks, but one general intellectual interest: to understand what could help the companies build insight on (and face) the challenges of digital revolution more effectively.

The authors in this specific publication are from USA, Chile, Italy, New Zealand, Korea, Switzerland, and Taiwan. The contributions are interdisciplinary.

The study by Bhargava and Tanghetti (from US, Chapter 9) analyzes the value creation due to the the diffusion of mobile apps (more than a hundred thousand) in the health area. According to their findings, MHealth technology has affected patients' information access and behavior, but not necessarily their health and well-being.

The researchers Godoy, Labarca, Somma, and Gálvez (from Chile, Chapter 3) studied, using a qualitative approach, the role of trust in ecommerce. Trust is an essential ingredient of human relationships, and therefore also economic exchanges. Trust is particularly relevant in uncertain social/economic settings. Without trust ecommerce cannot develop at its full potential. The study was able to show some relevant corporate blindspots that should be addressed by retailers, but also the different strategies that consumers deploy to overcome relationship uncertainty (and lack of trust) in ecommerce.

Hsiao and Karmarkar (from USA, Chapter 4) investigated how digital technology has affected the role and practice of product management in technology-intensive companies. Products are substituted by processes and platforms, which may connect customers with multiple service or product providers. In these new economic ecosystems even the electronic devices like smartphones become service bundles. The study shows how, in this context, the key skills and activities involved in the role of product management change radically.

Lee and Liang (from Taiwan, Chapter 1) reported on a survey of 265 CIOs from major Taiwanese companies. Their findings describe the new digital business practices, the nature of the evolving workplace, the new organizational forms connected to technology adoption. They also explored factors expected to influence technology adoption decisions: dynamic environment, dynamic capabilities, and the fit between the above two factors.

Mari (from Italy, Chapter 7) explored, with the use of literature data and different cases, how companies can overcome the barriers to adopting a relational approach to consumer branding, within the framework of social media marketing. Companies can use social media for listening and learning what matters most for their customers, but also interact with them and their communities, to become a valuable part of their everyday world. Brand equity in the era of social media is made by passion and community, not just through awareness and meanings. The practice of digital social transformation for these brands is, though, not simple or uni-directional. It requires a deep understanding of the relationship building process and a sound governance of the decision, data and practices involved.

Accoto, Valtolina and Mandelli (from Italy, Chapter 8) researched the social activities of a B2B community with the case of BTicino. My Open is a social support platform (15,000+ members) for the company's complex ecosystem of stakeholders (installators, system integrators, software houses, and developers). The case analyzes the complex process of building the community and the different factors that drove its success. Particular attention was given to the role of data and community analytics, and the capability to use social intelligence to drive management decisions, transforming a social practice into valuable business outcomes.

Fuduric (from Switzerland, Chapter 10) addressed the changing nature of marketing in social media times, and analyzed and classified the different approaches to social media marketing strategies. She developed a scheme that could be beneficial not only to academic researchers, but also practitioners by enhancing their understanding of the various types of social media strategies that could be valuable to their businesses.

Papadimitriou and Marcuzzo (from Italy, Chapter 5) investigated the dynamics of adoption of Facebook by the students at Bocconi University (a major academic institution in the country). According to their findings the most diffused social network is here to stay. Its usage is not a fad; it has become a relevant and valued habit. Age, network size, and perceived usefulness are major factors in predicting usage. The authors also report that perceptions concerned with privacy do not play a relevant role.

Kim, Park, Rhim and Choi (from Korea, Chapter 6) explored the complex area of product-service combination in mobile communication markets. PSS (Product–Service System) is a new way of conceiving and designing products, to maximize customer satisfaction. In the era of service-dominant marketing, the possibility to augment the value of the offering through an enhanced package that combines the attributes of product and the attributes of service may bring about the difference in competition. Understanding what most successful strategies for this combination is crucial. The study produces this knowledge outcome, which can be applied to very different industries.

Wu and Srinivasan (from New Zealand, Chapter 2) studied patterns and explanatory factors of information diffusion in two types of online social networks (OSN): one text oriented (Twitter) and one visually oriented (Flickr). By contrasting these OSNs across three differently oriented accounts, the authors observed the information diffusion over time by examining some critical social network metrics. Their findings can be very valuable to help organizations optimize their use of social networks for marketing and management objectives.

In synthesis, the different contributions show valuable and varied perspectives on the complexity of the new digital transformation in place, but also offer actionable frameworks to support the complex transformation of management in these turbulent digital times.

CHAPTER 1

A SURVEY ON BUSINESS AND INFORMATION TECHNOLOGY IN TAIWAN: ANNUAL REPORT 2014

YA-CHING LEE AND TING-PENG LIANG

Abstract

The Business and Information Technologies (BIT) project, lead by researchers at UCLA Anderson School of Management, investigates the impact of new information technologies on business practices and industry structure (Karmarkar and Mangal, 2004). The BIT project is being conducted internationally: SDA Bocconi (Italy), SOM-IITB (India), Theseus Institute (France), The World Internet Institute (Sweden), EIM (Germany), IESE (Spain), PUC (Chile), Korea University (Korea), CEIBS (China), IIT Mumbai (India), and SDA Bocconi (Italy). The global perspective is expected to unveil the reality of business practice affected by technological change. This study reports the BIT project results in Taiwan. The survey was sent to senior information systems managers or chief information officers who make independent decisions on information and communication technology systems. For business organizations, questionnaires were mailed to over 2,000 companies by systematically sampling the database of the largest 5,000 corporations in Taiwan. For government organizations, questionnaires were mailed to central government offices, local authorities, and state-owned enterprises. For each surveyed organization, we chose a correspondent who is either an alumni or an acquaintance of the principal investigators in order to increase the questionnaire response rate.

The CIOs (and related positions) were requested to complete the survey either by mail, fax or online, where the survey instrument was also made available. About 265 responses were received. This report addresses business practices, the evolving workplace, changing organizational forms, and technology adoption. In addition to the original BIT questionnaire, we added questions to further explore factors expected to influence technology adoption decisions: dynamic environment, dynamic capabilities, and the fit between the above two factors.

1.1. Introduction

1.1.1. *Domestic trend in Taiwan*

The Business and Information Technologies (BIT) project, led by researchers at the UCLA Anderson School of Management, investigated the impact of new information technologies on business practices and industry structure (Karmarkar and Vandana, 2004). Special focus was on "the internet phenomenon" that essentially drove the rapid advances of information technologies. The BIT project was conducted internationally: SDA Bocconi (Italy), SOM-IITB (India), Theseus Institute (France), The World Internet Institute (Sweden), EIM (Germany), IESE (Spain), PUC (Chile), Korea University (Korea), CEIBS (China), IIT Mumbai (India), and SDA Bocconi (Italy) were some of the research institutions involved in the BIT study. Results from BIT partners are expected to unveil the reality of business practice affected by technological change across the world.

The BIT study in Taiwan followed the changes that occurred in private and public sectors over an extended time horizon. The project consisted of two major components:

- A questionnaire-based survey in Taiwan conducted annually starting in 2006 targeted senior information systems managers of organizational units (from private and public sectors) that make independent decisions on information and communication technology systems. The survey will address business practices, the evolving workplace, changing organizational forms, and technology adoption. In addition to the original BIT questionnaire, the authors added questions to further explore factors expected to influence technology adoption decisions such as market pressure, customers' expectations, organization climate, and dynamic environment.

1.2. Results

The survey was sent to senior information systems managers or chief information officers of various organizations. For business organizations, questionnaires were mailed to over 2,000 companies; these companies were chosen by systematically sampling the database of the largest 5,000 corporations in Taiwan. For government organizations, questionnaires were mailed to central government offices, local authorities, and state-owned enterprises. For each surveyed organization, the authors chose a correspondent who was either an alumni or an acquaintance of the principal investigators in order to increase the questionnaire response rate. The CIOs (and related positions) were requested to complete the survey either by mail, fax, or online, where the survey instrument was also made available. About 251 responses were received. Details of the sample are discussed in Appendix A. Results obtained by analyzing these responses are discussed in Sec. 1.2.1.

1.2.1. *Technology adoption/infrastructure and budget trends*

As shown in Fig. 1.1, a large number of companies already had or planned to have websites and e-commerce (83.7%; have was 80.5% and plan to have was 3.2%), wireless hardware and software (88.9%; have was 85.7% and plan to have was 3.2%), and collaboration and portal tools (67.4%; have was 55% and plan to have was 12.4%) within the next three years. Among these technologies, business intelligence (15.9%), e-learning (14.3%), and collaboration and portal tools (12.4%) were the most popular technologies on company budgets and slated for adoption within the next three years. Technologies that organizations did not plan to purchase in the next three years included biometrics (53%) and digital receipts (47.4%).

As shown in Fig. 1.2., website and e-commerce were widely adopted in service sectors (79.1%), and manufacturing sectors (82%).

Comparing service (86.8%) sectors, and manufacturing sectors (84.4%), only 84.4% of manufacturing sectors already had wireless network tool. 1.6% of manufacturing sector companies planned to purchase it in the next three years (see Fig. 1.3). Similarly, over half of manufacturing (78.6%), and service sectors (76.8%) already had SAN and NAS (see Fig. 1.4).

Manufacturing sectors (83.6%) already had enterprise resource planning. Additionally, 79.8% of service sectors already had Enterprise Resource Planning, and 3.1% of service sectors planned to buy it in the next three years (see Fig. 1.5).

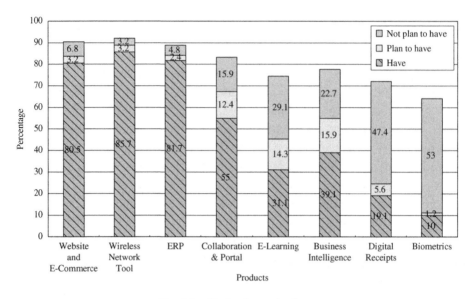

Fig. 1.1.   Technology adoption.

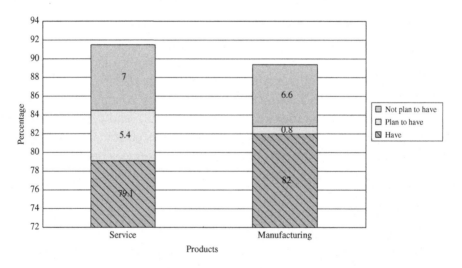

Fig. 1.2.   Website and e-commerce adoption.

1.2.2. *Internal organization*

Overall, the proportion of employees facing a screen and using teleconferencing was decreasing. Demand for intelligence in information at executive levels was decreasing. Demand for IT skills at lower levels in the organization was also decreasing. Collaborative work due to technology was decreasing somewhat. In addition, in order to keep up with changing technologies, employees needed to retrain

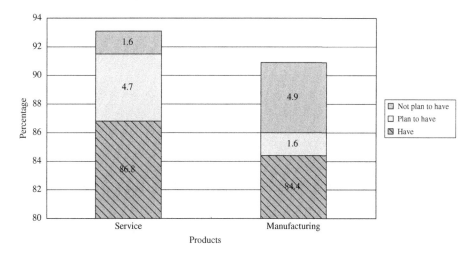

Fig. 1.3.   Wireless network tool adoptions.

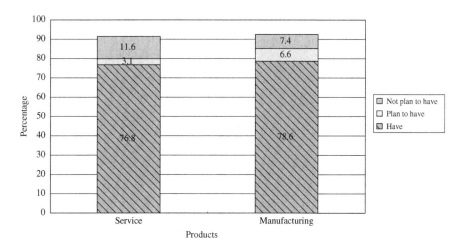

Fig. 1.4.   SAN and NAS adoptions.

constantly. However, the number of middle level managers was not felt to be decreasing, with only 19.2% of organizations reporting that this was taking place. These trends are shown in Figs. 1.6 and 1.7.

Codes for the trends are as follows:

1. Proportion of employees facing a screen is increasing.
2. Use of teleconferencing is on the rise.
3. More employees are telecommuting.
4. Demand for intelligence in information at executive levels is increasing.
5. The need for IT skills at lower levels is going up.

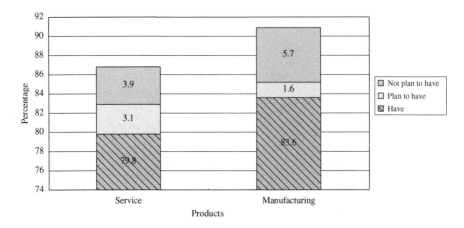

Fig. 1.5.   Enterprise resource planning adoptions.

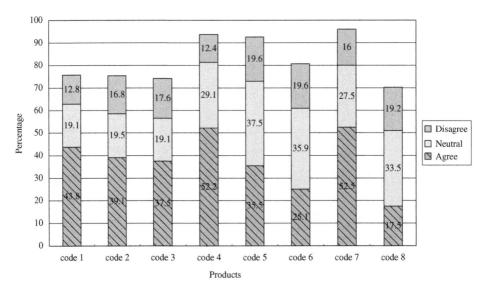

Fig. 1.6.   Internal organization workforces.

6. Collaboration between workers from use of internet-based technologies
   is increasing.
7. Workers need to retrain constantly to keep up with changing technologies.
8. The number of middle level managers is decreasing.

The most significant trend was the increasing of the monitoring of customer facing interactions, as reported by over three-quarters (61.8%) of the organizations. Organizations were becoming geographically dispersed. Incentives were

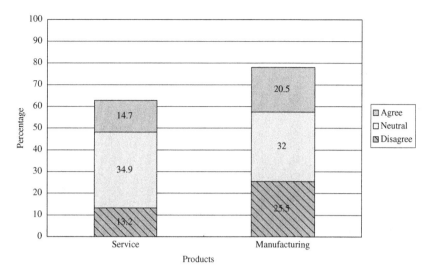

Fig. 1.7.   Level managers numbers trends.

based on monitoring of productivity. New decision-making tools and online technologies becoming available and automated monitoring of workforce productivity were decreasing. Additionally, organizations were becoming flatter; the span of control for most managers was widening. These trends are shown in Fig. 1.8.

Codes for the trends are as follows:

1. New decision-making tools and online technologies are becoming available.
2. The organization is becoming geographically dispersed.
3. Incentives are based on monitoring of productivity.
4. The monitoring of customer facing interactions is increasing.
5. Automated monitoring of workforce productivity is increasing.
6. The organization is becoming flatter.
7. The span of control for most managers is widening.

The monitoring of customer facing interactions was becoming common across two sectors (manufacturing sectors (58.2%), and service sectors (65.1%)). These trends are shown in Fig. 1.9.

53.5% from the service sectors and 52.5% from manufacturing sectors agreed that organizations were becoming flatter. These trends are shown in Fig. 1.10.

The most often outsourced business processes were IT functions programming (47.4%), including outsource partially (16.3%), and outsource significantly (31.1%). Accounting was outsourced by 37.8% of the organizations (partially was 14.7% and significantly was 23.1%). IT network management

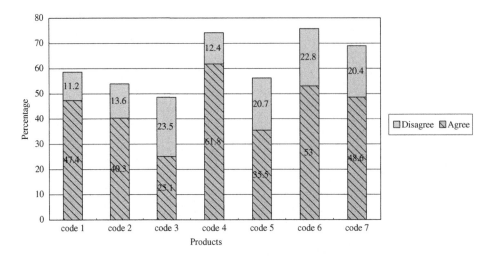

Fig. 1.8.   Internal organization structure.

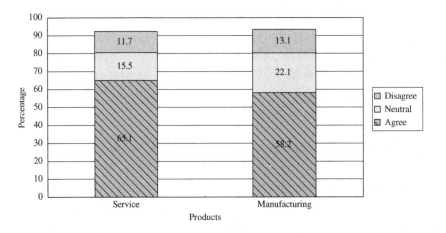

Fig. 1.9.   The monitoring of customer facing interactions is increasing.

(27.1%), payroll (33.1%), and order fulfilment (28.7%) were high rate on not outsourcing now and on not planning to outsource in the next three years. (Fig. 1.11) However, one particular piece of information was noteworthy: over one-quarter of organizations reported that this outsourcing question was not valid for their organizations.

IT functions programming was the most often outsourcing business processes in manufacturing sectors (57.4%) *vis-à-vis* service sectors (38%). These trends are shown in Fig. 1.12.

These results were based on a little more than half of the original sample size. Only 50% of organizations responded to the questions regarding the budget for

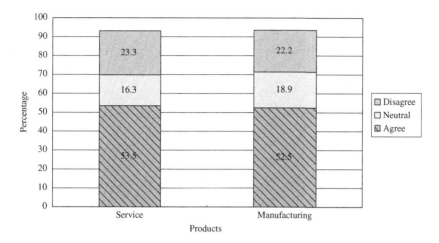

Fig. 1.10.   Flat organization trends.

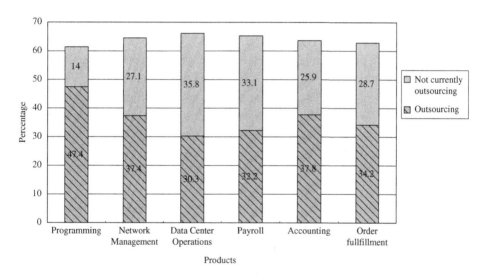

Fig. 1.11.   Business process outsourcing trends.

organizations' non-IT functions, and 51% responded to the questions regarding offshore outsourcing. These facts may be interpreted as indicating that a large percentage of the organizations do not currently outsource.

1.2.3. *Trading partner relationships*

A half of organizations that were using technology for communicating with their trading partners, 34.7% of them indicated that they had or were in the process of buying electronic data interchange (EDI), 34.7% indicated sourcing and

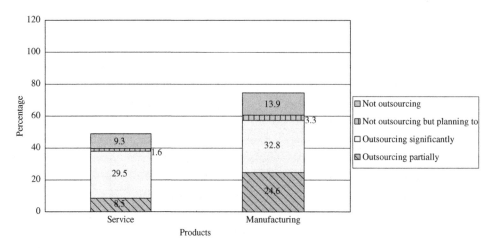

Fig. 1.12.   Outsourcing for IT functions programming.

procurement management; and 28.3% indicated web-enabled communications. These data are shown in Fig. 1.13.

Among these applications, EDI, sourcing and procurement management, and web-enabled communications topped the list with adoption rates of 24.3%, 26.3%, and 20.3% of the respondents, respectively. As Fig. 1.13 also shows, e-compliance (5.2%) and collaborative forecasting (4.4%) were communication technologies that most organizations planned to purchase in the next three years. The technology applications which many organizations did not have and did not plan to purchase in the next three years were e-compliance (23.1%) and collaborative forecasting (21.5%).

Across all sectors, sourcing and procurement management was the most commonly used technology. 36.1% of manufacturing sectors, and 33.3% of service sectors use this technology to communicate with their trading partners. These results are shown in Fig. 1.14.

EDI communications technologies (37.5%) was the most-adopted trend (About was 24.3%, are in the process of buying was 10.4%, and plan to buy in next three years was 2.8%). 34.9% of service sectors (have was 20.9%, are in the process of buying was 10.9%, and plan to buy in next three years was 3.1%), 40.2% of manufacturing sectors (have was 27.9%, are in the process of buying was 9.8%, and plan to buy in next three years was 2.5%) had or planned to have this technology (Fig. 1.15).

Of the organizations surveyed, 15.5% were using direct purchasing, 5.6% were using catalogues, and 12.7% were using long-term purchasing contracts. Collaborative purchasing (0.4%) and auctions/e-auctions (0.8%) were the least used (Fig. 1.16).

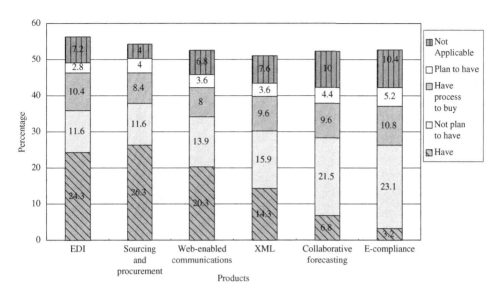

Fig. 1.13.   Communicating with their trading partners.

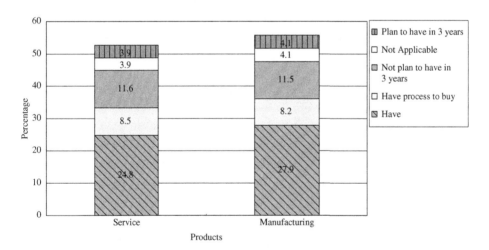

Fig. 1.14.   Sourcing and procurement management communications technology adopted.

Direct purchasing was commonly used in 19.7% of manufacturing sectors and 11.6% of service sectors (Fig. 1.17).

As shown in Fig. 1.18, various economic and operational results were impacted by technologies. The highest cost reductions were in internal communications (31.5%, which includes decreased: 23.5% and decreased significantly: 8%), production (30.3%, which includes decreased: 21.9% and decreased significantly: 8.4%), and consultancy and collaboration (30.3%, which includes decreased:

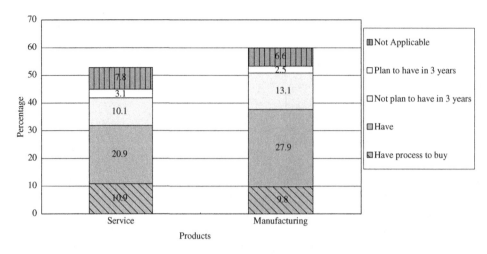

Fig. 1.15.   EDI communications technology adopted.

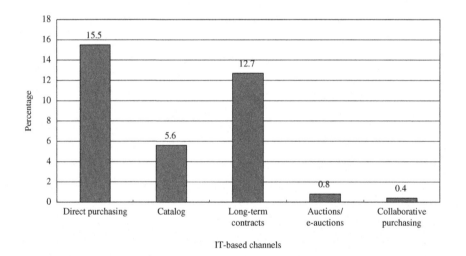

Fig. 1.16.   IT-based channels for purchasing.

20.7% and decreased significantly: 9.6%). In addition, use of technologies drove up the customer service (33.5%, which includes increased: 31.9% and increased significantly: 1.6%) and market share (30.7%, which includes increased: 30.3% and increased significantly: 0.4%).

Technology also impacted strategic areas in organizations. Understanding of customer satisfaction for current products and services (41.4%), knowledge of competitors' products and services (33.5%), and understanding of future product expectations (37.1%) and of customer buying behavior (38.3%) improved because of technology usage (Fig. 1.19).

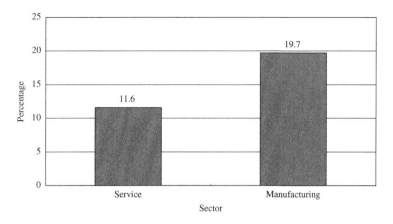

Fig. 1.17. Direct purchasing across sectors.

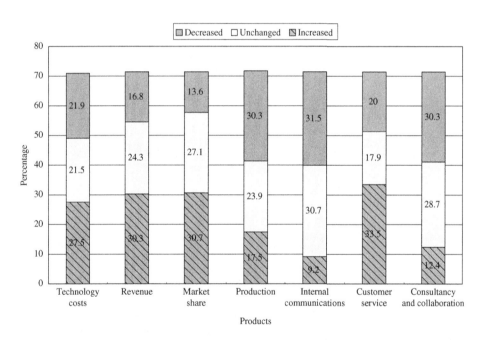

Fig. 1.18. Operational business results.

1.2.4. *Globalization*

Organizations were increasing their geographic reach in terms of trade in other countries (increasing or somewhat increasing in 24.7% of the organizations). They were also increasing their production or service bases in other countries (increasing or somewhat increasing in 14% of the organizations) (Fig. 1.20).

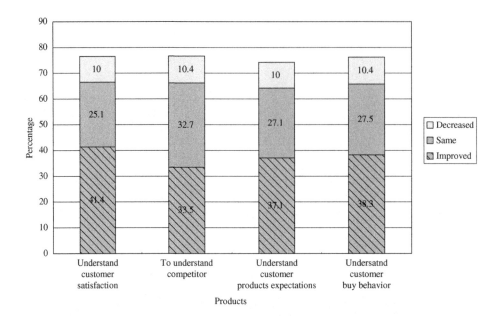

Fig. 1.19.   Technology has impacted strategic areas.

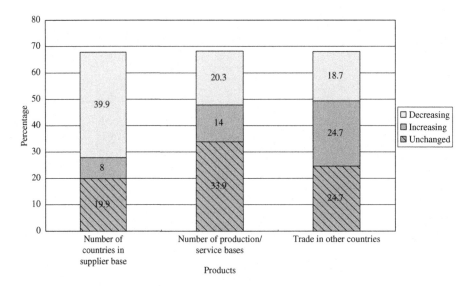

Fig. 1.20.   Geographic reach 1.

The average distance to suppliers, branches/distribution centers globally (36.3%), number of languages on the website and in brochures (36.3%), and distance to suppliers/vendors (41.4%) were decreasing. (Fig. 1.21).

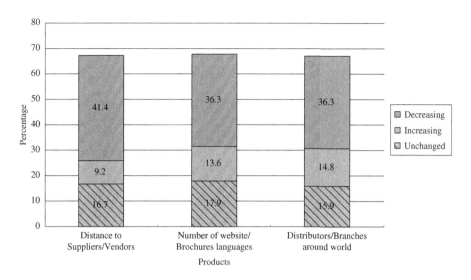

Fig. 1.21.   Geographic reach 2.

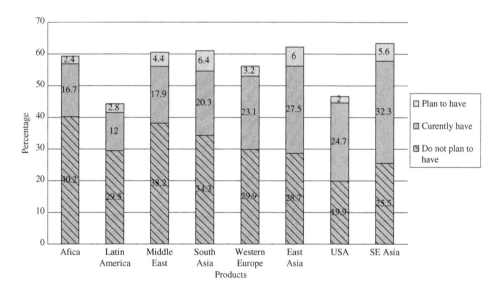

Fig. 1.22.   Business regions.

With regard to global terms of the regions to which organizations had expanded or were planning to expand to, over half of the organizations had or planned to have operations in SE Asia (37.9%), the USA (26.7%), and East Asia (33.5%). Close to a one-third of the organizations did not plan to have operations in Africa (40.2%) or Middle East (38.2%). These results are shown in Fig. 1.22.

Acknowledgments

This paper is particularly supported by "Aim for the Top University Plan" of the National Sun Yat-sen University and Ministry of Education, Taiwan, ROC.

Bibliography

1. Karmarkar, U.S. and Vandana, M. (2004), "The business and information technologies survey, Annual report 2003–2004", available at: http://www.anderson.ucla.edu/documents/areas/ctr/bit/Annualreport.pdf.

Appendix A: Survey Respondent Sample Characteristics

Background Information	Item	Amount	Percentage
Industry type	Manufacturing	44	17.5
	Service	21	8.4
Employee	Less than 50	18	7.2
	50–100	10	4.0
	100–500	35	13.9
	500–1,000	174	69.3
	1,000–5,000	13	5.2
	More than 5,000	1	0.4
IT employee	Less than 50	249	99.2
	More than 50	2	0.8
Revenue	100 million–1 billion	12	4.8
	1–5 billion	33	13.1
	5–10 billion	5	2.0
	More than 10 billion	7	2.8
Budget	100 thousand–1 million	6	2.4
	1–5 million	19	7.6
	5–10 million	8	3.2
	10–50 million	17	6.8
	More than 50 million	7	2.8
Budget (%)	Less than 5%	13	5.2
	5–10%	2	0.8
Taiwans's Information technology (IT) spending	Increase	21.52 billion	0.03

About the Authors

Ya-Ching Lee

Telecommunications, Indiana University, PhD, Professor and Director, Institute of Marketing Communication. National Sun Yat-sen University, Kaohsiung, Taiwan. Major research: Digital Marketing, Electronic Commerce, Media Management, Technology Adoption.

Ting-Peng Liang

Decision Sciences, The Wharton School, University of Pennsylvania, PhD, Director, Electronic Commerce Research Center. National Sun Yat-sen University, Kaohsiung, Taiwan. Major research: Decision support system, Strategic system and Professional information system.

CHAPTER 2

PATTERNS OF INFORMATION DIFFUSION IN ONLINE SOCIAL NETWORKS: WHAT SNA METRICS CAN REVEAL

MINGHAN WU AND ANANTH SRINIVASAN

Abstract

In this chapter, we report on a study of patterns of information diffusion across a variety of online social networks (OSNs). Specifically, we are interested in how diffusion patterns vary based on the choice of social networking media (text versus pictures) and context (international versus national, information consumption versus resulting action by network participants). We collected data from three different examples of network sites using both media over a three week period. By examining traditional network metrics, we outline some preliminary results from our study.

2.1. Research Motivation

The field of social network analysis (SNA) has existed for several decades focusing on issues such as network characteristics, metrics to study networks, and network evolution. In particular, there are a number of network phenomena studies available for the purposes of exploring diffusion activities from different perspectives. Crane (1972) discusses the fact that communities are positively associated with the development of knowledge. Valente (1995, 1996) and

Abrahamson and Rosenkopf (1997) mention that social networks are helpful to enhance innovation diffusion. Friedkin (1998) notes that social networks are correlated with the developments of interpersonal influences. In order to understand the mechanisms and principles of information diffusion, many researchers analyze diffusion patterns and characteristics within various research settings. In academia, Small (1973), White and McCain (1998), Carter *et al.* (2007), and Hu and Racherla (2008) analyze knowledge diffusion and creation in co-citation and co-authorship networks. On the other hand, Reagans and McEvily (2003), Cowan and Jonard (2004) and Morone *et al.* (2006) explain knowledge diffusion in a business relevant context, such as a patent citation network. All of these studies help us understand the foundations of knowledge diffusion through networks and provide a platform for investigating the phenomenon with current technologies that are commonly employed to facilitate interaction in networks.

People use online social networks (OSNs) to develop and maintain interpersonal relationships with their friends as well as acquaintances. Users of OSNs are also able to disseminate user-generated content about a multitude of topics. There are increasing numbers of studies reporting on information diffusion activities in OSNs. Java *et al.* (2007) studied usage and community structures in Twitter. Mislove *et al.* (2007) examined differences among network structures and users' positions in Flickr, LiveJournal, Orkut, and YouTube. Cha *et al.* (2009) studied the information propagation of user-generated content in Flickr. Oh *et al.* (2008) investigated the diffusion of user-generated contents in YouTube. With the widespread acceptance of social networking technologies among individuals and institutions, there is considerable research interest to understand and characterize phenomena that are directly attributable to the use of these technologies.

This research focuses on understanding information diffusion in OSN structures and the differences that exist with variation in the type of media used in such diffusion within broader network populations. Specifically, our aim is to (1) structurally study the diffusion patterns in an informant's egocentric network, (2) distinguish the properties and characteristics of information dissemination in both textual based and visual based OSNs; and (3) examine the properties and characteristics of information diffusion that exist in networks that focus on very different contexts. We do this by

- Using SNA metrics and network analysis properties to explore the pattern of information propagation in the textual based OSN and the visual based OSN for selected accounts.
- Differentiating the characteristics and properties of information diffusion between the textual based OSN and the visual based OSN.

- Differentiating the characteristics and properties of information diffusion among accounts that operate for very different purposes.
- Identifying the characteristics and properties of information diffusion in a specific time period.

In the rest of the chapter, we describe the research method that we used to collect data and outline the results that we have obtained thus far.

2.2. Research Method

In order to address the research questions above, we undertook to study two specific OSNs, namely Twitter and Flickr. The former is a text based social networking site with information consisting largely of user generated content in text form. The latter is a visual based social networking site with information consisting largely of content that is visual (picture) based. Further, we looked at these two OSNs across three different accounts, namely BBC World News, World Wildlife Fund (WWF) and Pure New Zealand. The cross-section of these accounts represents three distinctly different contexts: an international news organization, an international non-profit organization focusing on the protection of wildlife, and a tourism oriented organization promoting various aspects of tourism in New Zealand. This variety allows us to look at contrasts such as high versus low frequency information generation (news versus tourism), fund raising that relies on the ultimate active participation of network participants versus information consumption (donations versus news), and international versus national focus (worldwide versus New Zealand). An examination of information diffusion patterns across such a diversity of sites will allow us to examine how these patterns vary and whether these patterns can be influenced to achieve the objectives of these sites.

We used a number of classic metrics that are developed in the SNA literature to examine the diffusion phenomenon across the OSNs that we investigated. These metrics allow us to understand the influence patterns in these networks and enable us to get a sense of how information is diffused across network participants in different contexts. Specifically, we looked at the following important SNA constructs in this study:

- Egocentric network: A local network which is created by a specific account in an online social network. For example, a local network is established by BBC World News's Flickr account.
- Core actor: This term refers to informant and focal actor in the egocentric network. For example, the core actor in the egocentric network BBC World News's Flickr account is BBC World News.

- First rank actor: Actors with degree centrality exceeding a predefined threshold are included in the first rank. The thresholds are varied depending on the network population. Generally, first rank actors are positively correlated with the intensity of information diffusion in an egocentric network on the basis of their degree centrality.
- Degree centrality: A measure of the total number of inbound (in-degree) and outbound (out-degree) connections that a node has in a network.
- Eigenvector centrality: A metric to identify the numbers of friends on contact lists of actors' neighbors. More than relying on the calculations of an individual actor's degree centrality, eigenvector centrality investigates the total degrees of a focal node's proximate neighbors.
- Subgroups: In this case, subgroup refers to the cluster that involves a particular actor.
- Reciprocity: A metric to measure the frequency and intensity of communication. In this study, reciprocity is also adopted to examine the volume of transmitted information.
- Clustering coefficient: A metric to identify the magnitudes of interpersonal communications among actors' proximate neighbors.
- Diameter: A metric to measure the distance for information diffusion across a network.
- Average geodesic distance: A metric to identify distances for interpersonal communications in a network.

Finally, we used the software tool NodeXL (Hansen *et al.*, 2010) to extract the required metrics from across the two OSNs (Twitter and Flickr) and the three accounts in each of the OSNs (BBC World News, WWF, Pure New Zealand). For the purpose of data analysis, we collected data over a three week period at six points in time (two per week) giving us a total of 12 snapshots.

2.3. Results and Discussion

We analyzed the data collected as described above to answer the following questions:

- What are the diffusion patterns between a textual based OSN and a graphical based social network?
- What are the advantages for a particular account?
- How do other accounts use these advantages for improvements?
- What are the reasons for key changes during a specific time period?
- What are the suggestions from these essential changes?

Table 1.1 shows the number of nodes in each of the networks. Tables 1.2–1.5 show how the various metrics compare with each other in terms of the OSN and the particular accounts under consideration. The data in these tables are the summarized results of running group comparison statistical tests. It is clear that text based OSNs such as Twitter encourages wide participation. However, visual based OSNs such as Flickr are important vehicles to convey better quality information through media richness. The choice of media for information diffusion is related to the objectives of the network. It may be possible to achieve specific network objectives by allocating resources appropriately to encourage the most effective means of information diffusion.

In this section, we discuss some implications of the research results. Outcomes of this research include summarized diffusion patterns for given combinations of OSNs and accounts, differences between textual-based social networks, and graphical-based social networks, distinctions among three accounts with different audiences and orientations.

Table 1.1.   Number of nodes in each network.

	Twitter	**Flickr**
BBC World News	34446	3381
WWF	71714	27458
Pure New Zealand	58467	4224

Table 1.2.   Picture-based (Flickr) versus Text-based (Twitter) OSNs: core actor properties.

	Flickr	**Twitter**
Egocentric network		
Vertices	Small	Large
Core actor's properties		
Reciprocity	Small	Large
Eigenvector centrality	Large	Small
Clustering coefficient	Large	small
Core actors' subgroups		
Diameter	Small	Large
Geodesic distance	Small	Large

Table 1.3.   Picture-based (Flickr) versus Text-based (Twitter) OSNs: first rank actor properties.

	Flickr	**Twitter**
First rank actors' properties		
Reciprocity	Small	Large
Eigenvector centrality	Large	Small
Clustering coefficient	Small	Large
First rank actors' subgroups		
Diameter	Small	Large
Avg. Geodesic distance	Small	Large

Table 1.4.   Site content and diffusion: core actor properties.

	BBC World News	**WWF Climate**	**Pure New Zealand**
Description of egocentric network			
Vertices	Low	High	Medium
Description of core actor's properties			
Reciprocity	Low	Medium	High
Eigenvector centrality	High	Low	Medium
Clustering coefficient	Medium	Low	High
Description of core actor's subgroup			
Diameter	Low	High	Low
Average Geodesic distance	Medium	High	Low

Table 1.5.   Site content and diffusion: first rank actor properties.

	BBC World News	**WWF Climate**	**Pure New Zealand**
First rank actor's average properties			
Reciprocity	High	Medium	Low
Eigenvector centrality	High	Low	Medium
Clustering coefficient	High	Low	Medium
Average properties of first rank actors' subgroups			
Diameter	Low	High	Medium
Avg. Geodesic distance	Low	High	Medium

2.3.1. *Patterns of information diffusion*

In our dataset, there are eight different diffusion patterns observed from a total of 36 egocentric networks. All these egocentric networks follow general diffusion patterns that have been observed in the literature (Small, 1973; Morone *et al.*, 2006; Carter *et al.*, 2007; Hu and Racherla, 2008). In a commonly observed pattern, information is initialized from a focal actor and then is received by its audience. Mislove *et al.* (2007) mention that the core actor in a network is essential to efficiently propagate information. However, other essential actors in these networks include first rank actors who have a relatively high degree centrality and betweenness centrality (Carter *et al.*, 2007; Hu and Racherla, 2008; Cha *et al.*, 2009). Mislove *et al.* (2007) identified these aggregated key actors as a tight core.

Therefore, in our observations, core actors and first rank actors as well as the interactions between them with other actors are considered as the most essential parts for diffusion. Actors at first rank have higher degree centrality and betweenness centrality. In order to understand these patterns, we categorize them into three types. Most egocentric networks are included in a first category that diffuses information via both focal actor and first rank actors. For this kind of a network, the core actor and first rank actors' abilities and characteristics as well as the structures of their subgroups decide the streams of major information in the egocentric network. In the second category, the performance of information diffusion is positively associated with the first rank actors and their subgroups. In this case, the core actor's contribution to the diffusion is limited. In general, both diffusion patterns demonstrate dependency on the core actor and first rank actors. Changes of core actor's and first rank actors' status will result in upgrade or downgrade of the entire process of information diffusion. Comparatively, elements of a third diffusion category include an additional key actor other than core actor and first rank actors. In the egocentric network of WWF Climate's Flickr account, actor 1 demonstrates ultimate social influence through representation of in-degree centrality to attract peripheral actors' attention. Friedkin (1998) considers a node with high in-degree usually as possessing substantial social influence. Therefore, in an egocentric network, an actor with outstanding in-degree centrality will positively boost the diffusion processes.

2.3.2. *Differences between OSNs*

The most intuitive distinction between Flickr and Twitter is the network size. For example, the populations of BBC World News's Twitter account are approximately 10 times larger than its Flickr account. The primary reason to explain this phenomenon is different amounts of registered members in both OSNs. According to Cha *et al.* (2009), Flickr obtains around 2.5 million users in contrast with 200 million users in Twitter based on a BBC News' report. Moreover, the accessing settings can be considered as another explanation for this particular issue. Twitter has raised its accessing criteria from publicly accessible to registered users only by removing the search textbox on the main page since September, 2011. However, Flickr maintains an open policy for its public users. As Oh *et al.* (2008) mention, user preferences and heterogeneity of resources have positive correlations with information diffusion. Based on the needs of large size populations, Twitter has a variety of resources on different topics and areas to satisfy users from different backgrounds. Moreover, the current version of Twitter provides the ability to post images rather than just plain text. The popularity of Twitter has improved through adopting this new feature.

As per our summary of results, users in Twitter demonstrate a greater degree of communication intensity than Flickr on the basis of high reciprocity for both core actor and first rank actors. This phenomenon can be explained by the configurations and designs of Twitter which create an environment to support the high degree interactions between core actors and their contacts. Users share and exchange information with each other through retweeting and replying to contacts' messages within the limitation of 144 characters plus embedded hyperlinks and photos. The Twitter interface is designed as a platform for interpersonal communications. Updated news, contacts' replies, retweets, and mentions are displayed on both sender and receivers' home page synchronously. Comparatively, the purpose of Flickr is the exhibiting of personal collections of photography within a specific topic to a group of users who are particularly interested in this area. This setting implies that Flickr is a content oriented OSN rather than Twitter which can be considered as a user oriented network. Moreover, the reply tag of Twitter also enables the convenience of interactions between core actors and direct contacts. Based on these settings, Twitter is considered better in interpersonal communications between core actors and their direct contacts than Flickr.

The findings also show that core actors' contacts prefer to communicate with each other frequently in Flickr rather than Twitter based on a high degree clustering coefficient. This phenomenon can be explained by the orientations of OSNs. Flickr users prefer to exchange information, commenting, and even critiquing the details and photographic techniques about a photo rather than directly questioning a core actor. In Twitter, users tend to ask the core actor the details about updated news on this actor's personal home page. However, the degree of interpersonal communications among first rank actors' contacts in Twitter are greater than Flickr. This finding is consistent with the literature (Jansen *et al.*, 2009) which identified mechanisms of information diffusion in Twitter following the principle of viral marketing. Undoubtedly, functions and settings of Twitter in this case provide necessary support for information distribution. Users are able to disseminate information through adopting mention and retweet tags. For both core actor and first rank actors, eigenvector centrality in Flickr is greater than Twitter. This suggests the existence of sufficient friends on core actor and first rank actors contact lists in Flickr's egocentric network rather than the networks of a Twitter account. In Flickr, actors distribute graphical information to share their experiences and news in visual representation. Compared with textual representation, information in visual format exhibits characteristics that are understandable, acceptable, and memorable. Therefore, graphical information is observed having sustainable attractiveness for subordinate members.

In conclusion, information diffusion in Twitter reaches larger audiences than Flickr. Information diffusion in the egocentric network of Twitter account is more productive than Flickr. Users are able to obtain more information through high degree reciprocity. For core actors, Flickr has advantages, over Twitter on the basis of a greater clustering coefficient. Comparatively, first rank actors of the Twitter account demonstrate sufficient capacities of information diffusion. Core actors in Twitter perform as salient elements to transit the information to their direct contacts as well as bridge communication for individuals or subgroups in most scenarios. On the other hand, information diffusion through both core actor and first rank actors' subgroups of the Twitter account consumes more resources and time due to distant diameter. However, a distant diameter in this case also implies greater coverage of current subgroups. In contrast to Flickr, first rank actors in Twitter usually reach more network members for information diffusion and exchange. Similar to in-group communications, the performances of information diffusion inside the subgroups of the Flickr account are considered more efficient than in Twitter due to small average geodesic distance.

Twitter shows its strength to establish high degree interactions between core actors with their contacts due to the characteristics of textual inputs, limitation of entry (140 characters), accessing conditions, and the availability of huge user populations. Information diffusion of an actor's egocentric network is able to reach a large amount of recipients with inefficient diffusion activities. Nevertheless, these statistics reveal that diffusion in Flickr reaches fewer populations, which implies a high degree of efficiency of interpersonal communications. As a visual based social network, Flickr mainly aims for displaying and exhibiting photos. Users connect to each other through commenting and recommending photo collections. Low degree reciprocity and interactions can be explained by fewer registered populations due to the existence of public access mechanisms. Moreover, in contrast to textual based contents, visual based contents are considered to have long vitality on the basis of great eigenvector centrality.

2.3.3. *Differences among the three accounts*

In this section, we discuss the characteristics and patterns of information diffusion among BBC World News, Pure New Zealand and WWF Climates. As described earlier, three accounts are selected in both Flickr and Twitter with different operating purposes and target audiences. BBC World News is a news agency aiming to provide updated news and information that covers entire industries and areas. Audiences of BBC World News include people who are looking for the latest news worldwide. Pure New Zealand is a commercial organization providing comprehensive information about travel, environmental, economic, and business information of New Zealand. Travelers, business investors, and visitors are the primary audiences of this account. WWF is the largest non-governmental organization around the world that focuses on conservation, scientific research, climate, and environmental issues. In contrast with other accounts, the audiences of WWF express more interest in receiving the information about nature and changes of living environment as well as ongoing projects of WWF.

In the overview of these three accounts, WWF Climates has the largest population, suggesting that climate and environmental issues have raised people's attention. The egocentric network of BBC World News in both Flickr and Twitter has the lowest size. In this case, the small populations of the BBC World News account only reflect the size of this particular account rather than the overall accounts of the BBC family.

As a portal for introducing New Zealand, Pure New Zealand's emphasis is on interacting with its followers through answering questions as well as giving suggestions in Twitter. This action can be explained by accumulating advertisements on New Zealand's scenery, cultures, and ongoing world class events, such as Rugby World Cup 2011. Contacts and followers of this account gain the information through social learning with the core actor. More than officially questioning the information of Pure New Zealand with the core actor, information diffusion is improved through exchanging and sharing first rank actors' travelling experiences, suggestions, and feelings with their direct contacts. In Flickr, Pure New Zealand aims to provide introductions of New Zealand via disseminating beautiful photos about New Zealand's scenery, cultures, and other attractions. These user-generated contents are provided by Pure New Zealand or other direct contacts. Core actor and its subgroups positively support information diffusion on the basis of short diameter and average geodesic distance.

On the other hand, the core actor of BBC World News demonstrates a low reciprocity with direct contacts based on implementing a different diffusion pattern. BBC World News obtains the highest eigenvector centrality of the three accounts. There are several reasons to explain this phenomenon. First, first rank actors are main characters for information propagation in the egocentric network. Second, people are curious about news that happens locally and internationally.

Third, information of BBC world News is attractive due to coverage of heterogeneous areas rather than concentrating on one topic. Followers are able to receive and disseminate information, which satisfies their taste, to their contacts. Performances of first rank actors in BBC World News's egocentric network are perfect. As mentioned above, BBC World News adopts other accounts in the same family (such as BBC Break News, BBC Night News) for news diffusion. Therefore, existing subscribers of these accounts are included as distributors for the diffusion process. Moreover, the stability of diffusion operations and precision of news are also ensured through adopting the first rank actors that derive from the same organization. Generally, information diffusion in BBC World News's egocentric network operates efficiently. First rank actors provide sufficient volume of information through high degree reciprocity. However, the finding shows that coverage of core actor and first rank actors' subgroups is small. This can be explained by the existence of lower network populations.

Summaries of WWF Climate suggest the existences of backgrounds and contexts are weak for information diffusion. In contrast with the two other accounts, the volumes of exchanged information in WWF Climate are at an acceptable degree. However, the rapidity and extent of information transmission are weaker than the other two accounts. Diffusion contents in this case can help in explaining this scenario. Dissimilar with BBC World News and Pure New Zealand, information of WWF Climate is professionally oriented. Users have sufficient knowledge and experiences in conservation and the environment and therefore might enjoy the discussion of posted contents. Ordinary audiences in the network prefer to read and learn the information that is provided by WWF Climate.

The summaries of diffusion patterns among the three accounts consolidate the observations of diffusion patterns between Flickr and Twitter. In this case, discussions of two major diffusion patterns are present, including core actor and first rank actors as key components. In the first diffusion pattern, WWF Climate and Pure New Zealand employ both core actor and first rank actors for information diffusion. The efficiency and coverage of information diffusion relies on the performance of core actor and first rank actors. On the other hand, information diffusion in BBC World News's egocentric network demonstrates a strong dependency on first rank actors. In this case, first rank actors' abilities and characteristics decide the performance of information diffusion. Additionally, the degree of reciprocity is proposed as a key metric to identify the volume of information diffusion and communication intensity.

2.3.4. *Changes over time*

Results of longitudinal analysis of the accounts with both social networks reveal interesting phenomena for discussion. Firstly, the populations of accounts in Flickr have gradually increased during the three weeks rather than same accounts in

Twitter. In contrast with Pure New Zealand, the populations of the BBC World News account display a decreasing trend across the three weeks. The Size of WWF Climate's egocentric network reduced slightly at the end of week 3, reaching the lowest populations in week 2.

There are a number of reasons for the undulations. First, information diffusion of the three accounts in Twitter demonstrates significant dependency on first rank actors' reciprocity. The diffusion patterns of both WWF Climate and Pure New Zealand's Twitter account suggest the existence of positive correlations between first rank actors and numbers of vertices of the egocentric network. Especially in WWF Climate, the decreasing population starts at the beginning of the second dataset in the first week, that is consistent with the decreasing reciprocity. For Pure New Zealand, the milestone for increments is discovered at the first egocentric network in the second week and matches the improvement of reciprocity. This finding suggests that the interactions are critical precedents to increased volumes of information transmission for most of the organizations in Twitter. Network members benefit from obtaining more interesting information via interacting with core actors. From the end of the second week, WWF Climate's first rank actors increased their reciprocity, which finally lead to population growth.

The second reason is related to the settings of OSNs. In September 2011, Twitter improved the threshold for content navigation by removing the search bar at the index page. This move restrains visitors who normally view information anonymously, as well as eliminates potential members who intend to explore the accounts with similar preferences and conformity before signing up. This mechanism also implies that Twitter encourages registration of new network members by allowing access. As a result, both BBC World News and WWF Climate show a descending trend for their populations.

Third, the evidence shows that the size of Pure New Zealand's egocentric network is inconsistent with the constraints of access. The populations of Pure New Zealand have increased across the three weeks under tight access conditions. More than the existence of high core actor's reciprocity, both environmental and intrinsic factors account for the increment for this phenomenon. The environmental factor refers to availability of important events or incentives to benefit the economies of the entire country. For example, Rugby World Cup 2011 in New Zealand can be considered as a reasonable justification. Intrinsic factors include support from government for promoting the brand of 100% pure as well as the environment for operating business and trade.

On the other hand, first rank actors of BBC News's Twitter account display an undulating pattern for reciprocity. The reciprocity reached a peak degree at 16% in the second egocentric network in the first two weeks. This can be explained as the existence of a relatively regular news updating schedule. The above phenomenon further suggests that selection of right contents and employment of an appropriate diffusion pattern improves the information diffusion even while the core actor's reciprocity is at a low degree.

In addition, diameters of first rank actors' subgroups are positively correlated with the numbers of vertices in a large dataset. For example, the diameter of first rank actor's subgroups in WWF Climate' account is consistent with the quantity of populations. The diameter decreases one step in the second week where the size of the network reached the lowest degree during the three weeks. The diameter reverts to eight steps in the case of growing network populations. In the case of Pure New Zealand, although the size of the egocentric network keeps growing during the three weeks, first rank actors demonstrate a strong communication intensity to maintain the distance for information diffusion across the network.

2.4. Conclusion

In this paper, we analyzed the patterns of diffusion across two types of OSNs: one which was text oriented (Twitter) and one which was graphically or visually oriented (Flickr). By contrasting these OSNs across three very differently oriented accounts, we observed the patterns of information diffusion over time by examining some critical social network metrics. This level of understanding about how information is shared across OSNs will help organizations make better use of social networks to achieve their objectives.

Bibliography

1. Abrahamson, E and L Rosenkopf (1997). Social network effects on the extent of innovation diffusion. *Organization Science*, 8(3), 289–309.
2. Carter, CR, R Leuschner and DS Rogers (2007). A Social network analysis of the journal of supply chain management: Knowledge generation, knowledge diffusion and thought leadership. *Journal of Supply Chain Management*, 43(2), 15–28.
3. Cha, M, A Mislove and KP Gummadi (2009). A Measurement-driven analysis of information propagation in the Flickr social network. In *Proceedings of the 18th Annual World Wide Web Conference (WWW'09)*, Madrid, Spain.
4. Cowan, R and N Jonard (2004). Network structure and the diffusion of knowledge. *Journal of Economic Dynamics and Control*, 28(8), 1557–1575.
5. Crane, D (1972). *Invisible Colleges: Diffusion of Knowledge in Scientific Communities*. Chicago: University of Chicago Press.
6. Friedkin, NE (1998). *A Structural Theory of Social Influence*. Cambridge: Cambridge University Press.
7. Hansen, D, B Shneiderman and M Smith (2010). *Analysing Social Media Networks with NodeXL: Insights from a Connected World*. San Francisco: Morgan Kaufmann.

8. Hu, C and P Racherla (2008). Visual representation of knowledge networks: A social network analysis of hospitality research domain. *International Journal of Hospitality Management*, 27(2), 302–312

9 Jansen, B, M Zhang, K Sobel and A Chowdury (2009).Twitter power: tweets as electronic word of mouth. *Journal of the American Society for Information Science and Technology*, 60(11), 2169–2188.

10. Java, A, X Song, T Finin and B Tseng (2007). Why we twitter: Understanding microblogging usage and communities. *In Proceedings of the 9th WebKDD and 1stSNA-KDD 2007 workshop on Web mining and social network analysis*, San Jose, California.

11. Mislove, A, KP Gummadi and P Druschel (2007). *Measurement and analysis of online social networks*. Proceedings of the 7th ACM SIGCOMM conference on internet measurement, San Diego, California, USA.

12. Morone P, R Sisto and R Taylor (2006). Knowledge diffusion and networking in the organic production sector: a case study. *In Euro Choices*, 5(3), 40–46.

13. Oh, JH, A Susarla and Y Tan (2008). *Examining the Diffusion of User-Generated Content in Online Social Networks*. SSRN eLibrary.

14. Reagans, R and B McEvily (2003). Network structure and knowledge transfer: The effects of cohesion and range. *Administrative Science Quarterly*, 48, 240–267.

15. Small, H (1973). Co-citation in the scientific literature: A new measure of the relationship between two documents. *Journal of the American Society for Information Science*, 24, 65–26.

16. Valente, TW (1995). *Network Models of the Diffusion of Innovations*. Cresskill, N.J.: Hampton.

17. Valente, TW (1996). Social network thresholds in the diffusion of innovations. *Social Networks*, 18(1), 69–89.

18. White, HD and KW McCain (1998). Visualizing a discipline: An author co-citation analysis of information science, 1972–1995. *Journal of the American Society for Information Science*, 49, 327–356.

About the Authors

Minghan Wu

Minghan Wu is a software test engineer with Paymark New Zealand which is an electronic fund transfer network in New Zealand. He graduated with a Masters degree in Information Systems from the University of Auckland Business School. Subsequently, he worked as a Technical Specialist at IAG Insurance in New Zealand before moving to Paymark.

Ananth Srinivasan

Ananth Srinivasan is a Professor of Information Systems and Digital Commerce at the University of Auckland Business School in New Zealand. He is also the Co-director of the Centre of Digital Enterprise which examines the role of digital technologies on people, organizations, and society.

CHAPTER 3

TRUST GAPS AND CORPORATE BLINDSPOTS IN CHILEAN B2C E-COMMERCE[1]

SERGIO GODOY, CLAUDIA LABARCA, NICOLÁS SOMMA
AND MYRNA GÁLVEZ

Abstract

Trust is an essential ingredient of human relationships and economic exchanges among them. On the other hand, blindspots are harmful omissions in strategy implementation due to reasons such as corporate inertia or management obsessiveness in pursuing a certain vision mismatched with reality. This article outlines the main areas in which customer trust is stressed in Chilean Bussiness-to-Consumer (B2C) electronic commerce (e-commerce) and how e-buyers circumvent the problems that arise in those areas of stress, from a communications perspective. We not only discovered compensatory strategies devised by users in overcoming those problems, but also some relevant corporate blindspots in that sector that should be addressed by retailers. Despite the strong growth of retail sales in that emerging Latin American country, Chilean B2C e-commerce is relatively weak and problems of trust may be an important cause.

Four areas of stress were outlined: previous perceptions about the firm, clarity and coherence of online information, security of personal data, and post-sales service. Within these, inter-channel communication incoherence, lack of integration

[1] "WIP/BIT Chile 3.0: Incidencia de las TICs en la confianza entre personas y organizaciones". National Science and Technology Fund Project (Fondecyt) N°1110098.

between retailers and outsourced logistics, and incoherent notions of trust emerged as the most important corporate blindspots harming the relationship with customers. On the other hand, we identified four compensatory strategies used by clients: selective auto-exposure, informal "certifications", online/offline hybridization and anticipation/incorporation of other people experience. This fills a gap in the existing literature, normally focused on unilateral actions of the e-vendor or on technological aspects of e-business. These results emerge from an inductive and qualitative approach, based on principles taken from Grounded Theory.

3.1. Introduction

Trust is an essential ingredient of human relationships and economic exchanges among them. This article outlines the main areas in which customer trust is stressed in Chilean business-to-consumer (B2C) electronic commerce (e-commerce), and how clients manage to surpass these difficulties. We believe that problems of ICT-mediated trust between e-sellers and e-buyers can be an important reason for this relative weakness.

The specific territory of relations and exchanges we will analyze is that of e-commerce of department stores, and the way these organizations relate to their customers within a wider arrangement of stakeholders such as employees, shareholders, suppliers, and other actors. The analysis was made in Chile, where retail in general and department stores in particular are especially dynamic and powerful, both in terms of sheer economic size (Chilean retailers became multinational companies and have expanded throughout South America) as well as in terms of shaping everyday life. We analyzed the major "brick and mortar" retailers, i.e. those companies whose main business come from physical stores and have implemented websites and call centers as complementary channels of sale and post-sales. These are B2C firms, oriented to individual consumers.

This chapter is divided into five parts. The first part summarizes the main advances in research on trust and e-commerce. The second exposes the methodology used, of qualitative and inductive nature. The third one, dedicated to the findings, identifies four areas that affect trust building in B2C commerce in Chile and describes four compensatory strategies used by clients to build trust, in scenarios of uncertainty. In the fourth place, these findings are discussed following the perspective of both clients and retailers, where corporate blindspots in B2C e-commerce are outlined as well. Finally, conclusions are outlined at the end.

3.2. Theoretical Framework: Definitions and Contributions

3.2.1. *B2C e-commerce and retail in Chile*

Big department stores are important actors within the Chilean retail sector along with supermarket chains and drugstores (which are not analyzed in this paper). We focus on e-commerce from retailers (or shops) to individual consumers (B2C). We neither address the virtual transactions between companies Business to Business (B2B) nor between individuals Peer-to-Peer (P2P). By e-commerce, we will understand business transactions mediated by computer technologies (McKnight *et al.*, 2002a, 2002b) and which are normally supported by other communication channels such as telephone systems (call centers) and face-to-face interactions (vendors or assistants in physical premises). This definition therefore contemplates e-commerce through the internet, which nowadays is gradually shifting from desktop PCs to mobile apparatuses.

As a relatively small developing country of 17 million inhabitants, Chile has relatively high levels of technologization both among its people and its organizations (Godoy and Helsper, 2011). Retail, meanwhile, is a very dynamic economic sector which accounted for 21% of GDP in 2007 (Ceret, 2010). However, there are some notorious paradoxes. One is the persistence of important gaps of access and use of ICTs, also known as digital divides. The digital divide among people has received considerable public policy attention since the 1990s. But there is an even sharper gap between big and smaller companies (SMEs) which causes important inefficiencies in the economy as a whole (Godoy *et al.*, 2008; Herrera *et al.*, 2009; Lever *et al.*, 2009). This is reflected, as discussed later, in disparities and lack of coordination between the large department stores analyzed and the smaller, fragmented providers of logistics subcontracted by the retailers.

Another paradox is the relative underdevelopment of B2C e-commerce, considering the high rates of technological access in Chile as well as its income per capita of $15,230 in 2013, a "higher middle" level according to the World Bank.[2] In 2008, B2C e-commerce was just $380 million in contrast to B2B's $14 billion (Lever *et al.*, 2009). This disparity can be partially explained by reasons such as low rates of banking among the general population, low digital literacy of web users, and poor logistics for the delivery of purchased goods (Godoy *et al.*, 2008, 2009; Godoy and Helsper, 2011). Yet, it is necessary to examine more in detail how these and other unexplored factors intervene in the phenomenon. Hence, the

---

[2] http://data.worldbank.org/country/chile, accessed on August 30, 2014.

interest to investigate "soft" variables, such as trust, which has been established as an essential ingredient for the smooth operation of markets, countries' prosperity, and the ability for markets to compete (Fukuyama, 1995).

3.2.2. Trust

Trust is a complex construct which has accumulated a large bibliography in the last 50 years from sociology, psychology, anthropology, computer science (thanks to the development of virtual environments), political science, and other fields (Bannister and Connolly, 2011). Its study has also acquired great relevance in fields such as e-commerce. There is no consensus on either the multiple definitions of the concept or its main dimensions, so there should be extra care when using it. Yet, it is more accepted that trust plays an important role in economic cooperation (Labarca, 2009, 2012). Some authors take a systemic perspective and understand trust as a mechanism for reducing complexity (Luhmann, 1979). This view assumes that the part that is going to interact with another (organizations, individuals, systems, and even machines) regards that interaction as a "black box" because it is not possible to know how the counterpart will act and react. Trust mitigates that uncertainty by the belief that the other will comply with one's expectations (Jarvenpaa *et al.*, 2000; Gefen, 2000; McKnight *et al.*, 2002a, 2002b; Shankar *et al.*, 2002; Teo and Liu, 2007, Bente *et al.*, 2012; Pestek *et al.*, 2011; Li *et al.*, 2012).

Another meaning of trust has to do with attributing to the other party one or all of the following attributes, relating the concept to trustworthiness rather than trust: ability, benevolence, integrity, honesty, goodwill, morality or predictability (Shankar *et al.*, 2002; McKnight *et al.*, 2002a, 2002b; Gefen *et al.*, 2003; Teo and Liu, 2007; Chen and Dibb, 2010; Godoy *et al.*, 2015).

In this chapter, we will apply the concise definition of Bannister and Connolly (2011: 139), somebody's disposition to become exposed to exploitation by their counterpart. This means overcoming uncertainty in the context of asymmetric interactions between an organization (supply side) and a multitude of individual and fragmented customers, both current or potential (demand side). Their interactions are affected by situational factors (such as social values or institutional protections to trade), propensity to trust (on which there is no consensus if it is due to the personality of who trusts or to situational factors) and the perceived risks associated to the interactions (*ibid.*). We chose this definition because it encompasses the concept of vulnerability and the willingness to take risks, which is adequate for the online environment. It also includes both the cognitive and behavioral aspects of trust — decisions are ultimately involved. Finally, this approach, although phrased somewhat negatively, is also associated with the trustor's positive expectation of not being deceived by his/her counterpart (Gefen *et al.*, 2003; Hardin, 2001, 2004; Kim, 2005; Mayer *et al.*, 1995; Onyx and Bullen, 2000; Zand, 1972).

The literature also distinguishes between "face-to-face" (offline) and online trust. There are two relevant differences between both: the object in which trust is placed and the factors influencing its construction and maintenance. On offline trust studies, the object is usually other individuals or organizations known personally and with which there is direct contact (Patil and Shyamasundar, 2005). In the online world and e-commerce, the object to be trusted expands to elements such as the website where the transaction takes place (Gefen, 2000; McKnight *et al.*, 2002a; Chen and Dibb, 2010; Godoy *et al.*, 2015), the internet in general (McKngiht, 2002), electronic networks in general (Shankar *et al.*, 2002) and the virtual trader or e-vendor (Jarvenpaa *et al.*, 2000; Gefen *et al.*, 2003; Teo and Liu, 2007).

As for the factors that affect confidence, the literature makes some relevant distinctions. First is about the variables applicable both to offline and online contexts, which do not depend on the individual who trusts, but are part of the environment and therefore are more difficult to modify. Among these are the generalized levels of trust existing in a country or context (also known as "willingness to trust", see Teo and Liu, 2007; Kim and Kim, 2011), the culture (Teo and Liu, 2007; San Martín and Camarero, 2011), and gender (San Martín and Jiménez, 2011). Other influential variables are the vendor's and/or the brand's reputation (Pestek *et al.*, 2011; Bente *et al.*, 2012; Jarvenpaa *et al.*, 2000; Shankar *et al.*, 2002; McKnight *et al.*, 2002a, 2002b; Teo and Liu, 2007). Company size is also relevant: bigger firms are often more renowned and, therefore, trusted (Jarvenpaa *et al.*, 2000).

At the specific level of online transactions, relevant factors include the levels of privacy and security of the website (McKnight *et al.*, 2002a, 2002b; Teo and Liu, 2007; Chen and Dibb 2010; San Martín and Jiménez, 2011; San Martín and Camarero, 2012; Karimov *et al.*, 2011; Pestek *et al.*, 2011). This category includes the presence of security seals on the website, normally provided by a third party certifier (Kim and Kim, 2011), the combination of techniques and tools available to the consumer to find information about products and services available online, known in the industry as e-CRM (Pestek *et al.*, 2011; Karimov *et al.*, 2011), the design of the website (San Martín and Camarero, 2012; Karimov *et al.*, 2011), the presence of audiovisual material, especially photographs of the products (Bente *et al.*, 2012), the quality of the online service (San Martín and Camarero, 2011), warranties of products (San Martín and Jiménez, 2011) and, finally, the reviews published by other consumers about products and services available online (Lee *et al.*, 2011).

3.2.3. *Contributions of the paper*

There are five relatively unexplored aspects of trust in e-commerce in the existing literature. First, most of the existing studies are quantitative, usually based on surveys of internet users (Shankar *et al.*, 2002; McKnight *et al.*, 2002; Gefen, 2003; Teo and Liu, 2007; Chen and Dibb, 2010; Tag, forthcoming). This type of analysis is based on standardized instruments, which allow generalizing findings at the expense of losing important nuances in trust building, particularly from the perspective of consumers.

Second, most of the studies are limited to online contexts alone. However, we found that e-commerce clients seamlessly integrate the offline 'real' world with the virtual one to build trust.

Thirdly, the role of trust is not constant along the process of online purchase. In fact, we found important differences, starting with the customer's prior perceptions about the company (i.e. corporate reputation), followed by the electronic search of information of the items, the entry of sensitive personal data on the website (credit card numbers, access passwords, and others), and finally, in the post-sales stage (which is crucial in e-commerce, as purchased products need to be delivered to the client).

Fourth, most of the existing studies focus on developed countries with high rates of overall trust. But, there is little information regarding countries like Chile, where 13% of overall trust was registered in the World Values Survey in contrast with the 40% average registered in North America and Europe in 2005–2007.

Finally, the literature about trust and e-commerce emphasizes on the actions in which the e-vendor incurs unilaterally, a rather outdated perspective based on concepts and theories of communication from the mid-20th century that assumed a relatively easy to manipulate mass society, in which an active sender transmits messages to a mass of undifferentiated, passive receivers (McQuail, 2005). This view is still influential in disciplines such as marketing and corporate communications, despite the fact that various authors have noted the increasing difficulties faced by organizations to interact in this way with their customers and other stakeholders (Argenti, 2009; Mandelli and Accoto, 2010; van Riel and Fombrun, 2007). Indeed, our findings suggest that buyers are very active and creative to build trust.

3.3. Methodology

Since the study of the relationship between trust and ICTs in retail is fairly recent and shows important gaps, we used an inductive methodological design of qualitative nature inspired by the principles of the Grounded Theory, which seeks to construct a theory based on empirical data collected during the course of an investigation. The purpose is to learn about a situation or process from the participants of the observed phenomenon (Glasser and Strauss, 1967; Strauss and Corbin, 1998; Creswell and Plano Clark, 2011; Bryman, 2008). We established the following data collection instruments: semi-structured interviews to e-commerce managers, focus groups of clients, website analysis, and participant observation of physical stores based on ethnographic techniques. This was complemented by analysis of secondary sources (including websites of customer complaints, such as www.reclamos.cl and those of the National Consumer Service, SERNAC[3]) and a purchasing exercise by which a small item was bought both through the physical store and the website which was later returned intact requesting the reimbursement. The subsequent analysis was conducted based on the extraction of the categories (coding) that emerged by applying the conceptualization made by Strauss and Corbin (1998). While all data collection techniques produced valuable information, the subsequent analysis will emphasize on the focus groups and interviews to e-commerce managers because these yielded the most interesting findings.

Originally, only two selection criteria were chosen to define the focus groups: gender (as males have different purchasing behavior and predisposition to shop than females) and frequency of online purchasing (distinguishing between e-buyers and non-e-buyers). As the study progressed, we decided to refine the distinction between buyers and e-buyers: the former were defined as those who had made at least one online purchase in the last six months, while the others bought less frequently, if at all. We also found that we needed to consider the age factor, since youngsters are more prone to buy online than their elders. As a result, eight groups were defined (numbered A–H) distributed by age, gender, and their frequency of online purchases in department stores (e-buyers versus non-e-buyers) as shown in Table 3.1.

Table 3.1.   Distribution of the eight focus groups according to segmentation variables.

	18–25 years, e-buyers	25+ years, e-buyers	25+ years, non-e-buyers
Men	A	C	F, G
Women	B	D, E	H

---

[3] http://www.sernac.cl.

3.4. Results

Although e-commerce is a global phenomenon, the factors that explain trust creation may vary among cultures (Gefen and Heart, 2006). Identifying the most important factors that affect trust among clients of B2C e-commerce in Chile highlights the variables that influence that process in that setting at least. This section is divided in two parts. The first one outlines the areas in which trust is stressed, and the second describes the compensation strategies devised by clients to overcome the problems of trust.

3.4.1. *Areas of stress*

Customer trust in B2C e-commerce in Chile is stressed in four main areas: previous perceptions about the firm, clarity and coherence of online information, security of data, and post-sales and multichannel integration.

(a) Previous perceptions about the firm

This first area of stress was the most evident from the focus groups of customers. In recent years, these perceptions have been operationalized under the concept of corporate reputation, understood as the degree of attraction (or rejection) expressed by an organization's clients and other stakeholders (Argenti, 2009; van Riel and Fombrun, 2007).

Albeit literature admits that reputation is nurtured in great deal by the accumulated direct interactions of the stakeholders with a firm, we found that in many cases, the firm's reputation was previous to the online experience of potential e-buyers. And this perception determined the attitude by which transactions were either conducted or not. In this case, a good reputation was related to a big size and a renowned brand regardless of whether the e-seller was a "brick and mortar" or an online one. In contrast, small, unknown, and less experienced companies were mistrusted.

(b) Clarity and coherence of online information

Many studies suggest that trust increases as information is perceived as more clear, complete, and coherent by customers. This is because uncertainty is reduced (McKnight *et al.*, 2002a, 2002b; Teo and Liu, 2007; Chen and Dibb, 2010). Yet, this literature says little about what type of specific information is valued by e-buyers, or whether it is useless, insufficient or incomprehensible.

Through the focus groups, customers revealed that their trust was reinforced when detailed and precise information about the products was made available. The wealth of detailed, complete product information online was a clear advantage in contrast to offline purchasing, where it is harder to get these data without the filtering (or bias) of salespersons:

— You see a product and all the characteristics are there, whether it's a heater or a bed: its brand, how long it is. You don't need to ask the salesman. 'Cause if you ask him too much, he'll put a bad face to you (group E).

— Aside from the fact that I can read (the information) many times, in the store they tell it to you only once and, if not, you become a nuisance... The salesperson tells you very general things, but in the internet you get more specifics, point by point (group D).

Note how these remarks contrast the information available online with that offline, where salespersons can be impatient, misinformed, or both. One of the interviewed managers even admitted that "our electronic e-commerce catalog for customers is so complete, that it is superior to what any salesperson can do in the (physical) store". Furthermore, many e-customers looked at the internet and made the purchase in the physical store after confirming that the article was in stock (see the section about the compensatory strategies below).

Additionally, many participants said that online purchases can be more trustworthy because the internet provided more complete and more balanced product information, including both positive and negative comments about the retailers and the products themselves. The experience of other e-buyers was especially valued.

But not all this wealth of information was positively valued. What was considered useful depended on the user's expertise and knowledge about the product: when these were low, participants said they preferred the assistance of a salesperson in order to properly understand and assess the available information. Besides, the impossibility of touching and feeling the products was a common complaint. Some participants explained that through the internet, it was difficult to be sure about the real quality of the goods, even when photographs were available — they could be distorted. The impossibility of touching, smelling, and manipulating the goods restricted the amount of information needed to create trust in the purchase, although this was more related to the product itself than to the store. This problem was especially acute in clothing, perfumes, and electronics.

More complicated was the existence of contradictory information in the website — for example, a different memory capacity of a computer being sold was once published in two isolated sections of the same site. The picture worsened in case of any inconsistencies among the different channels of contact with the client (i.e. website, call center, the physical store, and/or advertisements), especially if a problem arose after the purchase was done. When such cases occurred, which was nevertheless rare (5.5% of complaints analyzed in the complaints site Reclamos.cl in Vela, 2012), trust was particularly damaged.[4] As some retailers operated their own call centers (in contrast to delivery, see below), outsourcing seemed not to be the main reason for this lack of coherence.

Indeed, there are deeper problems of integration between the online operations of the big department stores in Chile and their physical ones. In a previous analysis of the sector, we already noted that some of these huge "brick amd mortar" retailers considered their e-commerce branches as just an extra physical store which came in addition to the existing ones, and ignored most of the specificities and potentialities of the web (Arriagada, 2007). Although this problem should be eventually surpassed as the organizations learn from their experience in B2C e-commerce, a few executives admitted during this study that salespersons in the physical stores resented their own firm's online operation because it diverted the sales commissions they earn per each item they sell (most of the income of salespersons in Chile is based on these variable commissions, over a very low base salary as described by Skoknic, 2008).

On the other hand, all the analyzed sites not only carried very similar information, but also looked very much alike. All included Facebook and Twitter, but these tools were used mostly for promotional purposes and not to interact with clients. These firms kept individualized record of clients, but did not use this information to enhance engagement or trust.[5]

(c) Security of personal data

The literature recognizes this factor as one of the most important ones in trust building (McKnight *et al.*, 2002a, 2002b; Teo and Liu, 2007; Chen and Dibb, 2010). E-commerce requires the user to upload very delicate personal data — national identity number, personal address, and passwords of credit cards and bank accounts.

Focus group participants were aware of the potential security risks of online transactions. Many were not only quite proactive in confronting them but also declared that internet in general and e-commerce in particular were reasonably

---

[4]There were even some isolated testimonies of call center operators ignoring how to proceed with a problem of dispatch, or outwardly blaming their own company for the existing difficulty. Although rare, these inconsistencies were probably highly harmful.

[5]Although not covered by this research due to its legal and technical characteristics, retailers faced another important trust problem due to what was only recently qualified as abusive credit contracts by the courts: As issuers of their own credit cards, some stores unilaterally raised the rates of interest and maintenance costs of their cards without consent of the clients. That was what the records were mostly used for. Yet, this problem has affected retail as a whole, not specifically the B2C e-commerce, so we chose not to include it in our analysis.

trustworthy.[6] Users also mentioned two technical traits of the internet that reinforced their trust: the supposed absence of human error and the traceability of communications and transactions.

> *I first look (...) if data will be transmitted through a secure channel. I always keep a copy of the e-mail confirming the purchase (...). Before pushing the "buy" button I look through all the data at least twice — the address, the e-mail address, the quantity bought. I check, I check all before buying, and afterwards I stay waiting for the mail confirming the purchase. Once it arrives, I say 'I'm at ease, I'll wait until Thursday when it comes home'. If it does not come that Thursday, then I recover that e-mail and I generally call by the phone and I say 'You know what? I am calling for purchase number 72348 which should have arrived yesterday but did not arrive'. That's what I do (group C).*

(d) Post-sales: dispatch and multi-channel integration

When the three previous obstacles to trust are surpassed, a fourth appears after the act of online purchasing: after sales service. Two issues emerged here from the perspective of the customer. The first is the dispatch of the product. The second is the coordination and coherence of the different channels by which the retailer contacts its customers.

Focus group participants reported how trust was reinforced because of positive experiences of dispatch after the online purchase in which the product arrived in one piece and in due time. The managers interviewed were fully aware of the need to satisfy the customer expectation, which combines both implicit and explicit promises. Customers expected the seller to be extremely clear in the conditions of the sale and dispatch, and a fast response in case of any inconvenience that may emerge:

> *— I bought something that did not arrive) so I put a complaint to the store, so they reimbursed me part of the money but that was okay... Those were the rules. I should have read them since the beginning, and I later realized the rules stated they reimbursed the value of the product, not the cost of dispatch (group C).*

Additionally, some participants valued the flexibility of online purchases to choose the moment and place of dispatch, and compared it to its offline counterpart. But many participants reported that Chilean retailers often failed in these aspects: late dispatches and lack of interest on solving any problem that arose after the act of purchase.

---

[6] Credit card fraud in e-commerce purchases is quite low in Chile: it ranged between 3% and 5% of internet users in 2003 and 2008, respectively according to the WIP Chile surveys (Godoy *et al.*, 2008).

To me, they take too long to solve (these) problems and, I you know, I prefer to go to the (physical) store and buy (the product) there. And if it turns to be faulty, I go and return it. Because it's finally much faster (to do it that way) (group B).

A bad experience in an emerging field such as B2C e-commerce in Chile can be particularly harmful in trust-building. In fact, they prevent repeating the experience of purchasing:

— They didn't return a defective product, I experienced that once. That was the only time I made a purchase by the internet. Since then, I kind of don't have too much confidence (group B).

The interviews with e-commerce managers and the analysis of websites and physical stores drew more light on the issue and complemented the clients' perspective. It emerged that the dispatch of goods bought online was outsourced to small freight companies. These were not always well integrated with the retailer's logistics systems due to their lower technological and corporate capabilities. This meant, for instance, that traceability of goods delivered was not possible. Furthermore, delivery could be overwhelmed by high demand. And despite management's preoccupation for complying with the implicit promise of a swift and safe delivery of the purchased good to the e-buyer, there was a widespread notion that as delivery was outsourced, this was "their" problem and not the retailer's own. Yet, customers did not make that distinction.

The picture worsened when the customer faced inconsistent information in the other channels of contact with the seller: the call center and the physical store (which is still highly relevant in Chilean B2C retail).

3.4.2. *Compensatory strategies*

Within these four areas of stress, customers engage actively in surmounting the difficulties that exist. We call these "compensatory strategies" (Godoy *et al.*, 2015). As mentioned, most of the studies about trust and online commerce put emphasis on the unidirectional actions carried out from organizations to potential clients, such as the design of websites and their contents. But, our findings show that e-buyers implement active strategies to collect, process and evaluate information, operate simultaneously in both the online and offline worlds at their convenience, and use their real and virtual social networks to reduce uncertainty in their decision-making, that is, to reinforce their trust towards purchasing. Customers are not only reflective (they learn from their own experience and from those who surround them) but also proactive (they make decisions ahead of time to minimize risks). We can group these strategies into four: selective auto-exposure, informal certification, online/offline hybridization and third-party confirmation (i.e. incorporation of others to their decision-making experience):

(a) Selective auto-exposure

Participants who were intensive internet users and e-buyers found particularly risky the moment in which they uploaded personal and financial information during the whole purchasing process. Therefore, a first strategy to operate confidently was to select favorable conditions under which such self-exposure to risk was made. Precautions ranged from using antivirus, selecting the type of computer used (their own instead of public ones, for instance), taking care to log off from the visited sites, contract credit card insurance and/or limit the amount that can be transferred from credit cards among other mechanisms.

Some strategies were relatively simple: "(I) Do not leave things (i.e. sites) open" (group A), "(You must) have a good anti-virus" (group B), "I block certain pages" (group B), "Do not enter from (a link taken from an) e-mail" (group B). Others, however, require additional services or special arrangements:

> *"I have (a special credit card) insurance. Then, if anything happens, I know I am insured... there is always a risk... (e-commerce) is not 100% sure" (group E).*

(b) Informal "certifications"

A second set of strategies consists of screenings by which the internet user collects information about some aspect of the online world, evaluates it, and "certifies" whether it is reliable or not. Certifying is essentially a cognitive strategy (it requires the collection and processing of information) which, however, may occasionally require physical actions. There are two types of certification: referred to the organization that provides the web page where the article is presented (which we will call "certification of the organization"), and those referring to the intrinsic characteristics of the web page.

Regarding the certification of the organization, the focus groups suggest that users do not trust all organizations in the same way. An organization depends on, in the first place, its corporate reputation (i.e. its pre-existing prestige) and whether it offers an offline support system as a complement to the website. For some participants, the nationality of the shop was also crucial and therefore so was pre-conceptions (or outright misconceptions) about these shops' countries of origin. While buying from North American websites was considered trustworthy, buying from some Asian sites was considered unreliable.

Additionally, internet users are attentive to the certification of the website. This means making sure that the site contains indicators, symbols or other design features considered to provide safety. Some participants carry out the certification based on general impressions of the site that may be not very accurate:

> "I window-shop in three large stores where I buy the most, but the last time I entered the website of (retailer's name withdrawn) not even how the site was built was trustworthy enough" (group C).

Others, however, show more expertise and sophistication in the criteria they use to certify a trustworthy website:

> "I am also attentive to technology, because whenever the time comes to put the credit card number, I look at the icons of the browser I use, (so to) make sure that it is a coded transmission, a secure system" (group C).

(c) Hybridization

A third strategy consists in combining the most reliable elements of both the online and offline realms. Hybridization implies the sociological concept of agency, by which users take actions to modify a relatively immobile structure (e-commerce, in this case). These actions (or agency to modify the structure) imply crossing a border between the two spheres, a border which is physical as well as symbolic. But above all, hybridization implies that even very proficient e-buyers observe the "real", offline world to secure transactions and therefore bridge trust gaps.

We found two ways of hybridization in which customers made a clear distinction between the act of seeking information about a product or service they wanted to buy (window-shopping) and the act of purchase itself. Window-shopping usually comes first, especially for items that are dearest. As shown in Table 3.2, there are two "pure" alternatives, either offline or online (A and B, respectively) in which these two consequential steps are taken separately in any of these realms. These "pure" choices are related to rather predictable factors such as age and income levels. But for the purpose of this article, we will only focus on alternatives C and D, which are the most novel:

Table 3.2. Matrix of hybridization strategies used by e-customers.

	Pure online or offline	Hybrid online–offline
Offline window shopping + purchase	A	—
Online window-shopping + purchase	B	—
Online window shopping + offline purchase	—	C
Offline window shopping + online purchase	—	D

In the hybridization "online window shopping + offline purchase" (alternative C in Table 3.2), the first step is to take advantage of the huge availability of online information about price, brand, and features of the articles considered for purchase. Such information can be sorted easily to compare among products and sellers, an annoying and complicated task in the offline world. In addition, the internet also allows knowing from the first moment if the item is in stock or not. A participant suggested that this possibility allowed him to make more reasoned purchases: "I Google products or pages... I think three times and then I go buying the issue personally" (group G).

Once the right item is selected by the internet, the purchase in the physical store is made. This is necessary to confirm that the information provided on the internet is true, that the product is in good condition, and to prevent delays and problems of dispatch:

"When you go personally (to the physical store), you can be sure that the product is a good one. But if you buy it (online and) comes to your house, and you open it, and (if) all is wrong, you get angry. So to avoid a bad time, it is a good option to go to the store and buy it there" (group A).

On the other hand, "offline window shopping-online purchase" (alternative D in Table 3.2) starts from the assumption that certain information cannot be obtained in a reliable way via the internet and so it is necessary to see, touch and even test the article personally:

"What happens is that in a store you can be sure (about, the product); in the internet they tell you 'pack XX', and you have no idea what it is, or what comes inside" (group A).

This problem is especially acute in some types of goods, mostly electronic, clothing, and large and expensive products. For example,

"I like very much to purchase electronics. Then, when I buy a TV set, I like to see the TV set. I even like to look at the back of the TV, to see how many connectors it has, how many other devices I can plug into to it"(group C).

After the "real" examination of an item, many users buy it online so to take advantage of discounts and other advantages of e-commerce:

"Sometimes I go easily to a store to see the product. And then I go home, see it (in the internet) and if I find it cheaper, I buy it immediately because I have already seen it — even if I have already gone to the store. But I saved those 15,000, 20,000 Chilean pesos" (group A).

(d) Third-party confirmation (Anticipation/incorporation of other people's experience).

The fourth strategy is to collect experiences and opinions of other users about products, websites or shops so as to anticipate any problem that may arise. There are two versions of anticipation, which differ regarding who are these "others" whose experiences and opinions are considered: what we will call the "anonymous third party" of the online world, and the "previously known" from the offline world.

The "anonymous third parties" are other internet users who express their opinions and buying experiences in different virtual spaces, which range from blogs and consumer forums such as Reclamos.cl, the National Consumer Service's website, SERNAC, or some seller's websites (domestic and foreign, such as e-Bay) that are enabled for such purpose. A good or bad reputation among the "anonymous third party" seems to be decisive. In a stark contrast to the real, offline world, in which individuals normally consider only the opinions of those they know personally, in cyberspace, e-buyers are happy to trust the opinions of perfect strangers:

—*"The evaluation (by others) is useful, because when you go to a website like Deremate there is an assessment from all the people who have bought there... You can find a record of how much the vendor has sold, and all the (clients') opinions are there, like 'Hey, you took too long to deliver', 'hey, your product was bad', or 'your product was good'" (group E).*

A second version of this type of strategy is based on the opinions and experiences of buyers that the internet user knows personally, such as relatives, colleagues or friends:

— *"If my dad needs something, he tells me 'find it' and, certainly, we both seek what he needs. And, well, then we purchase it if we find what he wants. But what happens is that, sometimes, they always depend on me to feel confident that what they are doing is OK" (group A).*

3.5. Discussion: Overcoming Blindspots in Chilean Retail

The results discussed above can be interpreted from both sides of the counter within the communications perspective that prevails in this study.

Let us start with the customer, often conceived as the passive receiver of the (commercial) messages delivered unilaterally by the firm. Our analysis confirms that such concept of communication is a grave misconception. Customers are, in contrast, very active in circumventing the difficulties faced when there is a need to purchase goods and services. Trust is stressed in at least four areas of B2C e-commerce transactions, yet users are quite imaginative in seeking mechanisms to reduce the uncertainty existing in those weak spots by means of selective auto-exposure, informal certification, online/offline hybridization, and third-party confirmation. The inherently bi-directional nature of the so-called web 2.0 is undoubtedly helpful, most notably when comparing product information online, as well as when they seek for advice and testimonies from perfect strangers who post their comments in cyberspace. Yet, customers are also keen to integrate and blend the offline and online realms to their convenience, something that sometimes is ignored by technological enthusiasts.

From the perspective of the seller, which in this case is a handful of big, powerful companies, an adequate analysis can be made referring to the concept of blindspots — "the underlying reasons for inaccuracies or flaws in the strategic-making process... (which explain) why analysts often misread the competitive environment and why internal scrutiny can lead to overestimates of a firm's competitive capability" (Fleischer and Bensoussan, 2003: 122). In other words, blindspots are harmful omissions in strategy implementation due to reasons such as corporate inertia, or management obsessiveness in pursuing a certain vision mismatched with reality. In this case, reality would be what B2C e-buyers expect from the e-sellers. In this sense, the most evident blindspots found were inter-channel incoherence (i.e. conflicting information among the website, call centers, physical stores, and advertisements), and lack of integration between retailers and outsourced logistics. While most e-commerce managers perceived delivery as somebody else's problem (they had outsourced this service to smaller and less advanced firms), from the perspective of the customers there was no such a distinction: any problem in the delivery of the products was perceived as a problem generated by the retailer. The situation worsened if a call center operator was either unable to solve the inconvenience or was indolent, or both.

A deeper interpretation of the focus groups and the interviews revealed a third blindspot: Incoherent notions of trust among retailers on the one hand and the customers on the other. In general, the executives declared that the trust relationship with their clients was based on cognitive and rational factors: Essentially, "to comply with the promise" in terms of what is informed in the website about price and product description, as well as the practical conditions of purchase and delivery. Although powerful and indispensable, this concept is not distinctive because all the analyzed sites not only carried very similar information but also looked alike. Furthermore, it ignores aspects of identity and emotional bondage which are increasingly important to generate trust among customers, such as corporate reputation, brand loyalty, and responding promptly and with care any doubts or complaints that may arise. In that aspect, there is indeed much space to differentiate.

This is ultimately related to the concept of communication or engagement with clients assumed by the firm, which can be characterized as rather unidirectional and aggressive, oriented towards sales. Although all websites included Facebook and Twitter, these tools were used mostly to send promotional messages but not as spaces for interacting and listening to clients. And despite some firms keeping individualized records of their clients (all of them are issuers of their own credit cards), this feature was not used to contact them in case of any difficulties that emerged, for instance, at the post-sales level. Furthermore, it annoyed many customers who were spammed with unwanted promotional e-mails.

3.6. Conclusions

From the communication perspective assumed by this chapter, and leaving aside technical and economic factors, we believe that problems of ICT-mediated trust between e-sellers and e-buyers can be an important reason for the relative weakness of B2C e-commerce in Chile. This article has outlined the main areas in which customer trust is stressed in Chilean B2C e-commerce, and how clients manage to surpass these obstacles because the need to purchase goods and services is not eliminated by the existing difficulties. We suggested that these difficulties were related to corporate blindspots affecting retailers, i.e. mismatches between what they do and their environment, in this case represented by the expectations of their clients. We arrived to these conclusions by means of an inductive, qualitative methodology based on principles of Grounded Theory that implied, among other things, interviewing e-commerce managers, focus groups of clients, website analysis, observation of physical stores, and purchasing experiments both online and face-to-face.

Although digital technologies allow processing enormous amounts of data about customers' profiles, expectations, complaints, demands, and consumption patterns, the firms involved (a rather concentrated oligopoly) do not take full advantage of these possibilities. The main reasons lie not in technology, but in failures of communication and engagement between organizations and their main stakeholders — the clients. Important discrepancies of expectations and concepts of trust emerged between the firms and their customers. In general, executives handled a rational and cognitive notion of trust in terms of accomplishing a promise of product features, price, and conditions of delivery. But, this notion was undistinguishable among rival sellers, aside from the fact that the websites themselves were remarkably similar to each other. For customers, this was an indispensable condition but by no means enough. Their trust required aspects of identity and of emotional bondage that went beyond a "cold" description of the terms of sales: they expected guidance, support, and sympathy in case of any difficulty. They found few of that, and resorted to compensatory strategies to reduce the subsequent uncertainty in order to get the demanded goods. From the other side of the counter, firms applied a vertical, unidirectional communication paradigm from a "sender" to a passive "receiver" of information. This explained why retailers ignored the potential of the so-called web 2.0.

But this article demonstrates that e-buyers are not passive subjects. They are instead very active to devise and implement the compensatory strategies to overcome gaps in trust. In other words, the construction of trust is bidirectional from the e-vendor to the buyer and vice versa.

Solving the communication gaps outlined in this article is not enough in itself to foster a radical growth of B2C e-commerce in Chile. There are other problems unrelated to communications that contribute to the relative weakness of this sector, such as low credit card penetration, weak integration of stores with delivery services (normally outsourced to small, fragmented companies), or poor inter-channel coordination. Yet, they shed unprecedented light from the perspective of the customers — often considered as passive receivers of unilateral communication messages delivered by e-vendors — which exceed purely technological considerations.

Acknowledgments

The project "WIP/BIT Chile 3.0: Incidencia de las TICs en la confianza entre personas y organizaciones" was funded by the National Science and Technology Fund Project (Fondecyt) No. 1110098. We also acknowledge the contribution of Paola Langer for her assistance in several phases of this research.

Bibliography

1. Argenti, P (2009). *Corporate Communication*, 5th ed. New York: McGraw Hill.
2. Arriagada, JC (2007). Uso de Tecnologías de la Información en el sector retail en Chile: el caso de Paris.cl (Editado por S. Godoy). Santiago: Business and Information Technologies (BIT) Project — Chile (Proyecto Fondecyt 1050769). Facultad de Comunicaciones UC/Instituto de Sociología UC/Escuela de Ingeniería UC/CETIUC/ Centro de Estudios de la Economía Digital CCS.
3. Bannister, F and R Connolly (2011). Trust and transformational government: A proposed framework for research. *Government Information Quarterly*, 28(2911), 137–147.
4. Bente, G, O Baptist and H Leuschner (2012). To buy or not to buy: Influence of seller photos and reputation on buyer trust and purchase behavior. *International Journal of Human Computer Studies*, 70(1), 1–13.
5. Bryman, A (2008). *Social Research Methods*, 3rd. ed. Oxford: Oxford University Press.

6. Chen, J and S Dibb (2010). Consumer trust in the online retail context: Exploring the antecedents and consequences. *Psychology and Marketing*, 27(4), 323–346.

7. Ceret (2010). Estudio Calidad del Servicio en la Industria del Retail en Chile, tiendas por departamento. Santiago: Centro de Estudios del Retail CERET, Ingeniería Industrial Universidad de Chile. Recuperado de http://www.ceret.cl/wp-content/uploads/2011/01/calidad-servicio-tiendas-por-departamento-version-resumida-ii-april-2010.pdf (consultado march 10, 2012).

8. Creswell JW and VL Plano Clark (2011). *Designing and Conducting Mixed Methods Research*, 2nd ed. Thousand Oaks, CA.: Sage.

9. Fleischer, C and B Bensoussan (2003). *Strategic and Competitive Analysis. Methods and Techniques for Analyzing Business Competition*. Upper Saddle River, New Jersey: Prentice Hall.

10. Fukuyama, F (1995). *Trust: The Social Virtues and the Creation of Prosperity*. London: Hamish Hamilton.

11. Gálvez, M and S Godoy (2011). La brecha digital correspondiente: Obstáculos y facilitadores del uso de TICs en padres, *Tecnología Y Sociedad No. 19*, 7, 199–219.

12. Gefen, D (2000). E-commerce: The role of familiarity and trust. *Omega*, 28(6), 725–737.

13. Gefen, D, E Karahanna and DW Straub (2003). Trust and TAm in online shopping: An integrated model. *MIS Quarterly*, 51–90.

14. Gefen, D and T Heart (2006). On the need to include national culture as a central issue in e-commerce trust beliefs. *Global Information Managment*, 1–30.

15. Gefen, D, RV Srinivasan and N Tractinsky (2003). The conceptualization of trust, risk and their relationship in electronic commerce: The Need for Clarifications, *Proceedings of the 36th Annual Hawaii International Conference on System Sciences*, 2003.

16. Glasser, B and A. Strauss (1967). *The Discovery of Grounded Theory: Strategies for Qualitative Research*. New Brunswick & London (reprint 2011)

17. Godoy, S (Ed.) (2008). *La empresa chilena en la economía de la información: Principales resultados de la segunda encuesta BIT-Chile 2007*, Santiago de Chile: Cámara de Comercio de Santiago/ Facultad de Comunicaciones UC.

18. Godoy, S and E Helsper (2011). La alargada sombra de la exclusión digital: una comparación entre Reino Unido y Chile (junto a Ellen J. Helsper), en *Un mundo conectado: Las TIC transforman sociedades, culturas y economías*, B van Bark (ed.). Madrid/Barcelona: Ariel/Fundación Telefónica.

19. Godoy, S, C Labarca, N Somma, M Gálvez and M Sepúlveda (2015). Circumventing communication blindspots and trust gaps in technologically-mediated corporate relationships: the case of Chilean business-to-consumer e-commerce. *Journal of Theoretical and Applied Electronic Commerce Research*, 10(2), 19–32.

20. Grabner, K (2002). The role of consumers in online-shopping. *Journal of Business Ethics*, 39, 43–50

21. Hardin, R (2004). *Trust and Trustworthiness*. New York: Russell Sage Foundation.

22. Hardin, R (2001). Conceptions and explanations of trust. In *Trust in Society,* KS Cook (ed.). New York: Russell Sage Foundation.
23. Herrera, S, G Lever, A Myrick and M Sepúlveda (2009). *Los internautas chilenos y sus símiles en el resto del mundo: Resultados del estudio WIP-Chile.* Santiago de Chile: Cámara de Comercio de Santiago/ Facultad de Comunicaciones UC.
24. Jarvenpaa, S, N Tracrinsky and M Vitale (2000). Consumer trust in an internet store. *Information Technology and Management,* 45–64.
25. Karimov, F, M Brengman and L Van Hove (2011). The effect of website design dimensions on initial trust: A synthesis of the empirical literature. *Journal of Electronic Commerce Research,* 272–292.
26. Kim, SE (2005). The role of trust in the modern administrative state: An integrative model, *Administration and Society,* 37(5), 611–635.
27. Kim, K and J Kim (2011). Third-party privacy certification as an online advertising strategy: An investigation of the factors affecting the relationship between third-party certification and initial trust. *Journal of Interactive Marketing,* 145–158.
28. Kotler, P (1967). *Marketing Management. Analysis, Planning and Control.* Englewood Cliffs, NJ: Prentice Hall.
29. Kotler, P (2010). Marketing 3.0: From Products to Customers to the Human Spirit.
30. Labarca, C (2009). Capital Social, Confianza y Desarrollo Económico: Hacia un enfoque integrador. *Revista Pozo de Letras.*
31. Labarca, C (2012). The state, market, and cultural norms in Sino-Chilean Relations. Doctoral thesis. Durham: Unbiversity of Durham. http://etheses.dur.ac.uk/3539/.
32. Lee, J, DH Park and I Han (2011). The different effects of online consumer reviews on consumers' purchase intentions depending on trust in online shopping malls: An advertising perspective. *internet Research,* 187–206.
33. Lever, G, A Myrick, J Soto and A Rodríguez (2009). *La economía digital en Chile 2009.* Santiago: Cámara de Comercio de Santiago (CCS).
34. Li, F, D Pienkowski, A van Moorsel and C Smith (2012). A holistic framework for trust in online transactions. *International Journal of Management Reviwes,* 85–103.
35. Luhmann, N (1979). *Trust and Power: Two works.* Chichester: Wiley.
36. Mandelli, A and C Accoto (2010). *Marca e metriche nei social media.* Lugano, Switzerland: UniversitàdellaSvizzera italiana.
37. Mayer, RC, JH Davis and FD Schoorman (1995). An integrative model of organizational trust, *Academy of Management Review,* 20(3), 709–734.
38. McKnight, DH, V Choudhury and C Kacmar (2002a). Developing and validating trust measures for e-commerce: An integrative typology. *Information Systems Research,* 334–359.
39. McKnight, DH, V Choudhury and C Kacmar (2002b). The impact of initial consumer trust on intentions to transact with a web site: A trust building model. *Journal of Strategic Information Systems,* 197–323.
40. McQuail, D (2005). *Mass Communication Theory,* 5th ed. London/Thousand Oaks: Sage.

41. Onyx, J and P Bullen (2000). Measuring social capital in five communities, *Journal of Applied Behavioral Science*, 36(1), 23–42.
42. Patil V and R. Shyamasundar (2005). Trust management for e-transactions. *Sadhana Academy Proceedings in Engineering Sciences*, 141–158.
43. Pestek, A, E Resic and M Nozica (2011). Model of trust in e-transactions. *Ekonomskaistrazivanja*, 131–146.
44. San Martín, S and C Camarero (2012). A cross-national study on online consumer perceptions, trust and loyality. *Journal of Organizational Computing and Electronic Commerce*, 64–86.
45. San Martín, S and N Jiménez (2011). Online buying perceptions in Spain: Can gender. *Electron Markets*, 267–281.
46. Shankar, V, G Urban and F Sultan (2002). Online trust: A stakeholder perspective, concepts, implications, and future directions. *Journal of Strategic Information Systems*, 326–344.
47. Shannon, CE and W Weaver (1949). *The Mathematical Theory of Communication.* Urbana (Ill.): The University of Illinois Press.
48. Strauss, A and JM Corbin, *Basics of Qualitative Research (1998): Techniques and Procedures for Developing Grounded Theory*, 2nd ed. Thousand Oaks, CA: Sage.
49. Skoknic, F. (2008). Los sueldos del retail, el boom que nunca existió. In *El periodismo que remece a Chile*. Abel Gilbert (ed). Santiago, Chile: CIPER, Ediciones Universidad Diego Portales.
50. Tag, TW (Forthcoming). The Role of Trust in Costumer Online Shopping Behaviior: Perspective of Technologu Acceptance Model.
51. Teo, T and J Liu (2007). Consumer trust in e-commerce in the United States, Singapore and China. *The International Journal of Management Science*, 22–38.
52. van Riel, C and C Fombrun (2007). *Essentials of Corporate Communication*. New York: Routledge.
53. Vela, L (2012). Análisis Del Entorno De La Industria Del E-Commerce En Tiendas Por Departamento En Chile Y El Rol Que Juega La Comunicación Estratégica Y Las Tics En La Relación Con Sus Stakeholders Y La Construcción De Confianza. Estudio adscrito al proyecto WIP/BIT Chile 3.0 elaborado por Martha Lizzy Vela Garzona para la obtención de grado de Magister en Comunicación Estratégica. Santiago, Chile: Facultad de Comunicaciones UC.
54. Zand, DE (1972). Trust and managerial problem solving. *Administrative Science Quarterly*, 17, 229–239.

About the Authors

Dr Sergio Godoy

Dr Sergio Godoy holds a PhD from the University of Westminster and a MBA from the University of Exeter in England. He specializes on the business of communications. He is the director of the Doctoral Programme in Communications at Pontificia Universidad Catolica de Chile (PUC).

Dr Claudia Labarca

Dr Claudia Labarca holds a PhD from the University of Durham in England and a Master in Corporate Communication from Universidad Autonoma de Barcelona in Spain. She is an expert on trust in business relations. She teaches at PUC's School of Communications.

Dr Nicolás Somma

Dr Nicolás Somma holds a PhD in Sociology from Notre Dame University in the USA. He graduated as a Sociologist at Universidad de la República Oriental del Uruguay. He is now based in the Institute of Sociology at PUC, where he teaches and does research about public opinion and social movements.

Prof. Myrna Gálvez

Prof. Myrna Gálvez holds a Master in Communication and Education from Universidad Autonoma de Barcelona in Spain and is a Journalist from Universidad Diego Portales in Chile. She teaches Information Technologies and their impact on everyday life at PUC's School of Communication.

CHAPTER 4

PRODUCT, PROCESS, AND PLATFORM MANAGEMENT IN TECHNOLOGY FIRMS

ANGELA HSIAO AND UDAY KARMARKAR

Abstract

In this chapter, we examine the evolving role of the "product manager" in high tech companies. This role encompasses multiple tasks and responsibilities, ranging from market research to process improvement. The role can be complex since it requires communication with many functional groups, including engineering and marketing. We surveyed product managers to determine the typical responsibilities of the role, the main activities involved, and the skills and capabilities that are important success in the job. It appears that the task requires a wide variety of skills, which cut across traditional functional areas. It also appears that often the authority vested in the role is often not commensurate with its responsibility.

4.1. Introduction

Product management in technology intensive companies is a role that varies from company to company, and sometimes even within the same company. A product manager's responsibilities range from making business development decisions to assessing market conditions and designing a service enhancement. The key skill sets required by product managers (PMs) can also differ substantially. For example, building an enterprise system requires a different set of capabilities from developing insights about customers for business to consumer (B2C) products.

In this project, the intent was to determine some of the common roles and responsibilities of PMs as well as identify some of the key skills needed to succeed as a product manager. The project consisted of two portions. We first conducted in-depth interviews with PMs to capture the important features and finer nuances of their roles. Based on these interviews, we created a short survey instrument that included both categorical and qualitative questions. The survey was sent to individuals who were PMs in technology intensive companies. Many of the individuals surveyed, though by no means all, were graduates of the UCLA Anderson MBA program. The survey was done in two rounds, and eventually yielded 36 usable responses. Characteristics of the respondents are summarized in Figures A.4.6 and A.4.7. Selected results from the survey are included in Appendix A (Figs. A.4.1–A.4.5).

4.2. The Product Manager

We note that the term "PM" is something of a carryover from traditional practice in product industries and can be a misnomer. Here, the role that we investigate could often more accurately be called a "Process Manager" or "Platform Manager". In some cases, there is indeed a product being managed. For example, it could be a device like a tablet, or a software product that is sold as such and installed on customer equipment. However, commonly and perhaps increasingly, there is no product as such, but rather a service that consists of software residing on a server that is not bought or installed by a customer. Rather, the customer accesses the server, and uses the service under some business arrangement. Here, the PM actually manages the service process which is largely if not completely instantiated as software. On occasion, the service may take the form of a platform, in that it may connect customers with multiple service or product providers. Or the platform may carry multiple services which can be accessed by some or all of the customers. Even a device, like a smartphone, may really be a carrier of a service, or be a platform for a service bundle.

One major point of difference is that the rate of change in a service process or platform can be much more rapid than a traditional physical product or even a software product. The nature of the management task may be much more fluid in the former case.

For the sake of simplicity, we will hereafter use the term PM as a catch-all term for the job category of interest. We will occasionally also use the term "product" to include products, processes (services), and platforms.

Then, the kinds of companies that we are considering are often described as "high technology" firms. However, strictly speaking, that label is not always accurate. A firm that provides an online service may depend on high technology assets, but may itself be no more than a sophisticated user of these technologies. A more accurate description of such companies might be that they provide products or services that are "technology intensive", often using digital, online information technologies. Again for simplicity, we will simply refer to these as "high technology" or "technology intensive" companies.

4.3. The PM Role

A PM is seen, and sees her/himself as the end-to-end owner of a product. However, the PM typically does not have "profit and loss" responsibility. An immediate conclusion is that there is the potential for a mismatch between the title and real responsibility, and between responsibility and authority. Furthemore, the PM usually does not execute on all the steps in a product development life cycle, or to manage every aspect of the product during its lifetime. Rather, the PM often takes the role of a communicator between all the business units required to take a product from concept to delivery. As one interviewee described it, "the PM is the hub in the middle of a wheel. Each spoke is a different team involved in the product, and the PM sits in the middle". Again, there are obvious conclusions that can be drawn about the potential mismatch between authority and responsibility, as well as the potential for diffusion of responsibility across the PM and team leaders.

To put this into a broader context: in many technology intensive companies, the product or service may require a high level of innovation during its development. Many companies, where this is the case, have gone to flexible organizational structures, and away from traditional hierarchies (Bernstein and Gino, 2014). After release of the product, the pace of change can be quite rapid with the changes themselves often being substantial. Furthermore, the direction of change may be highly unpredictable. The need to adapt the product to changes again means that a traditional hierarchical structure for product management can be counter-productive.

To understand the key skills and activities involved in the role of product management, we map the product management role to the product development life cycle and outline the responsibilities within each step.

Product discovery: During this phase, the PM identifies opportunities and evaluates the feasibility and profitability of the opportunity. Product ideas may come from diverse sources. Senior managers may see strategic opportunities, perhaps including new markets, that fit strategically with the capabilities and competitive positioning of the company. Seeing gaps in the product line, engineering or R&D, marketing, sales or customers. Evaluation methods range from NPV calculations, SWOT analysis, market share analysis to user interviews, and observation. One key capability of PMs at this stage is the ability to understand both the articulated and unarticulated needs of the user, often times through building empathy with the problem the product will solve. Once the business justification for the idea has finalized, the PM moves towards the design stage.

Product design: Depending on the type of product, this step can involve building UI wireframes or working with a design team to create mockups for review. Prototypes or other experiments are also common to express and test ideas. User engagement often continues in this step as many companies pursue tight feedback loops iterating quickly between users and development. Development of user stories and the involvement of engineering for design often feed into a product requirements document (PRD), the most common output of this step.

Product development: This is the stage at which the level of engagement in PMs differs the most across different organizations. Some PMs take on a project manager role working closely to manage schedule and deliverables while others work with designated project managers. During development, the PM maintains a focus on prioritizing and delivering the most useful product to the customer while working within the bounds of resource constraints (i.e. engineering hours, cost). Near the end of the development process, the PM also starts any pre-launch activities such as developing marketing material, conducting user acceptance testing (UAT), and product reviews.

Product launch: Once the product exits development, the product is launched as a service or as a product. If it is a custom development, it would be delivered to the customer. Product launches may be executed as a small beta test used to collect early feedback or a full-fledged launch to the public. Either way, the PM is responsible for analyzing and tracking metrics on product performance. Often, once a product is launched, the PM will continue to develop new features or versions of the product starting the process once again.

Product maintenance: When a PM retains responsibility for the products, he is responsible for various aspects of maintaining the product which range from correcting process problems and malfunctions to improving performance of specific steps.

Product enhancements: Any product (process, service) typically requires continual review, improvement, and enhancements. First of all, it is important to establish a process for product improvements. Many firms have put such processes in place, but many have not. So, it may be necessary to make a business case for the resources that are needed. Enhancements may range from changes similar to maintenance to significant new functionality and perhaps new releases. As part of a PM's role, this can vary in difficulty. If the product is successful enough, it is not difficult to acquire the resources needed to make the enhancements. However, for products which are still in a growth phase or still acquiring an adequate customer base, it may be difficult to find resources. Enhancements are rarely seen as being technically very interesting. If firms do not have a strong process in place, the task of persuasion and negotiation can be tougher at this stage.

4.4. Requirements for the PM Role

In both the interviews and the survey, communication was cited as the most important skill for a successful PM (Fig. A.4.1). This could be communication to key stakeholders such as upper management, communication with customers or cross-functional communication between teams.

A very important set of skills surrounds the tasks related to conceptualizing and defining the product (service process). A key aspect is the statement of technical requirements for the product, often captured formally in a PRD. The process of product development and design includes specifying the functionality to be available, often stated in terms of use cases, or use stories. Related to usability and service delivery are the issues of defining the user interface, and the details of the service process from the user's perspective. PMs may or may not play a role in setting out the technical specifications with regard to how the functional requirements are to be implemented in terms of the platform and process (software). But in the least, familiarity and literacy with respect to the technologies and tools are valuable assets (Figs. A.4.2–A.4.4).

Determining what product to build requires consensus building and persistence. The PM may need to "pitch" the value of the product to justify the project, so strong persuasion skills are also highly valued. Skills in team management are important. Related skills that were mentioned included negotiation and conflict resolution (Fig. A.4.1).

The ability to really understand the value of the product is also very important. We all know about products that seemed to "miss the market" or never took off as expected. It is a difficult challenge to manage, but a correct understanding of consumer expectations and needs is one factor that could help insure the success of a product. This means not only gathering feedback during the product design phase but also through the development process.

The role of product management can be a stressful one as the position requires one individual to "wear many hats". Interviewees described it as "grueling and intense" with the amount of work and number of skills needed to complete the job. However, interviewees also enjoyed the variety of the tasks and skills needed in the position and felt the ultimate reward of seeing a product go from concept to development to launch was worth the effort.

4.5. Summary and Conclusions

The role of a PM in high technology companies in the digital world is a crucial role. At this time, the role as defined in many companies appears to be in a process of evolution. As a symptom, the organizational location of this position can be in marketing, in engineering, or in a separate product organization (Fig. A.4.5). A major issue with the job description and its reality in many companies is that the responsibility and authority that go with the position are not well aligned. In smaller organizations, this may not matter all that much since functional divisions are not that rigid. In medium sized organizations, it is often possible to find champions in senior management who can help with difficult issues. However, in larger organizations, the presence of more formal processes can become barriers if the role of PM is not well constructed and defined. We expect that this role will continue to undergo evolution and refinement, and it is likely that it will be a key position in many high technology firms at a level below the senior management, or Director level.

Acknowledgment

The authors thank Amy Tzu-Yu Chen for assistance in conducting the survey.

Bibliography

1. Bernstein, EF and BS Gino (2014). *Opening the Valve: From Software to Hardware (A)*. HBS Case Study 9-415-015, Boston, HBS Publishing.

Appendix: Selected Survey Results

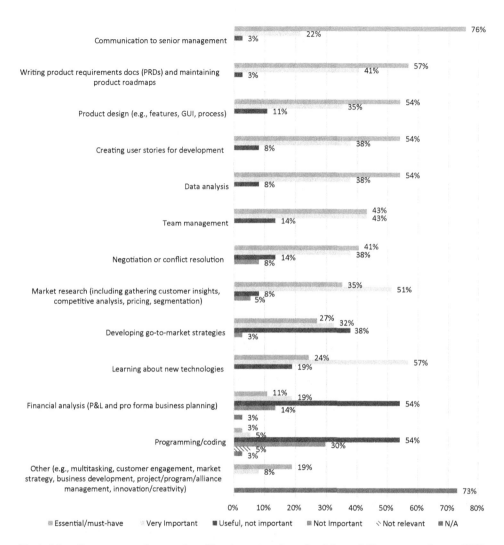

Fig A.4.1.   Responses to the question: How important is each of these skills to your role as a PM?

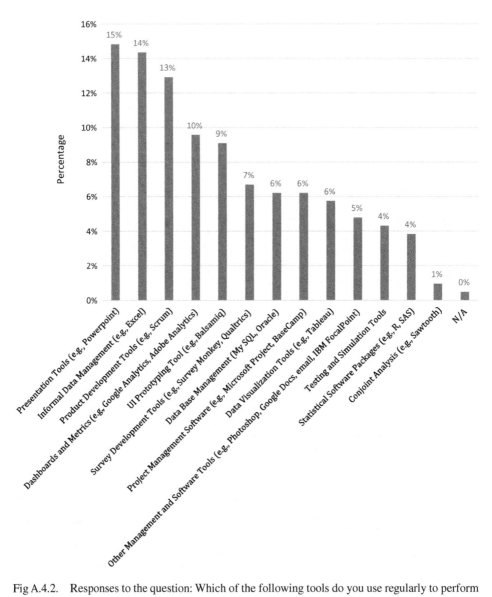

Fig A.4.2.   Responses to the question: Which of the following tools do you use regularly to perform your daily job?

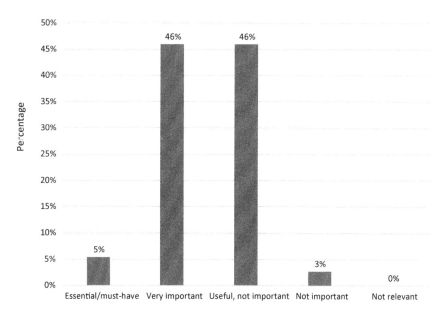

Fig A.4.3.   Responses to the question: How important is a technical background for a PM role?

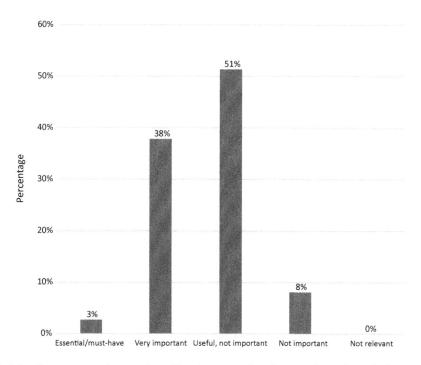

Fig A.4.4.   Responses to the question: How important is prior experience in a similar position important in order to be hired into or to advance into a PM position?

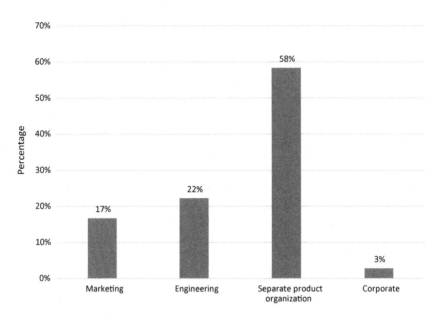

Fig A.4.5. Responses to the question: At your organization, in which department is your role located?

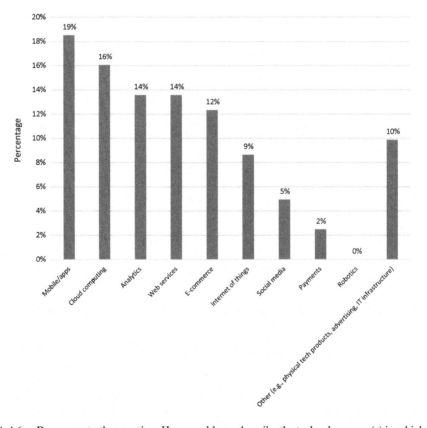

Fig A.4.6. Responses to the question: How would you describe the technology area(s) in which you work? Please choose all that apply.

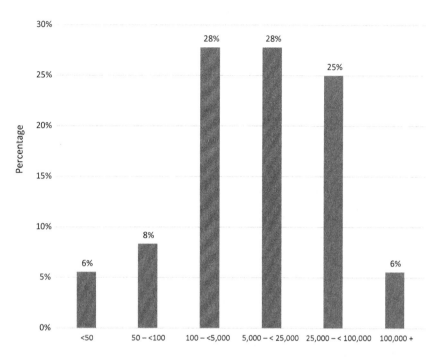

Fig A.4.7.   Responses to the question: How many employees does your firm have in the US?

About the Authors

Angela Hsiao

Angela Hsiao is a 2014 graduate of UCLA Anderson School of Management where she focused her studies on technology and entrepreneurship. She also holds a B.S. in Computer Science from UCSD. She has worked at a number of technology companies including Amazon and Adobe. She is currently a Senior Product Manager at Oracle Corp.

Uday Karmarkar

Uday Karmarkar is a UCLA Distinguished Professor, and the LA Times Chair Professor of Technology and Strategy at the UCLA School of Management. He previously taught at the Graduate School of Business at the University of Chicago (1975–1979) and the Simon School at the University of Rochester (1979–1994), where he held the Xerox Chair in Operations. Professor Karmarkar has published over 100 research papers and articles, has founded two academic journals, and serves on several editorial boards. His research interests include the information economy, service industrialization, technology management, and competitive strategy. He has undertaken projects in technology management, industrial marketing, manufacturing systems, supply chain management, and service strategy with over 50 firms in the U.S., Europe, and Asia. Professor Karmarkar holds a B.Tech. from IIT Bombay and a PhD in Management Science from M.I.T. He served on the Advisory Board of IIT Bombay until 2007, the Advisory Board of the SJM School of Management, IITB till 2011, and is on the Board of Directors of the IITB Heritage Fund (USA). He has received the Distinguished Alumnus and Distinguished Service awards from IITB and the Distinguished Service Award from M&SOM (Informs). He received an IBM faculty award in 2004. He was elected an Honorary Institute Fellow of IITB in 2008, and a Distinguished Fellow of MSOM in 2014. Professor Karmarkar was on the International Council (Ministry of the Economy) reviewing the Digital Strategy for Chile 2008–2010. He has been an Advisor to or Director of several companies in both traditional and new technology sectors.

CHAPTER 5

FACEBOOK USAGE AND PERCEIVED PRIVACY: AN EMPIRICAL STUDY AT A MAJOR ITALIAN UNIVERSITY[1]

THANOS PAPADIMITRIOU AND ALBERTO MARCUZZO

Abstract

The authors investigate Facebook usage by means of data that they have collected using a survey at a Major Italian University. The authors show that usage is unaffected by how long users have used Facebook. The authors also examine a number of plausible determinants eventually showing that age, network size, and perceived usefulness all play an important part in explaining usage. Surprisingly, perceived privacy does not.

5.1. Introduction

The success of any internet site is determined by usage (Anderson, 2009). None more so than for Facebook, the world's largest social network site (SNS). Facebook usage and its implications is a topic of high scientific and social interest. In this paper, we examine how usage is affected by user characteristics (duration of membership, age, friend network size) and perceptions (interestingness,

---

[1] This is a revised and updated version of a previously published work by that has appeared on Volume 5, Issue 1 of the *International Journal of Virtual Communities and Social Networking*.

usefulness, privacy). Perceived privacy is a particularly interesting factor to deci-
pher since on one hand, we see persistent and vocal concerns regarding Facebook's
collection and commercial exploitation of user data (Levy, 2014), on the other
hand, the SNS' growth seems to know no limits. To achieve our goal, we largely
rely on the final year data of a three-year-long study we conducted at a major
Italian University, namely, Bocconi University in Milan.

5.2. Previous Research

5.2.1. *Of network effects and fads*

The brief history of the internet is peppered with episodes of revolutionary products that eventually turned into fads. The obvious point in case is the dotcom bubble of the late 90s. According to Kunz (2008), the ultimate cause of the fatally
inflated valuations of companies such as pets.com or eToys.com was blind trust in
network effects and, in particular, in Metcalfe's law (Shapiro and Varian, 1999),
which in its general form postulates that the value of a network increases more
than linearly (n^2, $n\log(n)$, etc.) with respect to its size. About 10 years after the
dotcom bubble, friendster.com, the world's first general purpose SNS, was first
adopted and then abandoned by users en mass, ending up being called "one of the
biggest disappointments in internet history" (Chafkin, 2007).

While network effects help explain the increase of SNS value as a function of
network size growth, Zipf's law and Dunbar's number point to forces that are actually inversely proportional to network size. Zipf's law (Briscoe *et al.*, 2006) states
that each additional member in any series of items (such as an additional SNS
contact or "friend") has a predictably diminishing value. Offering an evolutionary
psychology viewpoint to the SNS topic, Dunbar (2010) suggests that there is a
cognitive limit on the number of people with whom one can maintain stable social
relationships. The value for that number ranges from 100 to 230, while a middle-of-
the-road estimate, often cited by many authors as "Dunbar's number", is 150
(Gladwell, 2002).

McAfee and Oliveau (2002) indeed point out that Metcalfe's law cannot be
regarded as "true ad infinitum" for there are "forces that put the brakes on network
effects, i.e. saturation, cacophony, contamination, clustering, and search costs".
The consequence, they argue, is that the growth of a network may eventually slow
down as it becomes too large.

However, network effects and their network-size related counterparts described
by Zipf's law and Dunbar's number are not the only factors that affect the fate of
a product. This problem runs deep in the marketing literature where two models
stand out, namely, PLC and diffusion.

5.2.2. *Product life-cycle (PLC) and diffusion*

According to the PLC model, the lifetime sales of a product follow a bell-shaped curve going through five stages: development, introduction, growth, maturity, and decline (Day, 1981). This model is widely used but has some important shortcomings: Many products never get past development and most successful products never die. Moreover, its stages can be further blurred when firms manage to reinvent themselves causing the life cycle to speed up, slow down, or even recycle (Ferrell and Hartline, 2010). Still, the PLC remains popular in the high-tech industry (Grantham, 1997) as it intuitively describes a number of market phenomena including that of a "fad" product, i.e. a product that exhibits a steeply sloped growth stage, a short maturity stage, and a steeply sloped decline stage.

A related but distinct module is "diffusion" that is defined as the process by which an innovation is communicated through certain channels over time among the members of a social system (Rogers, 2003). Innovation adopter categories (the classification of members of a social system on the basis of innovativeness) include innovators, early adopters, early majority, late majority, and laggards. Generally speaking, diffusion encompasses the adoption process of several individuals over time and in Fig. 5.1 we can see how it can be overlaid over the PLC.

Surprisingly, few authors have used diffusion in the SNS context: To our knowledge, only Firth *et al.* (2006) tried to model the diffusion of internet-based online communities to predict final community size and their peak times.

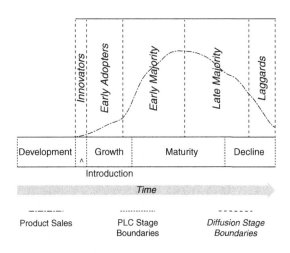

Fig. 5.1. PLC and Diffusion.

5.2.3. *The usage life-cycle*

Porter (2008) put forth the usage life-cycle (ULC) as a model to track the usage evolution of a web application. According to Porter, as time passes, "social web" users go through a cycle consisting of five stages: unaware, interested, first-time use, regular use, and passionate use. In the SNS context, the most relevant and difficult transition is from first-time use (sign-up) to regular (repeated) use, whereby, if users are not motivated by new content or new features, they will not reach the repeated usage stage and, as a result, will use the service less as time passes. The SNS usage distribution through the various ULC stages over time approximates that of a normal distribution. Hence, the ULC establishes a relationship between usage and time.

However, in contrast to the PLC and diffusion models, no academic study has verified Porter's model. Besides, at least one of its assumptions can be easily challenged: could passionate use be the terminal stage of usage? We can't agree with that since using an SNS is actually like using any other product or service: Decline will eventually settle in as it does with other high-tech products (Grantham, 1997).

5.2.4. *Platforms*

Our discussion so far has revealed that existing adoption and usage-related models diffusion are not adequately capturing all the characteristics of an ever-evolving SNS like Facebook.

According to Cusumano (2011), an SNS is a "technology platform" (Cusuman and Gawer, 2002) that facilitates communication. In the case of Facebook, users and application developers participate in the platform by creating content that users consume. Taking this idea further, Suarez (2004) believes that platforms describe a special case technology dominance that is affected by two major groups of factors: firm-level and environmental. The second group of factors is largely exogenous, so we focus on the first one that includes a firm's complementary assets and credibility, installed base, and its ability to strategically manoeuver. Since an installed base is directly tied to usage, exploring the latter becomes a key consideration in assessing the viability of an SNS and its position against other competing SNS or other software services in general.

5.2.5. *SNS usage: Importance and impact*

Boyd and Ellison (2008) reviewed the SNS literature and identified impression management, friendship performance, network structure, online/offline connections, and privacy issues as its main themes. These themes are closely tied to prior (offline) social network literature.

According to Eldon (2010) and Schonfeld (2009), major SNSs generate revenue through brand advertising, performance advertising, and the sale of virtual goods and subscriptions to the "fire-hose" (i.e. access to the full stream of public messages sent within an SNS). These revenue sources are closely tied to continuous active usage. In fact, it is only through continuous active usage — and not just sign-ups or simple occasional usage — that users keep joining the pages of paying companies, keep using third-party applications, keep buying virtual goods, and keep feeding the fire-hose. Moreover, continuous active usage plays another fundamental role. It is the ultimate driver of "friend-generated" content that lends SNSs consistent renewal, relevance, and authenticity.

Pagani and Hofacker (2010) examine the impact of network effects on active and passive usage through usefulness. They find that network size has a positive impact on perceived usefulness (Davis, 1989), which in turn increases passive use (sign-ins) and, to a lesser extent, active participation. Pagani and Hofacker demonstrate that the higher the number of users in an SNS, the brighter its prospects.

Bakshy *et al.* (2012) tell us that while close friends strongly influence the information an SNS user shares, their overall impact is dwarfed by the collective influence of numerous more distant contacts — what sociologists call weak ties. Hence, it is a user's diverse collection of weak ties that most powerfully determine the information that he or she will be exposed to.

The works of Li and Bernoff (2011), Fraser and Dutta (2008), and Fraser (2012) show that SNSs are causing a gradual shift of power from companies to customers, the latter using SNSs to review and rate products and services and — in the process — generating a very potent electronic word of mouth (Dellarocas, 2003; Qualman, 2009; Utz *et al.*, 2009; Trusov *et al.*, 2009).

Hence, it should not come as a surprise that according to research firm BIA/ Kelsey, local media advertising spending on SNSs in the United States will increase from $2.1 billion in 2010 to $8.3 billion by 2015 with similar increases expected around the world (Cheung *et al.*, 2009).

Closing our discussion on SNS usage, it is important to note that we have not come across a study that explicitly examines SNS usage and especially one that examines usage as a factor of long-term viability.

5.2.6. *Facebook conquers the world*

Thanks to the enormous amount of publicity that Facebook has received, its origin and story are already known to many. Yet, before we continue, we think that a concise review of what Facebook has achieved will be useful to both establish its importance in SNS world and to explain why until recently its success and future prospects have been taken for granted.

It took as many as 38 years for radio to reach 50 million users, 13 for television, four for the internet, while it took about three years for Facebook to reach 100 million (Qualman, 2009). On June 30th, 2012 had already reached 955 million users (Facebook, Inc.: FORM 8-K, 2012) and shortly after passed it the 1 billion user mark.

Facebook is the internet's most visited website in many countries around in the world (Alexa, 2014) and in terms of monthly time spent per person, Facebook is the undisputed worldwide leader. In the United States, Facebook users are spending more time on the site than on Google, Yahoo, and Microsoft websites combined (May 2012 — Top Online Sites and Brands in the US, 2012).

Facebook's dominance of the SNS space is overwhelming since 92% of all SNS users in the US use Facebook (Hampton *et al.*, 2011) and has more unique visitors than all the other major SNS combined (Twitter, LinkedIn, MySpace, Tumblr, Google+, and Pinterest) (Lipsman, 2011). Beyond these cumulative figures, finding more information on Facebook diffusion and usage quickly becomes problematic.

Actually, Facebook, that until recently was a privately held company, has insistently resisted all calls to share this or other user-related information with anybody other than its own affiliates. This policy could be now changing though, as Facebook is in the process of creating positive publicity with respect to the extent, depth, and commercial value of the information it holds that is a proxy for its market value (Simonite, 2012).

Despite this amazing run, the anticlimactic fate of previously successful web services (as discussed earlier), coupled with Facebook's recent market troubles (Rodriguez, 2012; Rushe, 2012; Womack, 2012) provide sufficient reason to cast doubt on the latent assumption that Facebook's success will be perpetual (Swift, 2012). Indeed, Facebook growth may taper off well before reaching each and every one of the world's 2.42 billion internet users (International Telecommunication Union, 2011) or, worse, its current users may start using the service less or even drop it altogether.

5.2.7. *Terms of usage and user consent*

Facebook's business model is founded on the monetization of its user data for various marketing purposes including market research and targeted advertising. As a result, a user signing up to use Facebook must agree to the SNS' terms of usage and data use policy (Scherker, 2014). By doing so, a user gives Facebook permission to monitor and track pretty much everything that they do or store on the SNS including their profile, postings, photos, friends, and likes. Actually, Facebook's monitoring policy is so aggressive that it even tracks information that a user "self-sensors" (Das and Kramer, 2013) such as posts that a user types but decides not to post. Some potential or existing users are being put-off but what they consider to be a blatant invasion of their privacy. Actually, a recent survey conducted by a market research firm in Ireland (B and A, 2013) shows that 48.3% of the users that have quit using Facebook did so due to privacy concerns.

5.3. Methodology

We have reviewed earlier three models that show some potential in helping us to better understand Facebook's current state and future usage prospects, namely, the PLC, diffusion, and the ULC. The first two are mature and well understood but are better suited to well-defined products or services and not necessarily to a constantly evolving web service. Indeed, Facebook is constantly reinventing itself. Today's Facebook may well be a different product from last weeks. On the other hand, the ULC is better suited to describe the use of a web service such as an SNS, but has its own limitations, the most important one being the lack of a stage that captures some form of usage decline. Additionally, intuitively attractive as it may be, the validity of this model has not been yet confirmed by an academic study.

Therefore, we cannot directly apply any of the above models to our work. Instead, we focus our efforts to understand which (if any) are the variables that affect usage. In this context, we want to understand if time, in particular, affects usage and if there are any tell tale signs that Facebook is a fad (in the PLC context that we discussed earlier). We use a hypothesis testing methodology on data that we have gathered at Bocconi University. We proceed with presenting our hypotheses and corresponding variables.

5.3.1. *Main variables and hypotheses*

The first hypothesis we want to test is whether Facebook is subject to the usage life cycle or not. The more time has passed since a user first signed-up with Facebook, the more the novelty factor may have worn out and the lesser the user is likely to actively use Facebook. As usage cannot decrease indefinitely, we expect this effect to have diminishing returns.

H_{1a}: *Facebook usage is affected by membership duration and its squared value.*

The second hypothesis we want to test is whether Facebook usage depends on the age of its users. As people with different ages have different lifestyles, it is legitimate to assume they also have different propensities towards Facebook usage. Similarly to membership duration, we expect this effect to have diminishing returns.

H$_{1b}$:   *Facebook usage is affected by user age and its squared value.*

The third hypothesis we want to test is the presence of network externalities. As Facebook is a networking service, we expect its value to increase with the number of its users. We assume this relationship to have a quadratic nature. At the individual level, network externalities are determined by the number of connections established by a user, i.e. by the number of its friends.

H$_{1c}$:   *Facebook usage is affected by the number of friends and its squared value.*

The fourth hypothesis we want to test is the effect of cacophony (information overload) on usage. As Facebook relies on friend-generated content (i.e. content generated by the friends of a user), cacophony should be limited with respect to other scenarios. However, are Facebook "friends" real friends whose thoughts we really care about?

Dunbar (2010) does not agree, especially in the case of users that have hundreds of Facebook "friends". Tokunaga (Tokunaga, 2011) explains that "individuals diverge in how they interpret the meaning of friends on SNSs; some use it to mean mere contacts, others only use friends to refer to people they have met offline, and there are those who apply the term to close friends only." It is hence likely that content generated by the inevitable acquaintances each user has is not noise-free.[2] Consequently, we can expect that

H$_{1d}$:   *Facebook usage is affected by the ratio of real friends over Facebook friends.*

Given its prominent role in the literature in accounting for the adoption and use of several technologies (Pagani and Hofacker, 2010), we want to test the effect of perceived usefulness on Facebook usage with the expectation of finding a positive correlation.

H$_{1e}$:   *Facebook usage is positively correlated with perceived usefulness.*

Finally, we want to test the effect of perceived privacy on usage. As Facebook publicly displays user-related information (such as photos, tags, and opinions), privacy concerns present a major issue that Facebook is confronted with and one that is confusing and annoying to its users (Liu *et al.*, 2011). Accordingly, we expect perceived privacy to have a negative impact on usage: The more the user feels his privacy is threatened, the less likely he should be to disclose personal information, thus using the service less.

---

[2] At the time of publication, Facebook has partially addressed this concern by implementing smart lists that can be used to filter content according to "friend" classification.

$\mathbf{H_{1f}}$: *Facebook usage is negatively correlated with perceived privacy.*

As a means to extend the horizon of our study, we also need to take into account user attitudes towards the future. In particular, do users *expect* to use Facebook more or less a function in the future? Hence, the next hypothesis:

$\mathbf{H_{2a}}$: *Future usage attitude is affected by membership duration and its squared value.*

Formulated in an analogous fashion, our remaining hypotheses follow:

$\mathbf{H_{2b}}$: *Future usage attitude is affected by user age and its squared value.*
$\mathbf{H_{2c}}$: *Future usage attitude is affected by the number of friends and its squared value.*
$\mathbf{H_{2d}}$: *Future usage attitude is affected by the ratio of real friends over Facebook friends.*
$\mathbf{H_{2e}}$: *Future usage attitude is positively correlated with perceived usefulness.*
$\mathbf{H_{2f}}$: *Future usage attitude is negatively correlated with perceived privacy.*

5.3.2. *The survey*

In order to carry out our hypothesis testing, we used data that we have gathered on Facebook diffusion and usage by means of an annual survey for three consecutive years (2008, 2009, 2010). The 2010 survey (or simply "survey"[3]) that serves as the basis of our analysis took place between June 10th and June 30th of 2010 by means of fielding a Qualtrics-based questionnaire (http://www.qualtrics.com) to the Bocconi graduate student population. We received a total of 127 complete and unambiguous submissions. The survey can be found in Appendix A, while a legend of how we matched survey questions with model variables can be found in Appendix B. Some notes on how we put the survey together follow.

When dealing with perceived usefulness and perceived privacy, we reused many of the questions of Pagani and Hofacker (2010) and Flavián and Guinalíu (2006), respectively so as to ensure comparability with their findings. Please refer to Appendix A for a detailed reference of questions reused.

When we asked our survey participants to recall a particular point in time, we helped them give us a more accurate answer by employing an aided-recall technique (David *et al.*, 2009). For example, when we asked them to recall when they had first signed-up to use Facebook, we suggested to them to look at the upload

---

[3]Our initial research interest was to track SNS adoption. By 2010 though, Facebook had already been adopted by each and every participant of our survey, so, we shifted our focus to Facebook usage. One of the co-authors also fielded the survey to a smaller sample at Bocconi in 2011 only to find that opinions had remained virtually identical and hence we opted to mark 2010 as the final year of this data gathering effort.

date of their oldest profile photo since this is generally one of the first things users do after joining Facebook.[4]

5.3.3. *Usage proxies*

With respect to active usage, our base assumption is that what really matters on the internet is attention, i.e. the "currency of the web" as Anderson (2009) puts it. It is exactly when users are concentrated into the SNS's content when they navigate through its pages that they eventually make those clicks that can be converted into money. Accordingly, the ultimate objective of this work is to investigate the determinants of users' attention inside SNS. However, as attention is a rather wide concept, we narrowed it down to "active usage".

Active usage itself is a concept that is subtle to define, let alone to measure. Pagani and Hofacker (2010) write about "active participation" as opposed to "simple use". In their work, what distinguishes active usage from simple use is users' participation, namely the time users spend typing or uploading something into the service.

We adopted a similar approach: We used four different proxies to measure participation and then used a data reduction technique (summated scale) to capture the different facets that define active usage and to overcome measurement errors (Hair *et al.*, 2005).

Four proxies were *Log-ons* (how many times a day users log on to the service), *Minutes* (how many minutes users actively use the service), *Status updates* (how many messages users post during a typical week), and *Comments* (how many comments users leave during a typical week).[5]

What we found is that Bocconi students log-on to the social network at least five times a day, spending about 40 minutes using the service, posting approximately two status updates a week and leaving around nine comments a week. These figures match those that Facebook itself reported during the same period, i.e. that on average its users log on to Facebook every other day and spend roughly 23 hours a month on the SNS, or 45 minutes a day (Facebook Newsroom).

As we can see in Table 5.1, our proxies are significantly correlated with each other, the only exception being log-ons: A high rate of log-ons does not necessarily imply that users use the service more once they have logged on. Accordingly, when reducing data by creating a summated scale we excluded log-ons from the

---

[4] At the time the survey was administered, Facebook had yet to implement the timeline feature which now displays the exact subscription date (A.5.4).

[5] Usage determinants and proxies appears in *italics*

Table 5.1.   Paerson correlations between usage proxies.

	Log-ons	Minutes^	Status Updates	Comments
Log-ons	1	0.117	0.089	0.127
Minutes	—	1	0.400**	0.437**
Status updates	—	—	1	0.676**
Comments	—	—	—	1

**Correlation is significant at the 0.01 level (2-tailed).

process. The final result leads to a statistically significant Active Usage measure as indicated by a Cronbach's Alpha of 0.759.

5.3.4. *Usage determinants*

With respect to the determinants of usage (independent variables), we chose to consider membership duration (H_{1a}), age (H_{1b}), network size (H_{1c}), the ratio of real friends over Facebook friends (H_{1d}), perceived usefulness (H_{1e}), and perceived privacy (H_{1f}).

Age was directly available as one of the questionnaire's items and ranges from 18 to 28. Membership duration (*Duration*), which ranges from 6 to 64 months, is derived from *Subscription date* taking July 2010 as a reference point and is measured in years. Network size is measured through the number of Facebook friends (*Friends*) and spans from a minimum of 48 to a maximum of 1,564 Facebook friends. The ratio of real friends over Facebook Friends (*Friends Ratio*) was obtained by dividing the number of real friends by the number of Facebook friends. Perceived usefulness items (Question 4.1) were summarized into a single factor by using a summated scale. The resulting measure was not reliable in strict statistical terms (Cronbach's Alpha = 0.578). Yet, we elected to use it anyway given that its role has been widely validated by the literature. Similar to *Usefulness*, the items for *Privacy* (Question 4.2) were summarized into a single factor by using a summated scale. This time, the measure is reliable with a Cronbach's Alpha of 0.689.

Finally, we tested for the presence of common method variance, i.e. variance that is attributable to the measurement method rather than to the constructs the measures represent (Podsakoff *et al.*, 2003). We achieved this by performing an exploratory factor analysis and by examining the unrotated factor solution (Harman's single-factor test). We were satisfied to see that the percentage of variance explained by any single factor was 26.8, a value well below the accepted cut-off ceiling of 50.

5.3.5. *Attitudes towards future usage and their determinants*

While fielding a test version of the survey, we had the chance to observe that participants had a great difficulty in using a cardinal measure to estimate future usage. Hence, we opted for an ordinal one ranging from "much less" to "much more" (Question 3.6). Whenever students declare they will decrease their usage in the future, they are said to have a *negative attitude* towards future usage. If instead they declare that they will increase their usage in the future, they are said to have a *positive attitude* and, finally, when they declare they will not alter their usage in the future, they are said to have a *neutral attitude*. In this way, we substantially extended the time horizon of our analysis increasing the membership duration observation window from 64 to 88 months.

Since they are expressed in a non-continuous scale, we could not directly relate attitudes towards future usage to the previously discussed usage determinants by means of an OLS regression. Hence, we had to transform the dependent variable into a dummy variable and use a LOGIT regression instead. *Fut_Attitude* therefore was to set to "1" whenever students express a negative attitude and to "0" otherwise.

5.4. Results

We are now ready to present our analysis and its results starting with some high-level observations on the data we collected.

The resulting sample of 127 respondents has the following characteristics: Gender is almost equally split between males (54% of the sample) and females (46%); age ranges between 18 and 28 years, though the majority of students (69%) are 23 or 24 years old; nationality varies a lot (19 countries represented in total), with Italians having the biggest share (74%). 100% of the survey participants use Facebook and only 41% stated that they also use another SNS. More specifically, LinkedIn is used by 30% of the interviewed students, Twitter by 13% and Myspace by 5%.

From Fig. 5.2, we can clearly see that Facebook diffusion at Bocconi is in line with the bell-shaped pattern of so many other innovations before (Rogers, 2003).

We continue with presenting our usage model and run an ordinary least square (OLS) model to see if our hypotheses are backed up by data. As we found that the requirement about the normality of residuals was not met, we employed the generalized linear model (GLM) methodology to obtain estimates of standard errors that are reliable, and thus usable to test our hypotheses.

5.4.1. *Usage model*

$$Active\ usage_i = \beta_{1,i} + \beta_{2,i}\ Duration + \beta_{3,i}\ Duration^2 + \beta_{4,i}\ Age + \beta_{5,i}\ Age^2\ \beta_{6,i}\ Friends + \beta_{7,i}\ Friends^2 + \beta_{8,i}\ FriendsRatio + \beta_{9,i}\ Usefulness + \beta_{10,i}\ Privacy + \varepsilon_i$$

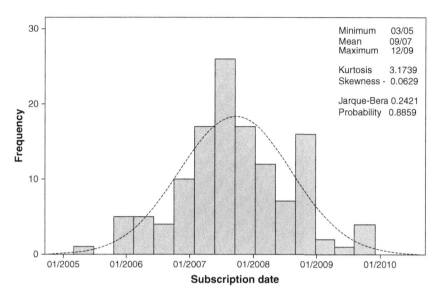

Fig. 5.2. Subscription date histogram.

The results of the two regressions (OLS and GLM) are reported in Table 5.2. Note that the two models lead to the same estimates of coefficients.

5.4.2. H_{1a}: Membership duration

We tested Hypothesis H1a by looking at the coefficients of *Duration* and *Duration²*. Neither one is statistically significant and hence the hypothesis is rejected. We were surprised by this finding since the literature review has pointed to a number of factors that can affect usage and that are directly or indirectly related to time including, novelty, fatigue, network effects, zip's law, and Dunbar's number. We will revisit this issue when we discuss our findings on Hypothesis H1b.

5.4.3. H_{1b}: Age

One can imagine that University students use Facebook intensively. Even more so when they start a new academic program and meet a lot of new people with whom they become Facebook friends. Then, as time passes and pressure for moving to the next academic or professional stage of their life increases, students may have less time to use Facebook. If so, one would expect to find a negative *Age* coefficient whose negative effect should be lessened by a positive *Age²* coefficient.

This time, the regression results endorse Hypothesis H1b: both coefficients are statistically significant and have the expected sign. There is still one problem though: this finding is particularly restricted in scope. If our intuition was right in

Table 5.2.   OLS regression results.

		Active Usage (OLS)	Active Usage (GLM)
Model coefficients	*Constant*	32.27306 (8,313315)***	32.27306 (8,313315)***
	Duration	0.007494 (0.029004)	0.007494 (0.029004)
	Duration²	−0.000246 (0.000422)	−0.000246 (0.000422)
	Age	−2.726995 (0.713600)***	−2.726995 (0.713600)***
	Age²	0.054303 (0.015237)***	0.054303 (0.015237)***
	Friends	0.001898 (0.000932)**	0.001898 (0.000932)**
	Friends²	−1.40E-06 (6.74E-07)**	−1.40E-06 (6.74E-07)**
	Friends Ratio	1.413602 (1.388611)	1.413602 (1.388611)
	Usefulness	0.305747 (0.109433)***	0.305747 (0.109433)***
	Privacy	0.066182 (0.095099)	0.066182 (0.095099)

* Significant at the 0.1 level.
** Significant at the 0.05 level. Convergence achieved after one iteration.
*** Significant at the 0.01 level.

the first place, i.e. that there is increased Facebook activity when people join a new social group, should we not see this phenomenon repeat itself when students graduate and leave the university (and very likely the city it is based in) to continue their career somewhere else? We will address this issue in the user attitudes section.

5.4.4. H_{1c}: Number of friends (network size)

We tested Hypothesis H1c by looking at the coefficients of variables *Friends* and *Friends²*. The literature review and, in particular, the references on Metcalf's law on one hand and Zipf's law and Dunbar's number suggest that the bigger a network gets, the more valuable it becomes, but, up to a point. If so, our regression must yield a statistically significant and positive *Friends* coefficient, as well as a statistically significant and negative *Friends²* coefficient, the idea being that the linear coefficient should be positive because of network effects, whereas the quadratic coefficient should be negative due to the inevitable dominance of cacophony and other related factors.

Indeed, the results confirm our conjecture: Coefficients have the expected signs while their statistical significance at a 0.05 level is guaranteed by their low *p*-values. This is in line with Hypothesis H1c as well as the findings of Pagani and Hofacker (2010) and McAfee and Oliveau (2002).

5.4.5. H_{1d}: Friends ratio (noise-free content)

We tested Hypothesis H1d by looking at the coefficient of the *Friends Ratio* variable. For reasons explained in the introduction, the ratio of real friends over Facebook friends is employed as a proxy for another ratio, namely, the ratio of interesting content over irrelevant content (noise). The idea here being that a higher ratio means more valuable content for users; thus, it should stimulate usage.

However, even though the *Friends Ratio* coefficient is indeed positive, it is not statistically significant, meaning that noise-free content, as measured by *Friends Ratio*, does not have a significant impact on active usage. One possible explanation could be that the concept of a *real friend* is subjective and prone to varied personal interpretations (Tokunaga, 2011) compromising the meaning and value of Friends *Ratio*.

5.4.6. H_{1e}: Perceived usefulness

Previous works (Davis, 1989; Pagani and Hofacker, 2010) have shown that perceived usefulness is a strong driver of new technology usage. It is only reassuring to see that our findings confirm this prevalent view: The coefficient of perceived usefulness (*Usefulness*) is positive and statistically significant.

5.4.7. H_{1f}: Perceived privacy

Our results also do not refute another prevalent belief regarding SNSs, i.e. that privacy concerns are negatively affecting Facebook usage. Yet, this time the evidence is not very strong as there is a negative, but not statically significant, correlation between usage and *Privacy* and usage. Our survey's students are aware of the privacy issues raised by Facebook but are not concerned to the point of limiting its use or abandoning it altogether.

5.4.8. Future usage attitude

Our analysis so far has yielded at least one thought-provoking finding, i.e. that membership duration does not affect usage. We will now see what happens when we extend the horizon by taking into account user attitude toward future usage, or just "attitude" for simplicity.

5.4.9. *Determinants*

This time we use a binary depended variable: Either a user is inclined to decrease their Facebook usage in the future (*fut_Attitude* = 1), or keep using the service at the same rate or higher (*fut_Attitude* = 0). Accordingly, the determinants of attitudes towards future usage are tested by means of LOGIT regression based on the following model.

5.4.10. *Usage attitude model*

$$fut_{Attitude} = \beta_{1,i} + \beta_{2,i} Duration + \beta_{3,i} Duration^2$$
$$+ \beta_{4,i} Age + \beta_{5,i} Age^2 \; \beta_{6,i} Friends + \beta_{7,i} Friends^2$$
$$+ \beta_{8,i} FriendsRatio + \beta_{9,i} Usefulness + \beta_{10,i} Privacy + \varepsilon_i.$$

The results of the LOGIT regression are reported in Table 5.3.

5.4.11. H_{2a}: *Membership duration*

In line with our previous findings, the effect of membership duration on attitude towards future usage is negligible. Hypothesis H2a must also be rejected. Once again, we do not see any relationship between membership duration and usage, let alone a clear sign of steep usage decline that would point to the possibility of Facebook being a fad.

5.4.12. H_{2b}: *Age*

In the case of age, the regression coefficients have the expected sign, but their overall effect on attitude towards future usage is not as definitive as we would have wished with *p*-values slightly above 0.10. One possible explanation is that whereas *Active Usage* captures several aspects of active usage, *fut_Attitude* does not. At the end, given the H2a result, we have decided to accept H2b, i.e. that age has a decreasing negative effect on active usage and future usage. In a future work, it would be interesting to explore if at a certain age or life stage users stop using the service or arrive to a stable, yet less intensive, usage.

Another issue worth exploring in the future could be to understand the cause of lack of correlation between usage and membership duration on one hand, and the presence of correlation between usage and age on the other. After all, time is the ultimate determinant in both cases.

Table 5.3. LOGIT regression results for Eq (4).

		fut_Attitude
Coefficients	*Constant*	−47.58547
		(34.13015)
	Duration	−0.270475
		(1.249022)
	Duration^2	0.140837
		(0.230739)
	Age	4.584313
		(2.932534)
	Age^2	−0.098571
		(0.061898)
	Friends	−0.002002
		(0.003671)
	Friends^2	2.85E−06
		(3.04E−06)
	Friends Ratio	−14.34805
		(6.060970)**
	Usefulness	−0.775920
		(0.403154)*
	Privacy	−0.652990
		(0.358513)*
Model statistics	LR-Statistic	23.15786
		Prob. = 0.005851
	Mc-Fadden R2	0.156931

* Significant at the 0.1 level.
** Significant at the 0.05 level.
*** Significant at the 0.01 level.

5.4.13. H_{2c}: Number of friends (network size)

In contrast to H1c, here the evidence that network effects have a fading positive effect as the network size grows is weak: although demonstrating some level of fit[5], the network size coefficients *Friends* and *Friends*^{2} are not statistically significant even at a 0.10 level. In other words, students do not appear to consider the size of their social network when they are asked to think about their future usage pattern. This is not entirely surprising since they may be — at least partially — unaware of the forces that come into play (Metcalf's and Zipf's laws as well as Dunbar's number and other factors of cacophony). In any event, we have to reject

H2c and note that additional research will be needed to resolve the dissonance with our H1c findings.

5.4.14. H_{2d}: Friends ratio (noise-free content)

The *Friends Ratio* coefficient is negative and significant, i.e. as Facebook friends gradually outnumber real friends, the ratio of valuable content over available content in the news feed decreases and users will be more inclined to decrease their usage in the future (negative attitude).

To explain why this trend is present in attitudes but not in current usage, we offer two possible explanations: Participants may indeed change their usage patterns in the future, thus giving importance to factors previously ignored, or, there may be a difference between what they think they will do and what they actually do. We think that the latter is more likely, as the former would indicate statistical correlation between *Friends_Ratio* and time that is not present in the data.

5.4.15. H_{2e}: Perceived usefulness

Perceived usefulness turns out to be a pretty influential determinant of attitude towards future usage, though its coefficient can be regarded as significant only at the 0.10 level. Still, the more students perceive Facebook to be useful, the less likely they are to have a negative attitude toward future usage. By combining this finding with the one on active usage, we can reasonably claim that usefulness is a good predictor of consumer acceptance (and usage) of new technologies.

5.4.16. H_{2e}: Perceived privacy

The last factor we analyzed is *privacy*. The negative and significant (at the 0.10 level) *Privacy* coefficient of the LOGIT regression suggests that the more students perceive their privacy to be safeguarded, the less likely they are to embrace a negative attitude towards future usage.

Yet, why is privacy a determinant for future usage attitude and not for current usage? Once more, it may be the case that what students actually do diverges from what they *think* they will do. The data indicates that students think that they will decrease their usage if they believe that their privacy will be threatened in future. In practice though, they continue using Facebook regardless of their privacy concerns.

5.4.17. Discussion

In this work, we have made several advancements along the research path pioneered by Pagani and Hofacker (2010) including that Facebook usage is determined by the age of its users, the size of their personal networks, the relative abundance of noise-free content, and its perceived usefulness. It does not depend on how students perceive their privacy to be safeguarded.

What do these findings imply for Facebook? We think the issue with user age is important. Facebook is a complex product with many attributes that collectively define its value proposition. Understanding how the appeal of these attributes changes with user age can open the window for a product that is more tailor-made. For example, Facebook could offer a set of predefined set of usage options to its users according to their stated age and interests.

We also think that Facebook would benefit if it would allow its users to easily filter and sort their friends according to a number of attitudes including when they befriended them.[6] For many users, it is not the 500th Facebook friend that matters the most but some of the earliest ones, maybe the first 20 or so. Such filters would allow users to better shield themselves from cacophony and usage fatigue.

Finally, probably the most counter-intuitive finding from the work is that actually Facebook does not need to substantially change the way it handles privacy despite the negative publicity that the issue has raised.[7]

5.4.18. *Limitations and future research*

The two main limitations of our work are data scope and data quality. Scope is really a question of resources and for a product with such worldwide appeal such as Facebook, any reasonable research effort will be limited in scope one way or another (excluding the work of Facebook's own data analysis group). We thought that our choice does provide valuable insight with respect to a very active population within the Facebook community. After all, Facebook started out in a University environment and student preferences had a formative and long-lasting effect to both its product features and overall approach (Kirkpatrick, 2010).

As far as data quality is concerned, with the benefit of hindsight, more robust proxies could have been chosen. This is particularly true with reference to noise-free content. Furthermore, the greatest leap in data quality could be reached by using first-hand data, namely, by directly accessing Facebook's internal statistics (Lewis *et al.*, 2008), or — if Facebook allows it — by independently fielding a Fabebook App that will ask permission from its users to access their data.

We also believe that significant research opportunities lie ahead in the study of effective web advertising within the realm of an SNS and Facebook in particular. For example, following the approach of Wang *et al.* (2009), one could

---

[6] The current smart list feature is very basic and non-parametrical in any fashion.
[7] As Sun's Scott McNealy famously said in response to a journalist's question back in 1999: "You have zero privacy anyway. Get over it." How true this sounds today in the context of our survey.

investigate the effectiveness of SNS advertising with respect to ad variation, message appeal, and goal directedness.

Finally, an important opportunity lies ahead in the general context of web services. The classic PLC model is not specific enough to capture the nuances of an evolving web service. In this respect, the ULC can provide us with future direction: The rate in which users adopt or drop a web service (including an SNS) has to be directly related to the level of its user population engagement.

5.5. Conclusion

Facebook was adopted by Bocconi students in a truly contagious manner. In spite of this, it is not a fad. Whereas fads go out of fashion as time passes, Facebook at Bocconi is not going out of fashion, at least not now or in the immediate future.

The survey draws a rather optimistic picture about Facebook usage at Bocconi University: Not only are students using it a lot, but their usage does not depend on membership duration as the analyses of active usage and attitudes towards future usage have shown: repeated usage does not result in boredom or indifference, but rather has become a habit.

Facebook is not a static immutable product, but an evolving platform that continuously transforms the user's experience. So far, Facebook has managed to change its interface every year, add new features every month, and incentivize external developers to create new applications every day. In effect, Facebook releases new versions of its product continuously and, as a result, manages to maintain a high degree of involvement across all levels of its user population.

Bibliography

1. (n.d.). Facebook Newsroom: http://newsroom.fb.com/ [May 21, 2012].
2. Alexa (2014). http://www.alexa.com/siteinfo/facebook.com [August 15, 2012].
3. Anderson, C (2009, January 31). *The economics of giving it away.* http://online.wsj.com/article/SB123335678420235003.html [January 12, 2015].
4. B and A, E (2013). *Household Sentiment Survey.* Behaviour & Attitudes.
5. Bakshy, E, I Rosenn, C Marlow and L Adamic (2012). The role of social networks in information diffusion. In *Proceedings of ACM WWW 2012, April 16–20, Lyon, France.* New York: ACM.
6. Boyd, DM and N Ellison (2008). Social networks sites: Definition, history and scholarship. *Journal of Computer-Mediated Communication,* 13(1), 210–230.
7. Briscoe, B, A Odlyzko, and B Tilly (2006, July). Metcalfe's Law is Wrong. *IEEE Spectrum,* 43(7), 26–31.

8. Chafkin, M (2007). How to kill a great idea!, from Chafkin, M (2007). How to kill a great idea! Inc. Magazine. http://www.inc.com/magazine/20070601/features-how-to-kill-a-great-idea.html [August 27, 2007].

9. Cheung, M, C Luo, L Choon and H Chen (2009). Credibility of electronic word-of-mouth: informational and normative determinants of online consumer recommendations. *International Journal of Electronic Commerce*, 13(3), 9–38.

10. Cusuman, M and A Gawer (2002). *Platform Leadership: How Intel, Microsoft, and Cisco Drive Industry Innovation*. Boston: Harvard Business School Press.

11. Cusumano, M. (2011, April). Platform Wars Come to Social Media. *Communications of the ACM*, 54(4).

12. Das, S and A Kramer (2013). Self-censorship on Facebook. In *Proceedings of the Seventh International AAAI Conference on Weblogs and Social Media*, 120–27.

13. David, AA, V Kumar, GS Day and R Leone (2009). *Marketing Research*, 10th ed. New York: Wiley.

14. Davis, FD (1989). Perceived usefulness, perceived ease of use and user acceptance of information technology. *MIS Quarterly*, 13(2), 319–339.

15. Day, GS (1981). The product life cycle: Analysis and applications issues. *Journal of Marketing*, 45, 60–67.

16. Dellarocas, C (2003). The digitization of word-of-mouth: promise and challenges of online reputation systems. *Management Science*, 49(10), 1407–1424.

17. Dunbar, R (2010). *How Many Friends Does One Person Need?: Dunbar's Number and Other Evolutionary Quirks*. Harvard: Harvard University Press.

18. Eldon, E (2010, March 2). *Facebook Revenues Up to $700 Million in 2009, On Track Towards $1.1 Billion in 2010*. http://www.insidefacebook.com: http://www.inside-Facebook.com/2010/03/02/Facebook-made-up-to-700-million-in-2009-on-track-towards-1-1-billion-in-2010/ [December 3, 2015].

19. *Facebook, Inc.: FORM 8-K*. (2012, 7 26). http://secdatabase.com/: http://pdf.secdatabase.com/700/0001193125-12-316895.pdf [July 26, 2012].

20. Ferrell, O and M Hartline (2010). *Marketing Strategy*, 5th ed. USA: South-Western College Pub.

21. Firth, D, C Lawrence and SF Clouse (2006). Predicting internet-based online community size and time to peak membership using the Bass model of new product growth. *Interdisciplinary Journal of Information, Knowledge and Management*, 1, 1–12.

22. Flavián, C and M Guinalíu (2006). Consumer trust, perceived security and privacy policy. *Industrial Management and Data Systems*, 106(5), 601–620.

23. Fraser, M (2012, 6 20). *Geopolitics 2.0: The Power of Social Media*. http://www.throwing-sheep.com/blog/?p=36.

24. Fraser, M and S Dutta (2008). *Throwing Sheep in the Board Room: How Online Social Networking will Transform your Life, Work and World*. New York: Wiley.

25. Gladwell, M (2002). *The Tipping Point: How Little Things Can Make a Big Difference*. New York: Back Bay Books.

26. Grantham, LM (1997). The Validity of the Product Life Cycle in the High-tech Industry. *Marketing Intelligence and Planning*, 15(1), 4–10.

27. Hair, JF, B Black, B Babin, RE Anderson and RL Tatham (2005). *Multivariate Data Analysis*, 6th ed. Upper Saddle River, New Jersey: Prentice Hall.
28. Hampton, KN, L Sessions Goulet, L Rainie and K Purcell (2011). *Social Networking Sites and Our Lives*. Pew Research Center's Internet & American Life Project: Pew Research Center.
29. International Telecommunication Union (2011). *Key Global Telecom Indicators for the World Telecommunication Service Sector.* http://www.itu.int/ITU-D/ict/statistics/at_glance/KeyTelecom.html [July 10, 2012].
30. Kirkpatrick, D (2010). *The Facebook Effect: The Inside Story of the Company That Is Connecting the World.* New York: Simon & Schuster.
31. Kunz, B (2008, August 18). *The trouble with Twitter.* Retrieved from Bloomberg: http://www.bloomberg.com/bw/stories/2008-08-18/the-trouble-with-twitterbusiness-week-business-news-stock-market-and-financial-advice.
32. Levy, A (2014). http://www.cnbc.com/id/102138902#.
33. Lewis, K, J Kaufman, M Gonzalez, A Wimmer and N Christakis (2008). Tastes, ties, and time: A new social network dataset using Facebook.com. *Social Networks*, 30, 330–342.
34. Li, C and J Bernoff (2011). *Groundswell: Winning in a World Transformed by Social Technologies* (Expanded and Revised ed.). Boston, MA: Harvard Business Review Press.
35. Lipsman, A (2011). http://blog.comscore.com/2011/12/state_of_the_us_social_networking.html.
36. Liu, Y, KP Gummadi, B Krishnamurthy and A Mislove (2011). Analyzing facebook privacy settings: User expectations vs. reality. *ACM SIGCOMM Conference on Internet Measurement Conference (IMC '11)*, 61–70.
37. *May 2012 — Top Online Sites and Brands in the U.S.* (2012, June 22). Retrieved from Nielsenwire: http://blog.nielsen.com/nielsenwire/online_mobile/may-2012-top-u-s-web-brands-and-news-websites/ [December 3, 2014].
38. McAfee, A and FX Oliveau (2002). Confronting the limits of networks. *MIT Sloan Management Review*, 43(3), 85–87.
39. Pagani, M and C Hofacker (2010). Use and participation in virtual social networks: a theoretical model. *International Journal of Virtual Communities and Social Networking*, 2(1), 1–17.
40. Podsakoff, PM, SB MacKenzie, JY Lee and NP Podsakoff (2003). Common Method Biases in Behavioral Research: A Critical Review of the Literature and Recommended Remedies. *Journal of Applied Psychology*, 88(5), 879–903.
41. Porter, J (2008). *Designing for the Social Web.* San Francisco: New Riders (Pearson).
42. Qualman, E (2009). *Socialnomics.* New York: Wiley.
43. Rodriguez, S (2012). Facebook's advertising growth slowed down a lot in the last year. *LA Times*.
44. Rogers, EM (2003). *Diffusion of Innovations*, 5th ed. Free Press.
45. Rushe, D (2012). Facebook shares fall below $30 as US authorities begin investigation into IPO. *The Guardian*.
46. Scherker, A (2014, July 23). *Didn't Read Facebook's Fine Print? Here's Exactly What It Says.* Retrieved from The Huffington Post: http://www.huffingtonpost.com/2014/07/21/facebook-terms-condition_n_5551965.html.

47. Schonfeld, E (2009). *Get Ready For The Firehose. Search Is About To Get Realtime, Real Fast.* http://techcrunch.com: http://techcrunch.com/2009/10/21/get-ready-for-the-firehose-search-is-about-to-get-realtime-real-fast/.

48. Shapiro, C and H Varian (1999). *Information Rules.* Boston, MA: Harvard Business School Press.

49. Simonite, T (2012). What Facebook knows. *Technology Review.*

50. Suarez, FF (2004). Battles for technological dominance: An integrative framework. *Research Policy*, 33, 271–286.

51. Swift, M (2012). Facebook shows relentless global growth. *San Jose Mercury News.*

52. Tokunaga, RS (2011). Friend me or you'll strain us: Understanding negative events that occur over social networking sites. *Cyberpsychology, Behavior, and Social Networking*, 14(7–8), 425–432.

53. Trusov, M, RE Bucklin and K Pauwels (2009). Effects of word-of-mouth versus traditional marketing: Findings from an internet social networking site. *Journal of Marketing*, 73(5), 90–102.

54. Utz, S, U Matzat and C Snijders (2009). Online reputation systems: The effects of feedback comments and reactions on building and rebuilding trust in on-line Auctions. *International Journal of Electronic Commerce*, 13(3), 95–118.

55. Wang, K, ET Wang and CK Farn (2009). Influence of web advertising strategies, consumer goal-directedness, and consumer involvement on web advertising effectiveness. *International Journal of Electronic Commerce*, 13(4), 67–95.

56. Womack, B (2012). *Facebook Audience Growth Slows To 5%, ComScore Reports.* http://www.bloomberg.com: http://www.bloomberg.com/news/2012-06-11/facebook-audience-growth-slows-to-5-comscore-reports.html [August 6, 2012].

Appendix A

The 2010 questionnaire administered to Bocconi University students follows:

(1)

1.1. Do you use Facebook?
☐ yes   ☐ no   ☐ I am not a member anymore

1.2. Do you use other social networks? Please indicate which ones
☐ I use only Facebook   ☐ Twitter   ☐ Myspace   ☐ LinkedIn

(2)

2.1. When did you first join Facebook (month/year)?
A hint: have a look at your profile pictures. Chances are that the oldest one was uploaded when you joined!

_____

2.2. How many friends do you have on Facebook?
Please, read it directly from our Facebook profile.

_____

(3)

3.1. On average, how many times a day do you log on to Facebook?

_____

3.2. On average, how many minutes a day do you spend actively using Facebook?

_____

3.3. On average, how many status updates do you post in a week?

_____

3.4. On average, how many comments do you make in a week?

_____

3.5. Compared to now, how much time do you think you will spend using Facebook two years from now?
Before answering, just take a second to imagine what you will be doing in two years!
☐ Much less   ☐ A bit less   ☐ Roughly the same   ☐ A bit more
☐ Much more

(4)

4.1. Please, express the extent to which you agree with the following sentences (1 = Strongly disagree, 5 = Strongly agree).

Facebook allows me to keep friends even if I have little time. (*)	1	2	3	4	5
Facebook allows me to get over my shyness. (*)	1	2	3	4	5
Facebook allows me to know more people than I could know without it. (*)	1	2	3	4	5
Facebook allows me to meet people with the same interests as mine. (*)	1	2	3	4	5
Facebook allows me to hide my personal defects. (*)	1	2	3	4	5
I find Facebook very useful. (*)	1	2	3	4	5

*Questions taken from (Pagani and Hofacker, 2010).

4.2. Please, express the extent to which you agree with the following sentences (1 = Strongly disagree, 5 = Strongly agree).

I think Facebook shows concern for the privacy of its users. (*)	1	2	3	4	5
I feel safe when I send personal information to Facebook. (*)	1	2	3	4	5
I think Facebook only collects user personal data that are necessary for its activity. (*)	1	2	3	4	5
Facebook does not send e-mail advertising without the user's consent. (*)	1	2	3	4	5
I think that Facebook will not provide my personal information to other companies without my consent. (*)	1	2	3	4	5
On Facebook, I know for sure what information about myself is public, and which one is visible only by my friends.	1	2	3	4	5
On Facebook, I feel in control of what information gets published on my wall (e.g., when people post on my wall or tag me).	1	2	3	4	5

* Questions taken from (Pagani and Hofacker, 2010).

(5)

5.1. Nationality

_____

5.2. Age

_____

5.3. Gender
☐ Male   ☐ Female

5.4. How many close friends would you say you have?
In other words, with how many people have you enough confidence to talk about your problems? Similarly, for how many people would you always find a couple of minutes to talk?

_____

Appendix B

The purpose of the following legend is to assist the reader to relate Facebook usage variables of interest with the questions of the 2010 survey.

Table A.5.4.   Variables and questions.

Variable	Origin
Subscription Date	Question 2.1
Log-ons	Question 3.1
Minutes	Question 3.2
Status Updates	Question 3.3
Comments	Question 3.4
Active Usage	Refer to the Usage Proxies Section
Duration	Refer to the Main Variables & Hypotheses Section
Age	Question 5.2
Friends	Question 2.2
Friends Ratio	Question 5.4 over Question 2.2
Usefulness	Summated scale of Question 4.1 items
Privacy	Summated scale of Question 4.2 items
Female	Question 5.3
Italian	Question 5.1

About the Authors

Thanos Papadimitriou

Thanos Papadimitriou is an SDA Professor at SDA Bocconi in Milan. He has received a PhD from UCLA Anderson in 2004 (with the aid of an Alexander S. Onassis Scholarship), an MS from UCLA in 1993, and a BS from MIT in 1992. His current research interests fall in the intersection of Operations, Information Systems, and Entrepreneurship. He has published on VLDB, ICDE, IJRDM, IJVCSN, IJPR, and on various trade journals. In addition to his academic activities, Professor Papadimitriou possesses considerable industry experience currently serving as the Managing Partner of mbriyo.

Alberto Marcuzzo

Alberto Marcuzzo is a Consultant at Bain & Company in Milan. He received his BS in 2008 and MS (with distinction) in 2010 at Bocconi University in Milan. He is interested in social media and their business applications.

CHAPTER 6

INTERACTION EFFECTS ANALYSIS OF PRODUCT–SERVICE SYSTEM BY CHOICE-BASED CONJOINT ANALYSIS

JINMIN KIM, KWANGTAE PARK, HOSUN RHIM
AND SUNG YONG CHOI

Abstract

Companies are developing new product or new service, and combining the existing product and service to meet the customer's needs. Product–service system (PSS) is a field where the products and services are combined to improve consumers' satisfaction. Well-integrated PSS enables to increase the utilization of the product and the service, so it can give higher level of consumer satisfaction.

Mobile communications market is a prime example of the PSS. South Korea's telecommunications market develops rapidly nowadays, and many consumers are taking advantage of the latest communication technologies, such as smart phone utilization.

We investigate the product–service interaction effects in South Korea's mobile phone service industry using Choice-based conjoint analysis (CBCA). We measure main and interaction effects of product and service integration. We collected a sample of size 171 from a college student group in Seoul, Korea. We find the positive interaction effects of product and service integration and show the direction of PSS strategy using main and interaction effect.

6.1. Introduction

In the modern economy, companies have placed more competitive environment than in the past. Competition with other firms in the market is becoming increasingly fierce, and consumers want even more requirements. Achieving sustainable growth to survive in this market has become very difficult. Companies are developing new product or new service, and to survive, they combine the existing product and the existing service to correspond to the needs of customers. Product–service system (PSS) is a field that combines the products and services that enable consumers to be satisfied.

Mobile communications market is a prime example of the PSS. South Korea's telecommunications market develops rapidly nowadays, and many consumers are taking advantage of the latest communication technologies, such as smart phone utilization. But, the growth has been slowing gradually, and thus, survival of each enterprise is becoming more intense. In the initial communication market, the choice of the consumer was dependent upon the brand of the manufacturer and the communication service. However, recently, the gap of performance is reduced, so consumers want new contentware and companies need a new marketing strategy to meet the needs of the customers.

Well-integrated PSS enables to increase the utilization of the product and the service, so it can give more satisfaction to the consumer. Instead of simply adding products and services, successful PSS strategy can create synergy effects by combining the value of products and services. That is, a combination of products and services should induce positive interaction, and will be able to bring greater satisfaction to the consumer.

In this research, we will attempt to demonstrate the effect of the PSS on the communication market, and introduce a product innovation strategy of enterprises. This paper is organized as follows. In Sec. 6.2, we will review the literature of the PSS and introduce CBCA. Section 6.3 describes the research model and analysis method. Section 6.4 presents the analysis result and the last chapter summarizes this study, and presents limitations and future research directions.

6.2. Literature Review

6.2.1. *PSS*

PSS is one of the strategies to meet what consumers want by combining products and services together (Goedkoop *et al.*, 1999). PSS initiated a strategic approach to service innovation in order to respond to the growing needs of consumers and has become an important strategy that companies have to try (Baines *et al.*, 2007). In

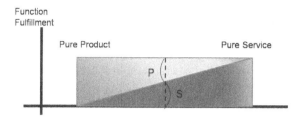

Fig. 6.1. The combination ratio of product and service (Baines *et al.*, 2009b).

about 15 years ago, the concept of the PSS was defined, and it is used as one of the company's strategies and has been developed (Goedkoop *et al.*, 1999; Manzini and Vezzoli, 2003).

Baines *et al.* (2009a) have studied the literature on the servitization utilized in the manufacturing and organized eight key information about the servitization. Servitization is a part of PSS and the innovation of organization and process. This innovation means that the change can deliver the integrated products and services that can increase customers' value. Eventually, manufacturers will be able to improve revenues through the use of competitive strategies based on the service. Baines *et al.* (2009b) analyzed a process model for the servitization, and summarized the challenges of the strategy to take advantage of the service from the manufacturers. Gebauer *et al.* (2012) studied the literature to help to perform a service strategy for the manufacturing firms. In this paper, they argued for the necessity of an integrated manufacturing strategy through the service of leverage to improve the financial performance.

PSS is to deliver new products to customers by integrating the properties of the products and services in one. P refers to the proportion of product attributes and S the proportion of service in Fig. 6.1. The proportion ratio can be varied by customers' needs (Goedkoop *et al.*, 1999). This means that a company can make a different access based on the configuration of the desired product of the consumer. So, a company can quickly respond to the needs of customers. Accordingly, by utilizing various attributes of products and services, the PSS strategy makes it possible to take advantage in various ways that each consumer wants (Alix *et al.*, 2009; Halen *et al.*, 2005; Mont and Tukker, 2006; Stoughton and Votta, 2003).

6.2.2. *CBCA*

Conjoint analysis refers to a method of mathematical analysis by representing the preference of the consumer with respect to the various properties to the utility function (Green and Srinivasan, 1978). In the late 1960s, conjoint analysis began to be used in the research field of consumer behavior, in the 1970s, it has been utilized in many areas of marketing. When developing a new analysis of the response of the consumer, analyzing the competitive structure among companies in the market, and making decisions about market segmentation, conjoint analysis has been used as supporting analysis method for decision-making (Green and Srinivasan, 1990; Riedesel, 1985; Wittink and Cattin, 1989).

Conjoint analysis is able to compare different products, so it can consider all of the attributes that can have any number of products. It also can take into account information about the low level for each attribute. Despite these complex structures, conjoint analysis helps to understand the significance through the individual preferences of the respondents and each attribute.

In this study, we used a CBCA that respondents select the most preferred profiles from several of the profiles (Louviere and Woodworth, 1983). Researchers are able to derive some interesting results from a more complex experimental design and analyze the simplest form of the main effects of traditional conjoint analysis (main effects) and possible interaction (interaction effects) (Anderson and Wiley, 1992; Lazari and Anderson, 1994; Louviere, 1988).

6.3. Research Model

6.3.1. *Wireless communication market in South Korea*

As wireless communications markets are activated, consumers are able to use a lot of products that we never imagined. Accordingly, as consumer's lifestyle has changes, the influence of the communication technology is more increased. In addition, the development of communication technology in Korea has excellent credibelity worldwide, and the mobile company has developed into a leader in the domestic consumer market as well as overseas. In recent years, the domestic smartphone market is dominated by Samsung, LG, and Pantech as domestic manufacturers and Apple as a foreign company. As shown in Table 6.1, it seems that technical differences do not appear.

Table 6.2 shows the market share of mobile service companies. Figure 6.2 and Table 6.2 show the market share of mobile service companies. SKT has the best portion of market share, 50%. KT has 31%, and LGT has 19%. The domestic mobile market share has been unchanged, and it can be very difficult that each company has big trouble to increase the portion of market share.

Table 6.3 shows Worldwide Smartphone Sales by Vendor and Table 6.4 by operating system in 1Q, 2013.

The purpose of this study is to identify the interactions between the properties of products and services through CBCA to build a differentiated strategy for each company.

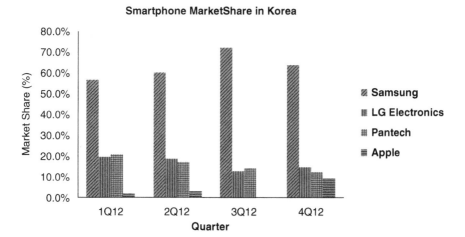

Fig. 6.2.   Smartphone market share in South Korea.
Source: Gartner.

Table 6.1.   Smartphone specifications.

	Galaxy S4	iPhone 5	Optimus G pro
Screen size	4.99 inch	4 inch	5.5 inch
Size	5.38" × 2.74" × 0.31"	4.87" × 2.31" × 0.30"	5.91" × 3.00" × 0.37"
Display	1920 × 1080 pixel, 441 ppi	1136 × 640 pixel, 326 ppi	1920 × 1080 pixel, 401 ppi
Display technology	AMOLED	RETNA	Full HD IPS
Weight	4.59 oz	3.95 oz	6.07 oz
Processor	1.9 GHz Quadcore	Dualcore A6	1.7 GHz Quadcore
Ram	2 GB	1 GB	2 GB
Platform	ANDROID 4.2.2	iOS 6	ANDROID 4.1
Front camera	13 million pixels	8 million pixels	13 million pixels
Rear camera	2 million pixels	1.2 million pixels	2.1 million pixels

Source: Manufacturers' website.

Table 6.2.   Mobile service subscribers in January 2013.

Service Company	Membership	Market Share
SKT	27,041,972	50%
KT	16,607,734	31%
LGT	9,989,927	19%
Total	53,639,633	100%

Table 6.3.   Worldwide smartphone sales by vendor in 1Q 2013.

Company	1Q13 Units	1Q13 Market Share (%)	1Q12 Units	1Q12 Market Share (%)
Samsung	64,740.0	30.8	40,612.8	27.6
Apple	38,331.8	18.2	33,120.5	22.5
LG Electronics	10,080.4	4.8	4,961.4	3.4
Huawei	9,334.2	4.4	5,269.6	3.6
ZTE	7,883.3	3.8	4,518.9	3.1
Others	79,676.4	37.9	58,537.0	39.8
Total	**210,046.1**	**100.0**	**147,020.2**	**100.0**

Table 6.4.   Worldwide smartphone sales by operating system in 1Q 2013.

Operating System	1Q13 Units	1Q13 Market Share (%)	1Q12 Units	1Q12 Market Share (%)
Android	156,186.0	74.4	83,684.4	56.9
iOS	38,331.8	18.2	33,120.5	22.5
Research in motion	6,218.6	3.0	9,939.3	6.8
Microsoft	5,989.2	2.9	2,722.5	1.9
Bada	1,370.8	0.7	3,843.7	2.6
Symbian	1,349.4	0.6	12,466.9	8.5
Others	600.3	0.3	1,242.9	0.8
Total	**210,046.1**	**100.0**	**147,020.2**	**100.0**

6.3.2. *CBCA*

In this study, we consider the properties of the products and services and study whether the integration of products and services will help in the positive interaction for consumers. In the telecommunications market, the properties of the products and services were selected as shown in Fig. 6.3.

We selected three attributes of product and one attribute of service. The product attributes are phone brand, screen size, and phone color. The first attribute, phone brand, means the performance and specifications. The second attribute, screen size, contains the different strategy of each competitor. The third attribute, phone color, is chosen in terms of design. And we chose the selection of mobile service provider as the service attribute. The more the number of attributes increases, the more diverse we can analyze. But, we considered only four attributes in order to simplify the model because the purpose of this study is to find out the application of conjoint analysis on the PSS. There is information about each attribute and the level shown in Table 6.5.

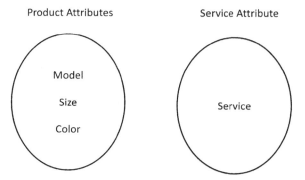

Fig. 6.3.   Attributes of product and service.

Table 6.5.   Experimental design.

Attributes	Levels
Phone brand	Galaxy, iPhone, Optimus
Screen size	4 inch, 5 inch
Phone color	White, Black
Mobile service	SKT, KT, LGT

Table 6.6.   Variables of each attribute.

X1	SKT	Brand	Galaxy, iPhone, Optimus
X2	KT	Brand	Galaxy, iPhone, Optimus
X3	LGT	Brand	Galaxy, iPhone, Optimus
X4	SKT	Size	4 inch, 5 inch
X5	KT	Size	4 inch, 5 inch
X6	LGT	Size	4 inch, 5 inch
X7	SKT	Color	White, Black
X8	KT	Color	White, Black
X9	LGT	Color	White, Black

In this paper, we try to understand the attributes of each product and service and the interactions between the attributes of the product and service. Table 6.6 shows the variables used. By specifying the parameters, each attribute was designed to require the analysis on the SAS program (SAS Technical Papers). Figure 6.4 shows an example of experimental design sets.

We collected 171 questionnaires targeting college students in Seoul. The survey was conducted on May 6–11, 2013. Demographic results of the survey targets are shown in Table 6.7. Pre-analysis necessary for research, survey statistics profile generation and after treatment were analyzed using the SAS 9.3 program.

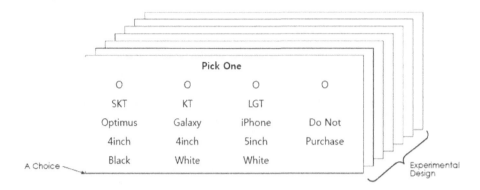

Fig. 6.4.   Experimental design set.

Table 6.7.   Demographic results.

Items	Details	#	%	Items	Details	#	%
Sex	Male	78	45.61%	Phone	Galaxy	90	52.63%
	Female	93	54.39%		iPhone	28	16.37%
Color	White	95	55.56%		Optimus	30	17.54%
	Black	67	39.18%		etc.	23	13.45%
	etc.	9	5.26%	Mobile	SKT	76	44.44%
Screen size	<4 inch	20	11.70%	service	KT	62	36.26%
	4–4.5 inch	58	33.92%		LGT	33	19.30%
	4.5–5 inch	52	30.41%	Fare	<50,000 won	25	14.62%
	>5 inch	40	23.39%		50,000–100,000 won	128	74.85%
	7 |E|	1	0.58%		100,000–150,000 won	18	10.53%

6.4. Results

The results were obtained through CBCA to the analysis of how to bring greater effectiveness to consumers by generating the preference for each attribute and the interaction of combined products and service when products and services are combined to deliver to the consumer. Table 6.8 gives the results of the investigation of the preference for products and services, including the interaction attribute. Also, the measurement zero is a reference level in the analysis. A positive value with respect to a reference level means better preference compared with the reference level, a negative value means lower preference than the reference level. For the

Table 6.8.   CBCA results.

		Parameter	Standard			Hazard
Parameter	DF	Estimate	Error	Chi-square	Pr>ChiSq	Ratio
SKT	1	1.1525	0.18295	39.6842	<0.0001	3.166
KT	1	−0.3089	0.18424	2.8111	0.0936	0.734
LGT	1	−0.98875	0.3378	8.5676	0.0034	0.372
Galaxy	1	−0.0994	0.17305	0.33	0.5657	0.905
iPhone	1	1.69294	0.38428	19.408	<0.0001	5.435
Optimus	1	1.14324	0.21315	28.7671	<0.0001	3.137
4 inch	1	−1.69294	0.38428	19.408	<0.0001	0.184
5 inch	1	−0.98875	0.3378	8.5676	0.0034	0.372
Black	1	−1.68394	0.37528	19.307	<0.0001	0.164
White	1	−1.25795	0.35841	12.3186	0.0004	0.284
SKT*Galaxy	1	−0.0994	0.17305	0.33	0.5657	0.905
SKT*iPhone	0	0	—	—	—	—
SKT*Optimus	1	1.14324	0.21315	28.7671	<0.0001	3.137
KT*Galaxy	1	−0.90653	0.20813	18.9712	<0.0001	0.404
KT*iPhone	1	−1.46251	0.22785	38.072	<0.0001	0.242
KT*Optimus	1	−0.28458	0.2755	1.067	0.3016	0.752
LGT*Galaxy	1	−1.68021	0.45302	13.7557	0.0002	0.186
LGT*iPhone	1	−2.14125	0.39498	29.389	<0.0001	0.118
LGT*Optimus	1	−2.49598	0.37706	43.8192	<0.0001	0.082
SKT*4 inch	1	−0.70419	0.1542	20.8551	<0.0001	0.495
SKT*5 inch	0	0	—	—	—	—
KT*4 inch	1	0.09682	0.24339	0.1582	0.6908	1.102
KT*5 inch	1	−1.46152	0.21585	38.072	<0.0001	0.192
LGT*4 inch	1	−1.22851	0.18822	42.6021	<0.0001	0.293
LGT*5 inch	1	−2.13225	0.38398	29.379	<0.0001	0.138
SKT*Black	0	0	—	—	—	—
SKT*White	1	0.43499	0.1368	10.1104	0.0015	1.545
KT*Black	1	−1.46141	0.23685	38.072	<0.0001	0.232
KT*White	1	−1.66544	0.22875	53.0065	<0.0001	0.189
LGT*Black	1	−2.04335	0.39388	29.479	<0.0001	0.218
LGT*White	1	−1.32547	0.60138	4.8579	0.0275	0.266

Analysis of maximum likelihood estimates

communication service, SKT is the most preferred and LGT is the worst. It seems a reasonable result at the 0.01 significance level to reflect the current market. For the phone brand, the iPhone is the best preferred and Galaxy is the worst according to SAS technical paper. Because the significance level of the Galaxy is not reliable, the result should be verified by further research. The result of brand preference shows that the preference of Galaxy and iPhone is declining and the preference of Optimus is growing. Finally, at the screen size, 5 inch is more preferred than 4 inch, and at the phone color, White is more preferred than Black.

At the results of the interaction, except SKT*Galaxy, KT*Optimus, and KT*4 inch, the values of the interaction are significant. This result means that there are synergy effects of interaction by combining product and service.

At the interaction of mobile service provider and phone brand, with respect to the communication service LGT, all data are shown to interact high. LGT*Galaxy (−1.68021) has the best score, that means consumers of LGT prefer the Galaxy the most, and then second the iPhone (−2.14125), and Optimus (−2.49598) the last. In the case of SKT and KT, the consumers of SKT prefer the Optimus (1.14324) to iPhone (0) and the consumers of KT prefer the Galaxy (−0.90653) to iPhone (−1.46251).

At the interaction of mobile service provider and screen size, SKT*4 inch (−0.70419) is smaller than SKT*5 inch as the reference level. That means the consumers of SKT like the big screen more. On the other hand, because LGT*4 inch (−1.22851) is greater than LGT*5 inch (−2.13225), the consumers of LGT prefer the smaller screen. The selection of screen size will vary with the selection of service provider.

At the interaction of mobile service provider and phone color, the consumers of SKT and LGT prefer White (SKT: 0 versus 0.43499, LGT: −2.04335 versus −1.32547), the consumers of KT prefer Black (−1.66544 versus −2.04335).

In the results as a whole, there are interactions between mobile service provider and the attributes of product. Utilizing an analysis of the interaction of the PSS can derive the fine differentiated marketing strategy for each company.

6.5. Conclusion

This study analyzed not only the value of product and service but also the interaction effects of PSS using CBCA. Synergy effects have occurred by combining the attributes of product and service, and we can use the effects to utilize the effective marketing strategy.

1. PSS is not to add the attributes of product and the attributes of service but to provide more values for customers with effective combination of the attributes of product and the attributes of service.

2. From the analysis of interactions, we can derive successful strategy for PSS.
3. This study can be applied to a variety of industries.

Bibliography

1. Alix, T, Y Ducq and B Vallespir (2009). Product–service value analysis: Two complementary points of view. *Proceedings of the 1st CIRP Industrial Product–service Systems (IPS2) Conference*, Cranfield University, 157–164.
2. Anderson, DA and JB Wiley (1992). Efficient choice set designs for estimating availability cross-effects models. *Marketing Letters*, 3(4), 357–370.
3. Baines, TS, HW Lightfoot, S Evans, A Neely, R Greenough, J Peppard, R Roy, E Shehab, A Braganza, A Tiwari, JR Alcock, JP Angus, M Bastl, A Cousens, P Irving, M Johnson, J Kingston, H Lockett, V Martinez, P Michele, D Tranfield, IM Walton and H Wilson (2007). State-of-the-art in product–service systems. *Proceedings of the Institution of Mechanical Engineers*, 211(10), 1543–1552.
4. Baines, TS, HW Lightfoot, O Benedettini and JM Kay (2009a). The servitization of manufacturing: A review of literature and reflection on future challenges. *Journal of Manufacturing Technology Management*, 20(5), 547–567.
5. Baines, TS, HW Lightfoot and JM Kay (2009b). Servitized manufacture: practical challenges of delivering integrated products and services. *Proceedings of the Institution of Mechanical Engineers, Part B: Journal of Engineering Manufacture*, 223(9), 1207–1215.
6. Gebauer, H, G Ren, A Valtakoski and J Reynoso (2012). Service-driven Manufacturing, Provision, Evolution and Financial Impact of Services in Industrial Firms. *Journal of Service Management*, 23(1), 120–136.
7. Goedkoop, MJ, CJG van Halen, HRM te Riele and PJM Rommens (1999). Product–service system, ecological and economic basics. The Report No. 1999/36 submitted to Ministerje van Volkshuisvesting, Ruimtelijke Ordening en Milieubeheer, 22–25.
8. Green, PE and V Srinivasan (1978). Conjoint analysis in consumer research: Issues and outlook. *Journal of Consumer Research*, 5(2), 103–123.
9. Green, PE and V Srinivasan (1990). Conjoint analysis in marketing: New Developments with implications for research and practice. *Journal of Marketing*, 54(4) 3–16.
10. van Halen, C, C Vezzoli and R Wimmer (2005). *Methodology for product–service system innovation: How to develop clean, clever and competitive strategies in companies*, The Netherlands: Koninklijke Van Gorcum.
11. Lazari, AG and DA Anderson (1994). Designs of discrete choice set experiments for estimating both attribute and availability cross effects. *Journal of Marketing Research*, 31(3), 375–383.
12. Louviere, JJ (1988). Conjoint analysis modelling of stated preferences: A review of theory, methods, recent developments and external validity. *Journal of Transport Economics and Policy*, 22(1), 93–119.

13. Louviere, JJ and G Woodworth (1983). Design and analysis of simulated consumer choice or allocation experiments: an approach based on aggregate data. *Journal of Marketing Research*, 20(4), 350–367.

14. Manzini, E and C Vezzoli (2003). A strategic design approach to develop sustainable product–service systems: examples taken from the 'environmentally friendly innovation' Italian prize. *Journal of Cleaner Production*, 11(8), 851–857.

15. Mont, O and A Tukker (2006). Product–service systems: Reviewing achievements and refining the research agenda. *Journal of Cleaner Production*, 14(17), 1451–1454.

16. Riedesel, PL (1985). Conjoint analysis is a worthwhile tool, but be sure data are valid. *Marketing News*, 19(19), 36–43.

17. Stoughton, M and T Votta (2003). Implementing service-based chemical procurement: Lessons and results. *Journal of Cleaner Production*, 11(8), 839–849.

18. Wittink, DR and P Cattin (1989). Commercial use of conjoint analysis: An update. *Journal of Marketing*, 53(3), 91–96.

19. SAS Technical Papers, http://support.sas.com/techsup/technote/mr2010f.pdf.

20. Apple website (http://www.apple.com/kr/iphone/specs.html).

21. LG mobile website (http://www.lgmobile.co.kr/mobile-phone/F240/LG-F240S/).

22. Samsung electronics website (http://www.samsung.com/sec/consumer/mobile-phone/mobile-phone/SHVE330SZB1SC-spec). Source: Manufacturers' website (Apple, LG mobile, and Samsung electronics website) in Table 6.1

About the Authors

Jinmin Kim

Jinmin Kim got his PhD, MS and BS degrees from Korea University Business School. Currently, he is an Assistant Professor of Production and Operations Management at Korea University Sejong Campus. He focuses his major research on Supply Chain Coordination and Service Strategy.

Kwangtae Park

Kwangtae Park is a Professor of Logistics, Service, and Operations Management (LSOM) at Korea University Business School(KUBS). He got his PhD degree from University of California, Berkeley and both his MS and BS degree from Seoul National University. He focuses his major research on service innovation and SCM.

Hosun Rhim

Hosun Rhim is a Professor of Logistics, Service, and Operations Management (LSOM) at Korea University Business School. He got his PhD degree from The Anderson School of Management at UCLA and both his MBA and BA degrees from Seoul National University. His research interests include completion in service operations and service productivity.

Sungyong Choi

Sungyong Choi is an Assistant Professor of Operations Management at Yonsei University. He got his PhD degree from Rutgers Business School and MS and BS degree from Michigan State University and KAIST. His research interests include various topics in stochastic inventory models.

CHAPTER 7

IMPACT OF SOCIAL MEDIA ON CONSUMER–BRAND RELATIONSHIPS

ALESSANDRO MARI

Abstract

This chapter bridges academic and managerial perspectives on the use of social media platforms for the creation of strategic consumer–brand relationships and their effect on brand equity. In particular, the chapter explores some of the recurring barriers that marketing managers have identified when discussing the implementation of relationship-based initiatives linked to marketing communications objectives. According to Fournier (1998: 344), the fact that brands are "animated, humanized, or somehow personalized" supports the idea that brands can be relationship partners. Kent and Taylor (1998) suggested that organizations have an opportunity to build dialogic relationships with stakeholders through the use of strategically designed websites. Although previous studies have investigated the potential of social media platforms for building and maintaining relationships with the public (Bortree and Seltzer, 2009; Park and Reber, 2008), there has been little empirical exploration on the evolution of consumer–brand relationships resulting from the advent of social channels (e.g., Mandelli and La Rocca, 2014). Social media platforms have had a remarkable impact in the evolution consumer–brand relationships. This phenomenon is expected to play a leading role in the creation of economic and social innovation during this decade (Tapscott, 2014). As Gummesson (2004: 139) noted, "when relationship marketing, CRM, and services marketing are combined with a network view, they become drivers of a paradigm shift in marketing." The reason for the shift is the advancement of information technology, which has resulted in the use of information to understand and enhance customer relationships. The author of the present chapter examines several cases to better understand the advantages of a total relational approach enhanced by digital technology.

7.1. Introduction to Social Media

In the area of communication, the advent of the internet and, more recently, of social media where internet users collaborate and share information and opinions is the critical phenomenon of the last decade. Depending on how one defines the term "social media", there are millions (if not billions) of users who participate in online communities as an ordinary ingredient of their social experience (Kozinets, 2010). In investigating this phenomenon, the literature has widely adopted the label of social media to identify a group of internet-based applications that build on the ideological and technological foundations of Web 2.0, and that allow people with common interests to gather together to share thoughts, ideas, and opinions (Kaplan and Haenlein, 2010). In recent years, websites have added functionality that enables users to easily participate in conversations and share content (for example, the diffusion of the Facebook 'Like' button), making the entire web more social. In this context, social media markets are conceived as being made by interactions and stories between people who use digital social platforms as a new form of communication media and a social environment (Mandelli, 2012). Unlike in the past, these users are not passively consuming published content; instead, they are actively communicating with one another (Mandelli *et al.*, 2010), which makes them media players. Under many circumstances, the online environment can be used as a medium for meaningful social exchange, where collectives of customers form new global niches and segments convene (Mandelli, 2008). Online connections and alignments are increasingly affecting our social behavior as consumers and social beings, but also as managers or employees. Online communities are not virtual because the people that we meet online have a "real" existence for their participants, and this has consequential effects on many aspects of behavior (Kozinets, 1998: 366). Therefore, online communities are communities (Kozinets, 2010). These communities, which have grown impressively in recent times, are no longer bounded by local, spatial, or temporal environments, and thus represent immense opportunities for market-oriented consumer interactions (Fielding, 2008). Social media is an invaluable research site that offers extraordinary opportunities for marketers to study the tastes, desires, and other needs of consumers as part of a specific community (Kozinets, 2010; Fielding, 2008). Social media are bringing consumers closer to companies, to the point that they can be conceived as part of the organization (Hanna *et al.*, 2011).

This evolution has led to the idea that brand managers can utilize social platforms to build and manage relationships with consumer communities (Schau *et al.*, 2009). This idea appears to have profound communication implications (Laroche *et al.*, 2012); indeed, managers must recognize that social media is little more than a technology-enabling tool.

7.2. Managing Relationships through Social Media

The recent explosion of interest in social media has led authors from many fields to release books and articles that have attempted to interpret the changes caused by digital technology (Mandelli and Accoto, 2012; Kietzmann *et al.*, 2011; Safko, 2010). On the one hand, these documents have invoked enthusiasm among countless professionals and researchers because they have highlighted the potential of the new technology. On the other hand, oversimplified analysis has reduced the complexity of this phenomenon and generated the belief that social media is a "magic formula" that solves the problems faced by entrepreneurs and companies in terms of generating new business. Incorrectly interpreted stories have led many corporate managers to suffer from Stendhal syndrome — freezing in front of this massive amount of "beauty" that they do not completely understand (Mari, 2014). I argue that the rise of the so-called "social media experts" has some connection with the deep meaning of social media. In a broad sense, in order to be truly "social", a brand must be able to effectively establish and maintain "relationships" with its consumers. According to many scholars, a firm's performance depends strictly on the nature and the quality of direct and indirect relationships it is able to develop with its counterparts (see Wilkinson and Young, 1994). Relationships are the new "currency" of the business world. The term "relationship" is defined as "a mutually oriented interaction between two reciprocally committed parties" (Håkansson and Snehota, 1995). The concept of "relationship" is not exactly new in marketing. When the term "relationship marketing" was coined by Berry (1983), interactions, relationships, and social networks received additional interest from researchers. Relationship marketing was defined as attracting, maintaining, and enhancing customer relationships (Grönroos, 1994). Interaction has been defined as the key construct at the heart of relationship marketing and social media marketing paradigm (Batt, 2008). Every company, as well as every individual, must initiate or maintain multiple and simultaneous relationships in any phase of life. Both individuals and managers don't live on a deserted island (Håkansson and Snehota, 1989). However, not all companies (and individuals) are able to create "high-quality" relationships that involve reciprocal respect, mutual trust, commitment, and satisfaction (Grönross, 2007). Although social media appears to have profound communication implications, managers must recognize that social media is nothing more than a communication-enabling tool. Ultimately, social media is simply a technology that enables consumers to become media agents (UGC) and communicate in a many-to-many fashion, while enabling companies to connect with their own communities to build and maintain relationships (Mandelli *et al.*, 2010). Therefore, social media is not a magic formula, but relationships are, whenever they are handled in a strategic way. I argue that whenever brand managers forget this, the expectations on the social media platforms and tools are deemed unreal. For a company, the relationship building process implies a deep understanding of the other party or parties in the relationship, primarily because each party is fundamentally different from each other party. Several scholars have viewed the relational side of marketing as an asymmetrical interaction process that requires an in-depth, personalized understanding and consumer needs and personality. This implies going beyond the "golden rule" of treating others as you would like them to treat you, which in the corporate environment was interpreted as "treat your customers as you (the manager) would like to be treated". However, I argue that managers need to treat customers as they wish to be treated and not as they, managers, would like to be treated by others. For large corporations, the only way to conduct one-to-one relationships with a high number of customers and bypass the complex practice of customer understanding is using digital technology to adopt a truly honest, social, and caring approach when communicating and serving clients. Ultimately, it is by becoming a social business or enterprise that a firm can effectively use the technology for customer relationship management (Mandelli and Accoto, 2012). It is not software such as analytic and monitoring tools or sales and customer care programs that make a company "social". Technology itself cannot turn a company's social media presence into an effective growth engine.

7.3. Importance of Long-Term Relationships in Social Media Era

The importance of building and maintaining long-term relationships with strategic consumers is further emphasized by the rise of such phenomena as global competition, sharing economy, service industrialization, and private labels. Increasingly, what differentiates one brand from another is not its visual ID or personality, but its overall relationships with consumers. It is quite limiting to assume that relationships reside in one corporate function; instead, relationships evolve anywhere there is a meaningful interaction. A company's marketing team is often considered the "relationship hub" that orchestrates all the actors involved in the relationship building process. Therefore, marketing becomes the art of building and maintaining meaningful relationships with strategic consumers. In that respect, relationships are a brand's most important asset regardless of the channel they initiate, evolve, or terminate. Every company should leverage key consumers as powerful marketers that are able to guide the company's decision-making process. Brand managers must have an active role in conversations with consumers and should aim to involve them in the company's internal processes. The democratization process of a relationship, in which brand lovers and brand owners have an equal relationship, is visible in the rise of crowdsourcing platforms like P&G Connect+Develop (co-creation platform for innovation), which function as relationship strengthening tools towards strategic partners. Consumers are forcing companies to become "social business". Social media users have increasing expectations regarding a company's ability to directly engage into conversations with them. For instance, questions asked on Facebook brand pages increased by 85% in 2013 compared with the year before (SocialBakers, 2013). It is not surprising that 50% of consumers expect to receive a response to a question posted on social media within one week; otherwise, they are likely to switch to another brand (KissMetrics, 2013). Whatever issue a company has to deal with, if not solved online it might turn in additional offline costs. In fact, 40% of unresolved social complaints result in costly call center calls (ClickFox, 2013). The main reasons why consumers worldwide write about brands online are: to offer advice (64%), praise (61%), criticism (52%), and to share content about a brand's product (51%) (Branderati, 2013). Generally speaking, a company must handle two types of interactions: positive and negative. Positive interactions originate from an act of affection shown by a user, while negative ones can derive from an initial stage of dissatisfaction. Besides helping to save costs, well-handled online conversations can turn negative opinions into positive ones (Grönroos, 2007), building the reputation of a good social business and stronger relationships with customers. Therefore, any interaction initiated from a consumer is an opportunity for the company to show its genuine interest in individuals. Whenever a brand neglects its customers, it runs a significant risk of losing them to its competitors. A study published by the software company Oracle (2011) showed that 89% of individuals have stopped doing business with a brand due to poor online service.

As many authors have pointed out, consumer–brand relationships are born through many acts and encounters and not via a single event (Grönroos, 2004). Time represents a key variable in the creation of quality relationship perception in the consumer's mind. Resources also play a significant role in the emotional connection development, as relationships are not "self-run". When a company establishes a presence on social media driven by clear relational-based objectives such as fostering dialog (Rybalko and Seltzer, 2010), promoting advocacy (Cova and Cova, 2002), facilitating support (Füller *et al.*, 2007), spurring innovation (Tapscott and Williams, 2008), building conversational leadership (Kozinets, 2002), or creating linking value (i.e. supporting many-to-many relationships, Cova, 1997), it can become quite costly to initiate and maintain relationships with strategic users. This is why many companies have initially underestimated the resources needed to manage conversations according to an "open leadership" approach (Li, 2010). The initial proliferation of brand accounts on every platform (for example, one profile for each country or language) was followed by a reduction of touchpoints due to a lack of internal resources.

Many businesses are struggling to reduce the customer acquisition cycle by shortening the communication funnel and driving consumers to the loyalty stage in the fastest possible way. Although marketing should focus on moving all customers up the ladder of loyalty (West *et al.*, 2010), this can only be achieved in a sustainable way if the company genuinely cares about human beings and builds solid win–win relationships (Smith, 2011).

Nowadays, companies are constantly reconsidering their online strategies due to the risk of seriously damaging their reputation, being labeled as "anti-social", or being unable to handle online conversations. Despite the common belief that keeping an existing customer is seven times cheaper than winning a new one (Bain and Company, 1999), companies have shown a reluctance to invest in relationships by creating online communities on social media platforms (Merlo *et al.*, 2013). This is mainly driven by the strong focus on immediate economic results, also enhanced by the recent global financial crisis, which is often preferred to the promise of stronger long-term results. However, several studies have shown that proactive participation in online brand-related conversations has a significant impact on brand advocacy and, subsequently, on the bottom line. Studies have shown that 71% of consumers who receive a response to a customer service request on social media "recommend" the brand to others (NM Incite, 2012) and spend 20–40% more with that company (Bain and Company, 2011).

A recent paper published by Merlo *et al.* (2014) explained how companies tend to focus on encouraging customers to recommend their brands by spreading positive word of mouth instead of fostering customer participation (or engagement). There are two main rationales for this preference. The first is the false belief that customer acquisition is more critical than customer retention for brand performance; the second is that brand advocacy is the main driver of increased customer loyalty. In the so-called "sharing economy" (Mathews, 2014), it is clear why customer advocacy is emphasized over customer engagement. However, the practices of actively and systematically encourage customers to volunteer constructive ideas and suggestions to improve product and service offerings is an "under utilized weapon in the marketer's arsenal" (Merlo *et al.*, 2014). Despite the huge availability of brand-related information on the internet, consumer advocacy is still considered to be a major factor influencing brand preference (Almquist and Roberts, 2000). In accordance with the research presented by Merlo *et al.* (2013), the benefits and positive returns of customer participation are underappreciated. Engaged customers are more likely to become repeat customers, buy more of a company's products and services, and ultimately deliver more profit (Fig. 7.1).

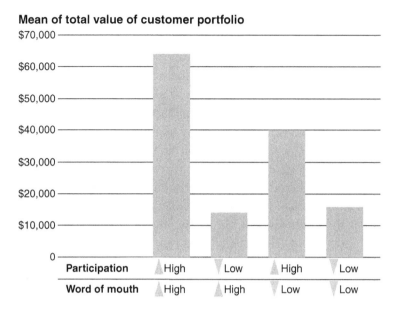

Fig. 7.1.   Value of participation and word-of-mouth — Merlo *et al.* (2014).

I believe that community commitment is an attitudinal antecedent of brand advocacy (and brand loyalty), and is therefore fundamental to the ultimate goal of building brand equity. In other words, an effective brand advocacy attitude is most easily found in consumers that have shown commitment and/or engagement toward a brand and its community. Since consumer attachment to a brand community translates into improved loyalty behavior (brand advocacy and brand loyalty), brand managers who are considering customer loyalty improvement strategies need to understand the value of managing an online brand community effectively.

By using service-logic variables such us providing the consumers with preferential treatment, social recognition, and social relationships, the aim of any brand should be to create a sense of community and community engagement; in other words, "brand community attachment". As noted by Thomson (2006), feelings related to attachment are an essential aspect of strong relationships between the consumer and the brand. Park *et al.* (2010) included self-connection as a characteristic that influences both brand attachment and relationship quality. Attachment is a construct that derives from psychology theories, where it was defined as an emotion-laden target-specific bond between a person and a specific object (Bowlby, 1979). Various studies have noted that the stronger the attachment, the stronger the feelings of connection, affection, love, and passion that the individual experiences. Brand community attachment is seen to have a strong effect on "emotional brand attachment", a construct that is created by self-brand connection and brand prominence. W. Park *et al.* (2010) defined brand prominence as "the extent to which positive feelings and memories about the attachment object are perceived as top of mind." The bond between the self and the brand requires time and experiences to develop; over time, thoughts, and feelings concerning the brand are integrated in the individual's memory. Thomson *et al.* (2005) noted that a strong attachment can also result in a higher probability that the individual will want to keep proximity to the attachment's object; indeed, separation from the object can even provoke pain in the individual. Park *et al.* (2008) confirmed the brand attachment model, discovering that both brand-self connection and brand prominence affect the attachment of an individual to a brand. In general, higher brand-self connection leads to higher brand attachment. Similarly, higher brand prominence leads to higher brand attachment. Hur *et al.* (2011) also demonstrated that emotional brand attachment construct is related to brand attitude strength, which is the positive attitude of a consumer to recommend a brand and become loyal. In synthesis, it is by offering services such as preferential treatment, social recognition, and social relationship to consumers that a brand builds a sense of community and customer engagement. Through participation in the company's initiatives and activities, a consumer feels connected to a brand and closer to its value and personality (brand prominence). This emotional connection will translate into positive word-of-mouth (brand advocacy) and repeated purchase (brand loyalty). These two factors, which are part of the brand attitude strength, can have a profound impact on brand equity, as well as on overall brand performance in the market place (Fig. 7.2). Villanueva *et al.* (2008) revealed that brand attachment precisely predicts companies' reported sales, brand purchase share, and market share.

7.4. Evolution of Consumer–Brand Relationships

The advent of social media and the diffusion of digital technology have created significant changes in the way consumer–brand relationships are conceived, both by consumers and by companies. This section discusses some of the major factors that have contributed to this development.

Personal versus public conversations. A few decades ago, interactions between consumers and companies were rare and occurred almost entirely in a one-to-one manner. Consumers had few available options for retrieving information from a company as communication channels were limited; they could perhaps contact a call center, drive to a store, and, more recently, write an e-mail. Interactions between companies (or intermediaries) and consumers were usually

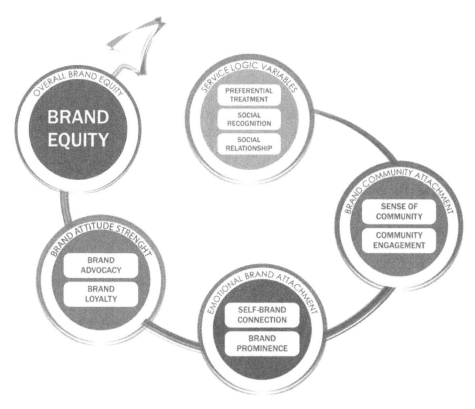

Fig. 7.2.   Brand community to brand equity.

private. Some recurring issues might have cost companies a lot of money as they needed to be addressed to different customers over and over again. Also, badly handled interactions would have had limited consequences for a company, as the fact could have been directly reported only to a small number of people. The likelihood of the outcome of such a conversation becoming public through traditional media was very low and was strictly proportional to its impact on the population. Nowadays, consumers have been empowered by technology and play an active role in conversations that increasingly take place on public platforms where everyone can form an opinion on the reported facts (Javornik and Mandelli, 2012). A company's social skills and its ability to detect consumer's needs and provide solutions can be evaluated by everyone. Soft skills are increasingly important, not only for the community manager, usually the brand's interface with consumers, but for any marketing professional. In particular, they are required to master both the technical skills needed to properly utilize the vast array of social tools, but also soft skills, which are needed to effectively build solid relationships through these social tools (Smith, 2011). Today, users can express their dissatisfaction online and their conversations can be easily shared, sometimes even going "viral". This extraordinary shift toward public brand-related conversations has forced companies to establish a presence in one or more social media platforms, regardless of their ability to effectively engage in a conversation. However, the opportunity for a user to show appreciation for a brand is significantly higher today than it was previously, if the company approaches all interactions as a way to show conversational leadership, demonstrating its commitment to the relationship.

Local versus global connections. Increased access to brands worldwide has encouraged the rise of global communities. Even small brands can now be distributed anywhere on the planet through e-commerce websites. The ability of brands to reach a global audience is certainly positive for many aspects, but it has also generated new challenges whenever the company is unable to deal with different cultures, values, and geographic areas. Those brands that manage online communities with a global approach and communicate in English on their platforms need to deal with issues such us misleading communications, low engagement from non-native speakers, and the inability to interact in languages other than English. Brands usually have different product line-ups in different countries, which can make it extremely complex to guarantee basic customer service to any online user. The risk for the brand is to turn the page platform into a well-organized press room that avoids "costly" spontaneous interactions due to the obvious complexity of being generated in a global environment.

Regular versus empowered consumers. One of the main objectives for companies in the online environment has been to aggregate groups of fans into communities based into social media platforms like Facebook or Twitter. In 2011, 46% of company executives in the United States said that an increase in brand advocates was one of the most important benefits of social media (Jive, 2011). This relational objective is coupled with the need to discover brand advocates and leverage them as a powerful marketing tool to promote product and spread brand communications. Advocates tell twice as many people about their purchase as non-advocates (Comscore and Yahoo!, 2006). A recent article from Harvard Business Review (Reichheld, 2006) estimated that a 12% increase in brand advocacy, on average, generated a two-fold increase in revenue and growth rate, plus boosts to market share. A company with 100,000 energized brand advocates can reach an average of 60 million people (Bernoff *et al.*, 2010). It is realistic to believe that any brand has at least one passionate consumer who will ideate, build, distribute, sell, and recommend its products. There are more than 60 million brand advocates in the US and billions worldwide (Zuberance, 2011). Globally, 80% of consumers recommend at least one brand, but the average number of brands that consumers recommended has increased significantly in all regions of the world (GfK Roper, 2006). Despite the proven importance of effectively managing advocates and experts, only 20% of brands have implemented programs with such intentions (Marketing Charts, 2013). As Godin (2014) explained:

"If you work for a company that you don't own, if you interact with customers, you're a brand ambassador. The person who runs the cash register or answers the phone or makes sales calls is a brand ambassador, in the world on behalf of the amorphous brand, whatever that is. [...] Organizations make two huge mistakes: (a) They don't hire brand ambassadors, they hire clerks and bureaucrats, and treat them and pay them accordingly; (b) They don't manage and lead brand ambassadors, don't measure and reward and create a cadre of people who can listen for the brand and speak for the brand."

Dispersed versus technology-enabled communities. Many authors have pointed out the significant benefits of an active group of consumers. Community is a core part of social thought (Muniz and O'Guinn, 2001). People are held together through shared emotions, styles of life, and consumption practices (Maffesoli, 1993). Community concept is an alternative form of social arrangements, also referred to as "neo-tribes" or "post-modern tribes" (Maffesoli, 1996), and is not new in brand management studies. Consumers desire an experience-based marketing that emphasizes interactivity, connectivity, and creativity (Cova and Pace, 2006; Cova *et al.*, 2007). This explains why people are often more interested in the social links that come from brand affiliations than they are in the brands themselves. In fact, 25% of users choose to engage with brands because they want join the community of brand fans (Technorati Media, 2013). Brand communities are not built on brand reputation, but on members' understanding of brand stories. Being communities dynamic, neither fixed or permanent, its meaning and concreteness are always being negotiated by individuals through narratives. Although this is true whether group members interact electronically, via face-to-face communication, or both (Komito, 1998: 105), we can argue that digital technology enabled the rise of these links between consumers. Consequently, the interaction between brands and consumers has also changed dramatically. Creating a linking value among consumers in order to establish a sense of community and spur collaboration has become commonplace in the social media environment (Cova, 1997). More than 3.5 billion brand-related conversations take place each day in the US (Keller Fay Group, 2007). Companies should always have an active role into these conversations, but the members of the community must also be free to interact and collaborate among themselves without any restriction.

Spontaneous versus Data-driven interactions. Some of the relationship barriers that companies face when establishing personal and long-lasting collaborations with strategic customers are a result of the complexity associated with the so-called "Big Data" phenomena. Companies must increasingly deal with tasks including the following: (1) data gathering — collection of real, systematic and inexpensive data about consumers; (2) data integration — integration of consumer data collected from multiple platforms; (3) data diffusion — distribution to the key people in the organization; (4) data intelligence — usage of data to improve the experience, content, and service delivered during any interaction with consumers; and (5) data update — organizing and polishing the collected data to constantly update user profiles. As consumers are consciously providing a large amount of personal data to companies through every registration — for example, related to a contest participation — they have increasing expectations on the way brands intelligently handle this information. For instance, if a user calls a customer service for information, he may wish to be automatically gathered as Mr. X. Also, he may expect the operator to know what kind of products he owns as well as the outcome of his previous interactions with the company.

7.5. Relationship Building Stages and Current Limits for Brand Managers

Relationships are dynamic; they develop and vary over time as a consequence of the interactions between the partners and of the variations in the surrounding environment. Relationships do not follow predetermined stages, although a common pattern can be found. The relational development model put forth by Knapp (1984) describes the full trajectory of human relationship development and deterioration. He stated that although the relationship cannot be precisely predicted, certain patterns are likely. This model is comprised of two sequential stages: Coming together and coming apart. In order to be effective, all of the steps in the relationship building process have to follow. Therefore, relationships should be considered as process phenomena (Hinde, 1995).

The process of coming together has five stages (Avtgisa et al., 1998): (1) initiating, in which first impressions of the two parties involved in the relationship are formed; (2) experimenting, in which the parties attempt to find some common ground between each other's lives; (3) intensifying, in which the parties test the potential of the relationship with varying degrees of self-disclosure; (4) integrating, in which the lives of the two people begin to merge; and (5) bonding, in which the commitment of the relationship is communicated to the rest of the world. Similar to human relationships, I believe that consumer–brand relationships follow a defined development process that is referred to, according to marketing terminology, as stages of: Awareness, consideration, involvement, engagement, and loyalty. Exactly like in the widely used communication funnel, brands have five stages, starting with awareness of a product and moving towards its consideration, involvement, engagement, and loyalty. If the relationship is not maintained and revitalized over time, it will probably decrease in intensity and

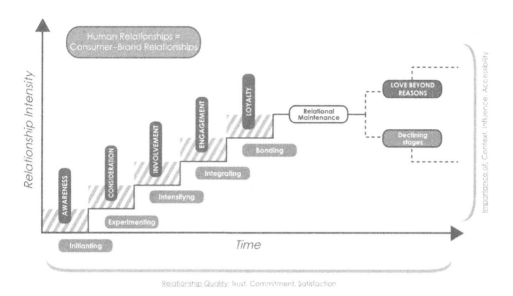

Fig. 7.3. Path to delightful relationship (Consumer–brand relationship development process). Adapted from Knapp (1994).

reach a declining stage in which the brand and the consumer move further and further apart (Fig. 7.3). The highest level of relational intensity can be reached in the "love beyond reasons" status (Roberts, 2004), where the love for a brand is such that his positive attitude towards the brand is sometimes purely irrational and not understood by external actors. An example is the Apple iPhone launch event, where the general public and media criticized thousands of brand lovers for queuing for several hours to buy the latest phone, which had similar characteristics to the previous version. This is definitely the point in people's minds where all brands would like to find a place. Particularly important for the definition of the relationship intensity is the context (and the location) in which the conversation happens. It would be rather different if this was initiated by a user in response to a technical issue, either for exposure to an advertisement or proactively by a company. This is similar to human relationships, in which the length and strength of the connection changes often depend on the context in which the initial contact is initiated (for example, meeting someone at a church versus at a rave party). In a social world, the influence of peers and family members is dramatically important; people increasingly come to know what kind of brands you own, use, and interact with. Judgment, criticism, and suggestions by other influencers will be inevitable when a romantic relationship is made public. Also, accessibility to information, technology, and resources plays a fundamental role in the definition of the relationship quality. The absence of a direct communication channel where a user can effectively communicate with a company can significantly influence the perception of the brand itself. For a romantic couple, a lack of accessibility could mean having a long-distance relationship or not having access to communication technology. Some of the most frequent issues that the author observed during the consumer–brand relationship development process come from the non-realization by the company that communication messages are more powerful if they take into account the stage that any consumer is in at a given moment. Also, the non-realization by brand managers that consumers engagement is something they should be aiming at only after the user knows the brand, has considered its values and benefits, has tried the product and have shown certain level of interest to it, makes the online communication particularly ineffective. Consider the example of an advertisement regarding a contest run by a new beauty product that offers tickets to events for those who share details of their beauty routine. This contest should, first of all, consider the consumer's level of familiarity with the presented brand. What stage of the relationship development process is the consumer at? The best way to initiate a relationship is usually introduce yourself, show your personality and values, and make clear what you can offer (that is, the "benefits"). Whenever a brand adopts a direct approach to engage with users that have zero familiarity with its products, there is a very high risk of having someone participate solely for economic reward. A brand might risk being perceived as a "stalker" given the sophisticated re-targeting technics available to managers today. In this case, the sole purview of a manager should be to create a word-of-mouth effect that lasts for the duration of a campaign, some basic PR to show that the company is active online, and not building strategic relationships.

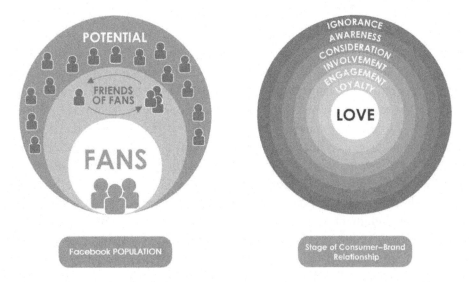

Fig. 7.4.   Fans versus brand lovers.

In the practitioners' perspective, the concept of "Facebook Fans" has further simplified the practice of building strong relationship within online communities. The common habit of acquiring as many consumers as possible via ads, even paying for fake "likes" whenever a marketing budget is not sufficiently high, has shifted the manager's focus towards hard metrics (for example, the number of followers, the number of fans, the number of shares) rather than on the quality of the relationship built inside the platform (Fig. 7.4). This trend was partially driven by brand managers' need to show sound returns of social media investments. The predominant use of numbers to measure the quality of relationships represents a myopic approach. Whenever a brand confuses fans with brand loyalists (or brand lovers), the long-term button-line results are severely biased. In this case, a brand might have millions of fans and still face issues such as engagement, sales, and retention. According to Facebook (Nielsen, 2012), the platform population can be split into fans, friends of fans (increasingly important for the so-called "social advertising") and potential fans. Consider a brand with 1 million fans on Facebook that wants to deliver content based on users' familiarity with the brand, their needs and wants, current interests, products owned, etc. Currently, a community manager, whether internal or external to the company, has no tools with which to effectively create diversified messages among his 1 million fans. This limitation is a reflection on the effectiveness of online communication.

One of the major challenges for companies is to guarantee continuity of the relationship development process. Since priorities in companies can change quickly, while the relationships takes time to evolve, it is not uncommon to observe a dramatic change in the online communication efforts of a brand, due to a lack of resources or interest by the top management. In every company, people, priorities, and the availability of resources change so frequently that the plan of building strong long-term connections can fall at any point. One way to prevent this is to include a consumer-centric strategy inside the overall company vision. Zappos.com, an online shoes and clothing shop acquired by Amazon, is a great example of such an approach. Zappos employees are encouraged to go above and beyond traditional customer service (Dubner, 2007). For example, when a woman called Zappos to return a pair of boots for her husband because he had died in a car accident, she received a delivery of flowers, which the call center rep had billed to the company without even checking with her supervisor (Chafkin, 2009). When a company decides to adopt an open approach to online conversations, it must consider that a certain level of consistency is needed over time. A general assumption coming from the managerial orientation of relationship marketing sees the relationships as something that can be imposed or withdrawn at will. Although there is a tendency for companies to believe and act as if this is true, there is enough evidence to suggest that whenever a relationship is dictated by the company, a process of consumer disaffection begins and negative business implications are expected. I argue that when a process of openness from the company is initiated, it is difficult to stop it without consequences on the consumer's perception of relationship quality.

Despite the growing interest in this area, managers are often required to take difficult calls that contrast with their regular communication-related decisions. On the one hand, there is a desperate need to create communication assets or experiences that are sufficiently attractive for consumers to be shared and for media agents to be covered. On the other hand, during such a period of scarcity, there is a need to focus on the initiative's return on investment (ROI) and on the process of prioritization and optimization of the company's resources. In evaluating the potentiality of launching a particular social media initiative, managers are increasingly confronted with questions related to the media coverage and audience reach. Through the estimated PR effect generated by the initiative in owned, earned, and paid media (Forrester, 2009), managers try to support the need of relational-based campaigns during the difficult task of showing top management the potential returns, at least in terms of media coverage and audience reach. Despite the market evidence that social initiatives are absolutely necessary to create a sustainable competitive advantage, which is greatly enhanced when brand community attachment is generated, the lack of data related to the initiative's ROI automatically de-prioritizes this powerful tool in favor of more measurable actions. Even in the rare case that a company collaborates with an agency that plans a social initiative perfectly in line with business objective, strategies, and messages, and is evaluated with proper metrics, its "PRability" effect is likely to fall over time as the idea becomes obsolete and is executed by other companies and in other industries/geographical areas. Furthermore, whenever a social media plan is evaluated as a standalone initiative — that is, not considered in a process aimed at developing relationships with strategic customers inside a so-called "consumer journey" (Edelman, 2010) — this tends to have a limited effect on the brand-consumer relationship and on the long-term business impact overall. This myopic view of social media has led companies to use "Social Media" platforms, not for their "social" characteristics but as PR machine tools to distribute press releases without any relationship-based objective. It is only after several steps in the social media environment that global brands have understood how much it costs to simultaneously manage thousands (if not millions) of relationships with consumers and prospects. Today, the need to create cost efficiencies is pushing those brands to reduce the number of fan pages or other corporate accounts.

7.6. New Technology Tools Available to Companies for Relationship Building

The greater number of communication technologies available has led to substantial changes in all organizational departments. The way people communicate has facilitated an increase in disintermediation and in new forms of relationships (Turnbull *et al.*, 1996). In particular, the internet is becoming a huge marketplace that contains market-relevant information and where interaction can happen at every moment and in every part of the world. However, researchers have underlined that, at least in some countries (such as Italy), the internet is enhancing communication rather than changing the fundamental nature of the relationship. However, the internet represents only a portion of the many technological changes driven by information and communication technology. In fact, many innovations in marketing and marketing communication driven by developments in ICT are often linked to a profound transformation of business processes and of the idea of organization itself (Achrol and Kotler, 1999; Karmarkar, 2004). One of the most radical innovations saw the explosion of data capture, storage, processing, and transformation. Parallel to a growing number of assets, there is the need for flexibility and accessibility of these resources. Consequently, these phenomena have transformed the relationships between companies and customers, but also between companies and agencies networks (such as advertising/PR/digital agency) (Mandelli and Mari, 2012). Stone and Shaw (1988) found that stored information may be used at the strategic level to strengthen relationships.

A recent report focused on data-driven practices of marketing industry professionals, called the Global review of data-driven marketing and advertising, found that data is becoming vitally important to ROI effectiveness and customer engagement (GlobalDMA, 2014). Results from more than 3,000 advertisers and marketers surveyed in 17 countries show that more than 80% of practitioners consider data to be important for the deployment of their communication efforts, and two-thirds have increased spending on data-driven activities compared to the previous year. For just over half of respondents, the key trigger driving investments in data-driven activities was demand to be more customer-centric. Desire to maximize effectiveness and efficiency of marketing, and understanding more about customers and prospects, were also mentioned as the main reasons for increasing future budgets on big data. When it comes to what would help advance data-driven marketing, managers indicated that expanded budgets (43.4%), deeper pools of experienced talent (42.1%), and improved organizational structures (33.0%) were required. Furthermore, the highest investment priority areas are data modeling and analytics skillsets.

Many players in the software industry have produced any kind managing platform to support managers handling a specific aspect of the overall relationship management process. The new challenge for the major software companies has become to offer a complete "customer system" that enhances managers' ability to manage a relationship in all its stages, from pre- to post-sales. Modules of this system include customer relationship management applications, analytics and monitoring tools, and social media management platforms.

Only a few years ago, Salesforce, one of the 10 largest software companies in the world, solely offered services from a sales force automation provider; it now offers tools for customer service, marketing, and community management, and has recently introduced analytics dashboards (Salesforce, 2014). As Marc Benioff, CEO of Salesforce (CNBC, 2014), pointed out:

> "Behind everyone of those applications, behind every voice activation, behind everything that is going on, whether it's in your home or in your business, there is a customer. And all those companies providing next-generation services [...] have got a new generation of 'customer systems' behind them. All of those apps, all those connected products, as well as their entire employees base. The way to manage all that customer information [in one place] is using Salesforce. It doesn't matter if they are doing sales, service [customer] or marketing, managing community, they need a customer success platform and that is what Salesforce is offering".

In underlining the importance of this revolutionary approach and its impact on the bottom line, Benioff also explained that:

> "Coca-Cola Germany re-built themselves using Salesforce; they have SAP on the back-end, of course, but on the front office it's all Salesforce. Their CEO said that they are growing faster and ever before in Germany because they have re-built using Salesforce as their Agile platform. Companies like Coca-Cola, Philips, LVMH, and others, the more they invest in mobility, social networking and in building the next generation of customer systems, the better they are doing and the faster they are growing. You can easily see the incredible results of these companies".

Salesforce's value proposition appears to be particularly convincing because it places consumers at the very center of its corporate strategy. I agree with the need for a "customer system", a platform that can integrate all the gathered data that allows anyone to retrieve the data in real-time for effective customer relationship management. As I have noted above, software cannot replace personal interaction, but it can certainly support consumer–brand relationship building.

Walmart's CMO, Stephen Quinn, stated during the ANA Masters of Marketing Conference 2014 that it is only recently that big data has started making sense in the organization. As he explained (AdWeek, 2014), "We have a customer knowl-edge platform that is our customer data that really didn't exist two years ago … In the past, (data sets have) been separate in order to build up that capability, but really it's been the last two years — even the last year — where we've had data to see horizontally what the customer is doing internally". According to Quinn, "the biggest challenge with data is still gleaning when or why shoppers switch over to competitors". MillerCoors' CMO, Andrew England, offered a different stance on data, saying, "We are less at a level of tracking individual consumers. We're at the level of trying to aggregate consumer behavior that we can then derive from" (AdWeek, 2014). Kraft CMO Deanie Elsner claimed that his com-pany is collecting 22,000 pieces of data from its 100 million online visits each year. The packaged-goods marketer uses the data to form 500 segments of con-sumers to buy ads against. Lisa Donohue, Starcom USA CEO, argued that mar-keters who get a grip on data have better insight into digital's full spectrum, including native advertising and social. As she said, "People are not spending enough time deciding what their infrastructure will be based on their business model … When you do that, then you can get to the data that matters that can drive business strategy" (AdWeek, 2014).

7.7. Connecting Content Strategy to Relational Strategy and Brand Strategy

Marketing and corporate communications managers are often confronted with the need to anticipate market trends. In order to be at the cutting edge of innovation, they are often willing to adopt technology that can generate visibility and a sense of innovativeness, despite the value delivered to consumers can be objected. Too often, a marketing goal becomes to distribute brand messages across the globe in the fast-est and cheapest way. This leads to the communication idea and the technological tools being chosen over the brand strategy. In other words, the communication cam-paign becomes a mere tactic with no (or even negative) long-term business implica-tions. At the very core of a content strategy, marketing managers should always focus their brand strategy on brand ideals. A brand ideal is the higher purpose of a brand or organization, which goes beyond the product and the service it sells (WPP, 2012). The overall brand purpose is often neglected and is not linked to the defined content strategy. According to Stengel (2011), former global marketing officer (GMO) at Procter & Gamble, "The ideal is the brand's inspirational reason for being. It explains why the brand exists and the impact it seeks to make in the world. A brand ideal actively aims to improve the quality of people's lives. It creates a meaningful goal for the brand — a goal that aligns employees and the organization to better serve customers". Stengel has extensively studied the inter relationships of people's bonding with brands and the growth in those brands' financial value. To do so, he used a database, provided by the agency BrandZ, which contains brand-equity-related information on more than 50,000 brands in 31 countries within 380 categories, from 1998 to the present. The implications of Stengel's study are relevant to any brand manager. One of the most profound finding is that brand ideals — that is, the higher-order benefit the brand gives to the world — drive the performance of the businesses that registered the highest growth in the mentioned period. The most successful businesses are those in which the brand ideals are deeply centered in one of the five areas of fundamental human values. These human values are considered to be "universal", as any human being generally wishes to actively experience happiness, to connect with one another in meaningful ways, to explore the surrounding world, to feel confident, and to positively affect society. Certain companies focus on the "eliciting joy" ideal, such as Coca-Cola, Emirates or MasterCard. Others, such as Skype, Nokia, and Facebook, have associated their brands with "enabling connection". Some brands, such as Google, Apple, or Red Bull, wish to "inspire exploration", while companies like Hugo Boss, Heineken, and Mercedes-Benz, aim to "evoke pride", giving people security or vitality. Yet others focus on "impacting society" in a broad sense; these include Chipotle, Dove, and Innocent. Although a brand might be directly or indirectly connected to several of the five universal human values mentioned earlier, it is important that one of the areas is dominant. For example, Facebook was created to enable connections among peers. Over time, the service has evolved to include many other features that have increased the users' perceived value in certain areas of pride (for example, you can easily share your entire life and receive a sense of appreciation from others), the area of joy (for example, play games, listen to music, or watch videos), the area of exploration (for example, the new feature called "Search Graph" that will revolutionize the way we retrieve social-related information) and the area of impacting society (for example, you can espouse social causes and donate money). However, almost all of Facebook's corporate communication, as well as any other marketing campaign, focuses on the brand ideal of "connecting people". It is strategically important that a brand stays true to its brand ideals along the journey, as this influences the way people perceive and think about the brand. Whenever a brand plays on several brand ideals at the same time, it is necessary to prioritize these ideals.

According to Stengel (2011), brand managers should be conceived as "business artists", leaders whose primary medium is brand ideals. The scope of these business artists is to discover (or rediscover) a brand ideal in one of the five fields of fundamental human values, to build a business culture around the ideal, to communicate the ideal across the organization and outside of it, to deliver a near-ideal customer experience, and to evaluate business performance against this ideal. Once a brand manager is clear on the brand ideals (that is, what the brand stands for), the next step is to create communication assets (and a campaign) to guarantee customer experience that supports the chosen ideal that will drive the business. An example is how Coca-Cola, which has long been associated with happiness, has transformed for a recent partnership with the James Bond movie "Skyfall" in a smart viral campaign (Fig. 7.5). Instead of focusing on the classic movie franchise's characteristics, Coke Zero challenged unsuspecting train passengers to "unlock the 007" in them for their chance to win exclusive tickets to the new film. However, the exclusive tickets were not free. Contestants had to go the extra mile and unlock their inner James Bond in less than 70 seconds to win. The humorous video spread across the web, showing Coca-Cola's need to share happiness around the world.

This is a good example of how brand ideals can be the focus of a marketing campaign, even if the link with the campaign's theme is not immediately apparent. Thinking in terms of brand ideals enables managers to create consistency in their actions and make their message easy to communicate. I agree that, in order to deliver brand essence consistently over time, the content strategy should be deeply linked to brand strategy and viewed through the lens of an overall relational strategy. This alignment between content, brand, and relational strategies must be considered in any channel and in any platform, whether online or offline.

To a certain extent, a manager can use brand ideals to directionally guide the brand's efforts toward a consistent product and communication innovation. The same applies in the digital environment (Fig. 7.6). A brand is a brand anywhere, whether the context is mobile apps or physical goods. Therefore, it is easy to find examples of mobile services that clearly play in connection to a specific

Fig. 7.5.   Coca-Cola '007 Campaign'.

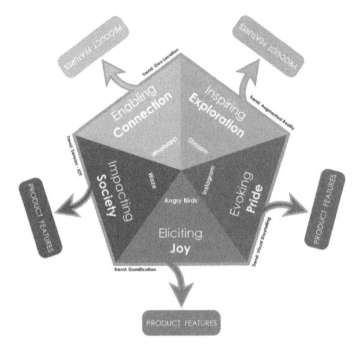

Fig. 7.6.   From brand ideals to app purpose — Adapted from Stengel (2011).

fundamental human value. The Shazam app, for example, recognizes music and media playing nearby. The app's purpose is to inspire exploration by discovering what a user is hearing at that moment. Once you have identified your brand (and, in this case, the app's purpose), it becomes straightforward to find your service value proposition, assess the landscape to identify competitors in that area, position your products considering Point of Parities (POPs) and Points of Differences (PODs), and make a clear prioritization of the new feature you intend to launch. On the latter point, Shazam has recently announced a new feature called "Auto Shazam" that can continuously recognize popular music and TV around a user, even if their phone is locked.

This means that if someone is unable to whip out their phone to Shazam a song, the phone will still be able to record it. As Shazam wrote on its update, "Flip the switch on the Shazam home screen to turn on Auto Shazam, and automatically recognize while you commute or watch a movie, even if you leave the Shazam app or lock your phone" (Cnet, 2013). This new feature is massively connected to the brand ideals and the app's purpose of "Inspiring exploration", and is consistent with the imaginary that the brand has got in the consumer's mind. Shazam might have launched other features that did not necessarily serve the purpose of letting users discover more of what they are experiencing in the physical world. However, it has rightly decided to prioritize product features that build the brand equity in that specific area, which is strategic for the company. Shazam could have created features in relation to any other brand ideal. If the scope is to enable meaningful connections, it could have created a community of people that are curious about the same music at the same time. Alternatively, if the scope is to create joy, it could have created a quiz game among the community members to guess the search song, and so on. Similarly to Shazam, also other services have a defined business strategy focused on brand ideals upon which they build their product innovation and marketing strategy. For example, Whatsapp is about connecting people in a convenient way, while Instagram allows you to express your personality to the world, Angry Birds delivers happiness, and Waze impacts society positively by reducing traffic.

7.7.1. *From brand ideals to app purpose — Volkswagen SmileDrive Case*

Any time a brand manager wants to add an additional touchpoint or asset to its campaign as a means of interacting with consumers, he or she should carefully evaluate the coherence of these with the brand ideals and brand strategy and under the perspective of a unique customer journey. A recent example of a branded mobile app that deeply connects its purpose to the brand promise and wants to form a deeper relationship with a strategic target comes from Volkswagen. The German car manufacturer presents its slogan — "It's not the miles, it's how you live them" — (eliciting joy) in the majority of its communication assets. Despite the different consumer perception of the brand, both in and outside Europe, the message Volkswagen wishes to emphasize appears to be clear and recognizable on every channel, platform, or tool being used for marketing purposes. The customer insight behind this campaign is that people spend increasing amounts of time in their cars, looking for ways to share their experiences and create meaning around everyday journeys (Fig. 7.7). In particular, consumers born between the early 1980s and the early 2000s (also known as Generation Y) are the hottest target for most brands; they are relatively easy to approach and willing to interact with the brand during their morning commutes. Based on this insight, Volkswagen has, in conjunction with its partner agencies, created the new mobile SmileDrive app (Mediacom, 2013).

This app provides an engaging new way for commuters to keep track of their drives; for example, by using the app to record distance traveled, time, and weather, and pass that info to friends and family. SmileDrive allows you to unlock "virtual badges" for going on extra-long rides or passing other drivers of similar cars. According to several sources (see Google Think Insight, 2013), the app generated 9,000 downloads within the first month from launch, with the average time driven

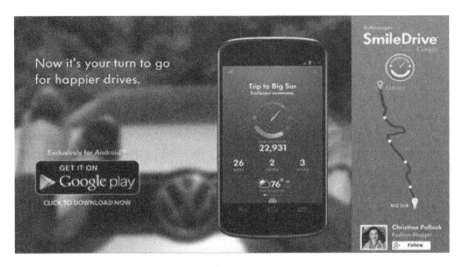

Fig. 7.7.   Volkswagen SmileDrive Case.

with the app being 73 minutes. Interacting with a branded app for an average of 73 minutes is uncommon, especially because this app was not solely distributed to Volkswagen's customers, but also to potential ones. Going beyond the definition of the value delivered through this app, which obviously changes from customer to customer, I find a relevant lesson coming from the way the consistency of the idea was assessed against the brand promise. The idea itself, used for a different brand, and therefore with different ideals, would have shown no impact in terms of overall brand equity contribution. In this case, the meanings the brand has generated towards its customers and potential ones are perfectly coherent with the previous campaigns (for example, see the "fun theory"), current messages, and among touch points.

7.8. Conclusions

Authors from a number of fields have attempted to interpret the changes brought by the latest technologies, while companies have moved into the field, starting to experiment, but often without a sound strategy. This has produced a peak of enthusiasm in the social media field, partially due to the oversimplification of the phenomena, with the increased belief that a magic formula for success has finally been found.

This chapter shows that complexity reigns supreme in online consumer–brand relationships, whereas companies often have no clue about the kind of actor they are interacting with. Within this complexity, I have identified social media as an enabling tool that enables direct, real-time interaction with consumers. This context requires a new mindset that helps managers identify all community members as single actors. Academics and practitioners around the world are realizing that marketing, which initially adopted the customer's perspective has ironically lost this focus (Rust *et al.*, 2004). Thus, it urges to refocus the effort on the relationships, not on the technology itself. Now an increasing amount of research is emerging, re-focusing attention on the customer perspective. As a new imperative in marketing practice, a focus on customer relationships is presented as an avenue to competitive advantage (Eisingerich and Bell, 2007; Grönroos, 2011). Relationship marketing, in one form or another, has been around for many years and will continue to prevail regardless of how technology develops (Smith, 2011).

Bibliography

1. Achrol, RS and P Kotler (1999). Marketing in the network economy. *The Journal of Marketing*, 63, 146–163.
2. Adweek (2014). How Four of America's Top Marketers Use Data Walmart's CMO notes strides in just the past year. http://www.adweek.com/news/technology/how-four-america-s-top-marketers-use-data-160871.
3. Almquist, E and KJ Roberts (2000). A mindshare manifesto. *Mercer Management Journal*, 12, 9–20.
4. Avtgisa, TA, DV Westb and TL Andersonc (1998). Relationship stages: An inductive analysis identifying cognitive, affective, and behavioral dimensions of Knapp's relational stages model. *Communication Research Reports*, 15(3), 280–287.
5. Bain and Company (1999). The Value of Online Customer Loyalty and How You Capture. www.bain.com.
6. Bain and Company (2011). Putting social media to work, 12/09/2011, http://www.bain.com/.
7. Batt, PJ (2008). Building social capital in networks. *Industrial Marketing Management*, 37(5), 487–491.
8. Bernoff, J, A Ray and J Wise (2010). Peer Influence Analysis — A Social Computing Report. Mass Influencers Are The Key To Achieving Scale In Social Media Marketing. https://www.forrester.com/.
9. Berry, LL (1983). Relationship Marketing. In *Emerging Perspectives of Services Marketing*, LL Berry, GL Shostack and GD Upah, (eds.). Chicago, IL: American Marketing Association.
10. Bortree, D and T Seltzer (2009). Dialogic strategies and outcomes: An analysis of environmental advocacy groups' Facebook profiles. *Public Relations Review*, 35(3), 317–319.
11. Bowlby, J (1979). *The making and breaking of affectional bonds*. London: Tavistock.
12. Branderati (2013). The age of advocacy and influence: 26 stats marketers should know, 14/06/2013. http://branderati.com/the-age-of-advocacy-and-influence-26-stats-marketers-should-know/.

13. Chafkin, M (2009). The Zappos Way of Managing. 01/05/09, Inc. Magazine. http://www.inc.com/magazine/20090501/the-zappos-way-of-managing.html.

14. ClickFox (2013). 15 Social Customer Service Statistics, 28/05/2013. http://www.sentimentmetrics.com/blog/2013/05/28/15-social-customer-service-statistics/.

15. CNBC (2014). Interview Salesforce CEO Marc Benioff, Mad Money. https://www.youtube.com/watch?v=lpYHRSE7mVA#t=337.

16. Cnet (2013). Shazam iPhone App Identifies Music When Phone is Locked, 19/12/13. http://www.cnet.com/news/shazam-iphone-app-identifies-music-when-phone-is-locked/.

17. Comscore and Yahoo! (2006). Engaging Advocates through Search and Social Media. http://www.businesswire.com/

18. Cova, B. (1997). Community and Consumption: Towards a Definition of the Linking Value of Products or Services. *European Journal of Marketing*, 31(3–4), 297–316.

19. Cova, B and V Cova (2002). Tribal marketing: The tribalisation of society and its impact on the conduct of marketing. *European Journal of Marketing*, 36(5–6), 595–620.

20. Cova, B and S Pace (2006). Brand community of convenience products: New forms of customer empowerment — the case my Nutella the community. *European Journal of Marketing*, 40(9), 1087–1105.

21. Cova, B and S Pace and DJ Park (2007). Global brand communities across borders: The Warhammer case. *International Marketing Review*, 24(3), 313–329.

22. Dubner, SJ (2007). Customer Service Heaven, Freakonomics. http://freakonomics.com/2007/05/17/customer-service-heaven/ 05/17/2007.

23. Edelman, D (2010). Branding in the digital age. *Harvard Business Review*, 88(12), 62–69.

24. Eisingerich, AB and SJ Bell (2007). Maintaining customer relationships in high credence services. *Journal of Services Marketing*, 21(4), 253–262.

25. Fielding, NG (2008). *Handbook of Online Research Methods*. London: Sage Publications.

26. Forrester (2009). Defining Earned, Owned And Paid Media, 16/12/2009. http://blogs.forrester.com/interactive_marketing/2009/12/defining-earned-owned-and-paid-media.html.

27. Fournier, S (1998). Consumers and their brands: Developing a relationship theory in consumer research. *The Journal of Consumer Research*, 24(4), 343–373.

28. Füller, J, G Jawecki and H Mühlbacher (2007). Innovation creation by online basketball communities. *Journal of Business Research*, 60(1), 60–71.

29. GfK Roper (2006). Global Brands Suffer Power Drain According to GfK Roper Consulting Annual Worldwide Study. http://www.prnewswire.com/news-releases/global-brands-suffer-power-drain-according-to-gfk-roper-consulting-annual-worldwide-study-58091862.html.

30. GlobalDMA (2014). The Global Review of Data-Driven Marketing and Advertising. http://www.cmo.com.au/article/558909/first-of-its-kind-report-benchmarks-global-data-driven-marketing-efforts/.

31. Godin, S (2014). Learning from the State Department. http://sethgodin.typepad.com/.
32. Google Think Insight (2013). Volkswagen SmileDrive. http://www.google.co.uk/think/campaigns/volkswagen-smiledrive.html.
33. Grönroos, C (1994). From marketing mix to relationship marketing: Towards a paradigm shift in marketing. *Management Decisions*, 32, 4–20.
34. Grönroos, C (2007). *Service Management and Marketing: Customer Management in Service Competition*, 3rd ed. Chichester: John Wiley & Sons.
35. Grönroos, C (2011). Value co-creation in service logic: A critical analysis. *Marketing Theory*, 11(3), 279–301.
36. Gummesson, E (2004). *Many-to-Many Marketing*. SE: Liber, Malmö.
37. Hakansson, H and I Snehota (1989). No business is an island. *Scandinavian Journal of Management*, 5(3), 187–200.
38. Håkansson, H and I Snehota (1995). *Developing Relationships in Business Networks*. London: Routledge.
39. Hanna, R, Rohm A and VL Crittenden (2011). We're all connected: The power of the social media ecosystem. *Business horizons*, 54(3), 265–273.
40. Hinde, RA (1995). *A Suggested Structure for a Science of Relationships. Personal Relationships*, 2, 1–15.
41. Hur, WM, KH Ahn and M Kim (2011). Building brand loyalty through managing brand community commitment. *Management Decision*, 49(7), 1194–1213.
42. Javornik, A and A Mandelli (2012). Behavioral perspectives of customer engagement: An exploratory study of customer engagement with three Swiss FMCG brands. *Journal of Database Marketing & Customer Strategy Management*, 19(4), 300–310.
43. Jive (2011). Jive Social Business Index 2011. http://www.prnewswire.com/news-releases/new-jive-study-unveils-social-business-is-top-executive-strategic-imperative-124700518.html.
44. Kaplan, AM and M Haenlein (2010). Users of the world, unite! The challenges and opportunities of Social Media. *Business Horizons*, 53(1), 59–68.
45. Karmarkar, U (2004). Will you survive the services revolution? *Harvard Business Review*, 82(6), 100–107.
46. Keller Fay Group (2007). Research Brief: 3.5 Billion Conversations a Day, 20/11/07. http://www.kellerfay.com/research-brief-3–5-billion-conversations-a-day/.
47. Kent, ML and M Taylor (1998). Building a dialogic relationship through the world wide web. *Public Relations Review*, 24, 321–340.
48. Kietzmann, JH, K Hermkens, IP McCarthy and BS Silvestre (2011). Social media? Get serious! Understanding the functional building blocks of social media. *Business horizons*, 54(3), 241–251.
49. KissMetrics (2013). How to Master Social Customer Acquisition. blog.kissmetrics.com/wp-content/.../great-customer-service-succeed.pdf.
50. Knapp, ML (1984). *Interpersonal Communication and Human Relationships*. Boston, MA: Allyn & Bacon.

51. Komito, L (1998). The Net as a foraging society: Flexible communities. *The Information Society: An International Journal*, 14(2), 97–106.
52. Kozinets, RV (1998). On netnography: Initial reflections on consumer research investigations of cyberculture. *European Management Journal*, 17(3). *Advances in Consumer Research*, 25(1), 366–371.
53. Kozinets, RV (2002). The field behind the screen: Using netnography for marketing research in online communities. *Journal of Marketing Research*, 39, 61–72.
54. Kozinets, RV (2010). *Netnography: Doing Ethnographic Research Online.* Los Angeles, LA: Sages.
55. Laroche, M, MR Habibi, MO Richard and R Sankaranarayanan (2012). The effects of social media based brand communities on brand community markers, value creation practices, brand trust and brand loyalty. *Computers in Human Behavior*, 28(5), 1755–1767.
56. Li, C (2010). *Open Leadership: How Social Technology Can Transform the Way You Lead.* Chichester: John Wiley & Sons.
57. Maffesoli, M (1993). *La Contemplation du monde.* France: Le Livre de Poche.
58. Maffesoli, M (1996). *The Time of the Tribes: The Decline of Individualism in Mass Society.* Thousand Oaks, CA: Sage.
59. Mandelli, A (2008). Consumer involvement in organizations in the "organization as communication" Perspective: A multidisciplinary research agenda. *OBS Journal*, 6, 111–119.
60. Mandelli, A (2012). Branding and control in markets as mediated conversations. *Sinergie rivista di Studi e Ricerche*, 89(Settembre–Dicembre), 147–165.
61. Mandelli, A and C Accoto (2010). *Marca e Metriche nei Social Media.* Lugano, CH: Università della Svizzera italiana.
62. Mandelli, A and C Accoto (2012). *Social Mobile Marketing.* Milano: Egea.
63. Mandelli, A and A La Rocca (2014). *From Service Experiences to Augmented Service Journeys: Digital Technology and Networks in Consumer Services. Managing Consumer Services.* New York, NY: Springer International Publishing.
64. Mandelli, A and A Mari (2011). The relationship between social media conversations and reputation during a crisis: The Toyota case. *International Journal of Management Cases*, 14(1), 456–489.
65. Mandelli, A and A Mari (2012). The impact of digital technology on service networks: studying a case in the advertising sector, In *The UCLA Anderson Business and Information Technologies (BIT) Project: A Global Study of Business Practice*, USA: World Scientific Publishing Company.
66. Mandelli, A, C Accoto and A Mari (2010). Social media metrics: Practices of measuring brand equity and reputation in online social collectives. In *Proceedings 6th International conference Thought leaders in Brand Management* (Università della Svizzera Italiana, Lugano, CH).
67. Mandelli, A, P Neirotti, A Canato, A Biffi, E Paolucci, M Cantamessa and C Parolini (2007). The Italy Business Information Technology Survey, U Karamtar and Y Mangal (eds.) *The Business and Information Technologies (BIT) Project: A Global Study of Business Practice*, USA: World Scientific Publishing Company.

68. Mari, A (2014). Is Social Media revolutionary?, BrandMates on Tumblr. http://brandmates.tumblr.com/post/80448384860/is-social-media-revolutionary.

69. Marketing Charts (2013). Use of advocates in branded online communities. http://www.marketingcharts.com/wp/online/use-of-advocates-in-branded-online-communities-seen-low-20145/.

70. Mathews, J (2014). The Sharing Economy Boom Is About to Bust, 27/06/14. http://time.com/2924778/airbnb-uber-sharing-economy/.

71. MediaCom (2013). The Connected Driving Experience. http://www.mediacom.com/en/news-insights/blink/issues/edition-6–2013/case-study-the-connected-driving-experience.aspx.

72. Merlo, O, A Eisingerich and S Auh (2014). Why customer participation matters. *MIT Sloan Management Review*. Cambridge, Massachusetts, pp. 1–9.

73. Muñiz, AM and TC O'Guinn (2001). Brand community. *Journal of Consumer Research*, 27(4), 412–432.

74. Nielsen (2012). Ads with friends: Analyzing the benefits of social ads, 03/07/2012. http://www.nielsen.com/us/en/insights/news/2012/ads-with-friends-analyzing-the-benefits-of-social-ads.html.

75. Incite, NM (2012). NM Incite State of Social Customer Service Report. http://soulofbrands.files.wordpress.com/2012/11/nm-incite-report-the-state-of-social-customer-service-2012.pdf.

76. Oracle (2011). Customer Experience Impact Report, Getting to the Heart of the Consumer and Brand Relationship. http://www.oracle.com/us/products/applications/cust-exp-impact-report-epss-1560493.pdf.

77. Park, CW, DJ MacInnis and J Priester (2008). *Brand Attachment: Constructs, Consequences and Causes*. Hanover, MA: Now Publishers Inc.

78. Park, H and RB Reber (2008). Relationship building and the use of Web sites: How Fortune 500 corporations use their Web sites to build relationships. *Public Relations Review*, 34, 409–411.

79. Reichheld, FF (2006). *The Ultimate Question: Driving Good Products and True Growth*. Boston, MA: Harvard Business School Press.

80. Roberts, K (2004). *Lovemarks: The Future Beyond Brands*. New York: Powerhouse Books.

81. Rust, RT, T Ambler, GS Carpenter, V Kumar and RK Srivastava (2004). Measuring marketing productivity: Current knowledge and future directions. *Journal of Marketing*, 68(4), 76–89.

82. Rybalko, S and T Seltzer (2010). Dialogic communication in 140 characters or less: How Fortune 500 companies engage stakeholders using Twitter. *Public Relations Review*, 36(4), 336–341.

83. Safko, L (2010). *The Social Media Bible: Tactics, Tools, and Strategies for Business Success*. Hoboken, New Jersey: John Wiley & Sons.

84. Salesforce (2014). Salesforce.com Becomes First Cloud Company to Enter Top 10 in Gartner's Worldwide Software Market Share Report. http://www.salesforce.com/company/news-press/press-releases/2014/04/140403.jsp.

85. Schau, HJ, AM Muñiz Jr and EJ Arnould (2009). How brand community practices create value. *Journal of Marketing*, 73(5), 30–51.

86. Smith, M (2011). *The New Relationship Marketing: How to Build a Large, Loyal, Profitable Network Using the Social Web*. Chichester: John Wiley & Sons.

87. SocialBakers (2013). Brands in All industries Increase Social Customer Care Performance (infographic). http://www.socialbakers.com/blog/1863-brands-in-all-industries-increase-social-customer-care-performance-infographic.

88. Stengel, J (2011). *Grow: How Ideals Power Growth and Profit at the World's Greatest Companies*. Rosewood Drive Dancers, MA: Crown Business.

89. Stone, M and R Shaw (1988). *Database Marketing*. Aldershot: Gower.

90. Tapscott, D (2014). *The Digital Economy Anniversary Edition: Rethinking Promise and Peril in the Age of Networked Intelligence*. McGraw Hill Professional.

91. Tapscott, D and AD Williams (2008). *Wikinomics: How Mass Collaboration Changes Everything*. New York: Penguin.

92. Technorati Media (2013). TechnoratiMedia's 2013 Digital Influence Report. http://technorati.com/report/?source=TRmenu.

93. Thomson, M (2006). Human brands: Investigating antecedents to consumers, strong attachments to celebrities. *Journal of Marketing*, 70(3), 104–119.

94. Thomson, M, DJ MacInnis and Park CW (2005). The ties that bind: Measuring the strength of consumers' emotional attachments to brands. *Journal of Consumer Psychology*, 15(1), 77–91.

95. Turnbull, P, D Ford and M Cunningham (1996). Interaction, relationships and networks in business markets: an evolving perspective. *Journal of Business & Industrial Marketing*, 11(3/4), 44–62.

96. Villanueva, J, S Yoo and DM Hanssens (2008). The impact of marketing-induced versus word-of-mouth customer acquisition on customer equity growth. *Journal of marketing Research*. 45(1), 48–59.

97. West, D, J Ford and E Ibrahim (2010). *Strategic Marketing: Creating Competitive Advantage*. UK: Oxford University Press.

98. Park CW, DJ MacInnis, J Priester, AB Eisingerich and D Iacobucci (2010). Brand attachment and brand attitude strength: Conceptual and empirical differentiation of two critical brand equity drivers. *Journal of Marketing*, 74(6), 1–17.

99. Wilkinson, IF and LC Young (1994). Business dancing: The nature and role of interfirm relations in business strategy. *Asia–Australia Marketing Journal*, 2(1), 67–79.

100. WPP (2012). Brand Ideals by Millward Brown. http://www.wpp.com/wpp/marketing/branding/brand-ideals/.

101. Zuberance (2011). Brand Advocate Data & Insights. www.zuberance.com/downloads/brandAdvocateInsights.pdf. [January 6, 2011].

About the Author

Alessandro Mari

Alex Mari is Digital Marketing Director at Sonova Group in Zürich (Switzerland), Founder of BrandMate (Brand Ambassador Community), and Lecturer of Social Media Marketing at the International University in Geneva (IUG). Alex is Global Entrepreneurship Fellow at the Central European University (Budapest, Hungary) and former marketer at Procter & Gamble, WPP and Telecom Italia. He has collaborated with the 'Digital Markets' project at the Institute of Marketing and Communication Management (IMCA) at University of Lugano (USI). His specialties are digital strategy, social business, social media planning, online advertising. His research interests are in the area of relationship marketing, consumer–brand relationships, brand communities. Alex earned a MSc in Marketing from the University of Lugano (USI).

CHAPTER 8

SOCIAL MEDIA IN B2B: MYOPEN COMMUNITY AT BTICINO

COSIMO ACCOTO, ENRICO VALTOLINA AND ANDREINA MANDELLI

Abstract

This chapter is a about a study of the creation and development of a B2B social community (MyOpen with 15.000+ members) as a social support platform for the BTicino business ecosystem (installators, system integrators, software houses and developers). The case analysis retraces the managerial and business issue originating the community (serving and innovating for niche markets while helping B2B clients through an efficient peer support dynamics) as well as the evolutionary stages experienced in more than a decade. It describes the use of a collaborative media environment related, in particular, to the development of market connections involving also open innovation practices and strategies. A key role in the evolution of MyOpen has been played by the capacity of building community analytics and social business intelligence to support business decisions. The practice of advanced analytics and intelligence insights of communities (from community digital analytics to community sentiment monitoring) has become important as the community has transformed into a relevant corporate asset in business development and innovation process. This case analysis has a descriptive rather than an analytic approach. It is particularly relevant for research studies and managerial discussions, since there is a lack of literature and knowledge about the introduction and the massive adoption of collaborative media in B2B market. It is also relevant in helping to understand the process of such strategic projects in large international companies like Bticino Legrand. The lessons that can be learned are mainly related to the evolutionary journey of a social support community and its adaptive mechanisms and dynamics related to the relationship between the company and its business stakeholders and ecosystems.

8.1. Introduction

This case is about the MyOpen community project at Legrand-Bticino, in which the use of collaborative media is related to the development of market connections and acts as an innovation platform. It is a case history with a descriptive rather than an analytic approach. It is valuable for research and managerial discussion, since there is a lack of literature and knowledge about the usage of collaborative media in B2B, and because it helps understand the process of developing such strategic projects in large international companies such as Legrand-Bticino.

8.2. Legrand Group

As global specialist in electrical and digital building infrastructures, Legrand's offering covers four fields: Control and command of electric power, cable management, power distribution and voice-data-image distribution (Fig. A.8.1). Operating globally, Legrand holds leading position in markets including France, Italy, and the United States, as well as in emerging economies such as Brazil, Russia, China, and India. In 2013, 68% of sales came from products ranked first or second in their markets. These strong national positions give Legrand major competitive advantages, including the ability: (a) to sell products suitable for most national markets — where installers work practices and consumer tastes can vary enormously, and where products, their operation and their installation must comply with specific standards; (b) to offer virtually all of the products needed for an electrical installation — often as an integrated system — from circuit protection panels to the connection of low-current sockets. Solutions like these help customers avoid the costs, risks, and delays associated with buying products from different suppliers; (c) to build on the familiarity and trust generated by its market-leading products among consumers, installers, and distributors, thus strengthening the position of products that are still challengers — and growing its business.

8.3. BTicino — Legrand

BTicino is an Italian company, part of Legrand Group and its identity is tightly interwoven with an advanced design culture (Fig. A.8.2). BTicino has always exercised a special leadership, anticipating changes in society — in its products, systems, and services — and new lifestyles at home and in the office. BTicino has always maintained a leadership position with regards to innovation, founded on the capacity to look beyond the standards to achieve new goals, to experiment with new processes, offer new solutions, present cutting-edge aesthetics, new technical, and social functions. The company has made significant moves in this direction, developing a sensibility that means constant improvement in the environmental performance of its products, in the pursuit of manufacturing certifications, in the development of energy-saving systems and in public awareness campaigns. From the very beginning, the focus on the industrial project as a whole has been a distinguishing factor of the company's *modus operandi*. In the immediate post-war period, BTicino contributed significantly to the modernization of the building heritage with innovative products that often anticipated market choices and evolution. BTicino has been the first manufacturer in Italy to conceive electrical components — from the "electrical panel" to the light switch — as industrial product design, not only in the perspective of standardized and low cost production, but also in terms of environmental significance, as components in a greater living system. BTicino was the very first company to introduce the concepts of aesthetics and comfort in an industry whose priority was the functional performance of products.

8.4. My Home — The Home Automation System

BTicino home automation is a system of integrated technology that makes it possible to use existing products in homes simultaneously, though they can continue to work separately (Fig. A.8.3). They are coordinated thanks to the digital solutions of home automation, so that they can respond efficiently to varying needs in home, saving time and optimizing energy savings. In the field of tertiary services and industry, the building automation system digitally controls and integrates different functions to rationalize resources and simplify their management. In 2001, to complement the range of electrical equipment, the revolutionary home-automation system My Home was introduced: advanced functions such as security (alarms, video entrance systems, video controls, access controls), comfort (advanced management of automatic devices and lighting, sound distribution), and energy savings (temperature control by zones, energy management for appliances) may be personalized and integrated, becoming more accessible and intuitive. The many user-friendly interfaces (traditional push-buttons, touch screen, controls managed by software on the personal computer) become an advanced tool to create a dialogue between the user and the technological systems. In addition, the flexibility of My Home makes it possible to select different levels of functionality, that can be modified any time as desired, to satisfy needs that may arise over time. The design of spaces and places for living is becoming increasingly complex. The application of its building automation solutions makes it possible to provide a flexible response to the client's needs, achieving an unprecedented synthesis of integrated tools to control, manage and supervise lighting, sound, comfort, and the security of things and persons. BTicino, using radio technologies, can boast of having a countless number of projects developed for monuments, museums, and venues for art and worship.

8.5. OpenWebNet — The Open Language

8.5.1. *The home automation connected to the internet*

It all began with the BTicino Home Automation offering when it started to be offered over internet backbone instead of the previous home automation system served as proprietary home communication protocol for domestic appliances (the classical home automation offering such as lighting, rolling shutters and all the other functions you can imagine in a contemporary home). In 2000, BTicino decided to connect over the IP internet protocol its home automation proprietary language. Before this period, all domestic appliances (and sensors and actuators related) were connected through a BTicino proprietary language. Starting from this period, BTicino felt the need to manage this infrastructure of home automation also through internet. To do this, it developed a gateway that is able to connect the internal network (and its proprietary protocol) to the internet. In practice, the gateway translates the information of the internal home network to the external IP network using a language that is called OpenWebNet.

8.5.2. *Why OpenWebNet?*

But for what reason was the OpenWebNet language born? The home automation systems of BTicino were initially oriented at domestic usage and to manage standardized automation features. But gradually, the market had begun to ask for customization of automation systems for not exactly household environments or standard functionalities. For example: there were requests for extension and customization of home automation systems for automated lighting of worship places, that would be able to meet special requirements related to religious rites and the specific times of religious celebration (for example, turning on the church lights with a remote control during various stages and special moments of the ceremony).

At the time, the marketing department of BTicino had not taken into consideration the possibility to use these systems in places not being households and to give this kind of opportunity to the company asking for the customizations Bticino should, under non-disclosure agreement, provide the specifications of the owned automation languages. Along with these, other requests for customization started to arrive — requests of other companies that intended to develop application for PDAs to manage the house in special conditions or for particular consumers. For example, there were requests for the development of applications for the home management of people with disabilities (in wheelchairs or with reduced mobility), or for customizations facilitating the opening of the shutters and turning on the house lights.

The requests for customization were even coming from luxury ships with installed BTicino home automation systems. These kinds of requests were niche, but potentially relevant and the company felt they should not be rejected. Nevertheless, their management resulted costly in terms of development time and in terms of continuous "non-disclosure" agreements to be signed by the various companies who asked to customize the BTicino home automation system and to access the proprietary language. Therefore, between 2003 and 2004, the R&D department of BTicino decided, in a creative and innovative manner, to adopt an alternative solution which consisted not in giving the specifications of the proprietary protocol (under non-disclosure agreement), but to release the OpenWebNnet language that, pushing down on the gateway, would allow everyone to develop customizations of the connection system.

The idea was to make the language public in order to allow the information system of home automation to be transferred and connected to third party systems so that, knowing the language specification, it was no longer necessary to have access to the proprietary protocol (which was preserved and remained as central in the architecture) and, at the same time, the third-party companies who wanted to customize the home automation systems could become autonomous and didn't need to burden BTicino with requests for interesting but niche customizations.

8.6. MyOpen — The Origin of a B2B Community

In those months, the idea of creating a site to convey requests for customization and where the business partners could find the specifications in order to customize their own BTicino solutions was born. The solution came neither from the Marketing nor from the Customer Service department, but from R&D department. In fact, the R&D department felt a strong need to find a solution to this problem and to take the opportunity of the customization requests that fell outside the envisaged lines of development. The R&D department (at Erba office) decided to adopt the solution of the open protocol and to create a website where the actors of the BTicino business ecosystem could find all the language specification and materials needed to independently develop solutions and customized home automation systems.

It was a localized and decentralized decision, which was taken independently by the headquarters considering the not-too-expensive investment of implementation. In 2005, it was decided to start the deployment of the open language solution (OpenWebNet). Supported by an open source infrastructure, in 2006, the online environment was created to welcome customers of Bticino home automation solutions. R&D department, together with the involvement of the IT department, created a platform on a PHP server called "MyOpen" community, where the OpenWebNet language was made available to interested parties, along with some initial information on home automation devices.

The website has been enriched with a forum, both in Italian and in English, that has formed the nucleus of the B2B community (branded with the orange color of BTicino). Unexpectedly and surprisingly, only one year later, MyOpen community could already count on more than thousand actively engaged members. Therefore, in 2007, this experiment, born in a decentralized and innovative way, could have been proclaimed a true success.

8.7. MyOpen — The Evolution of a B2B Community

Since its launch, the community continued to grow, month after month, but in 2008 something happened so relevant that changed the outlook on MyOpen by the Legrand Group and the central management. At that time, Apple began to push a model into the market which consisted in developing apps by a large community of developers. In the wake of this opening of the company at Cupertino, after only six months, thanks to the community and the opening of the previous years of the language, BTicino had an app to manage home automation. This app was not developed directly by BTicino, but by a company which was active in the community. Thanks to the community, BTicino had an app available for home automation in modality and timing that would have been impossible if there had not been the open community and the language.

This fact attracted the interest and attention of the top management of Legrand by ensuring that the community was no longer just a marginal experiment — spontaneous and open — but it represented a tool and an asset potentially disruptive and differentiating in the scenarios of "open innovation", brought to the fore by the approaches of Apple and more generally the movement of open innovation. The successful experiment of MyOpen as a community for information exchange and social support (peer-to-peer help) assumed a new light by developing app automation in record time. Bticino had been able to anticipate its competitors and to anticipate the trend of open innovation by cutting all the infrastructure and timing of routine development.

In normal conditions, Bticino would have taken no less than two years to develop and make available to its customers an app for home automation. In just six months, the company was able to bring to market a differentiating solution beating in the race both external competitors and internal R&D team. From this episode, that means, the acquisition of the awareness of the possibility to adopt the same approach (open innovation), the step was short and the management of the

Legrand group decided, at this point, to support adequately and in a structured way the MyOpen community project.

So in 2009 the decision, with more significant investments, to change the technological infrastructure that had supported the community so far — going from an open source php server to a professional community platform management such as Telligent and to rebrand the community, choosing a brand as neutral as possible, even if in connection with Legrand Group. In 2010 together with the new platform and the rebranding, Bticino changed also the nature of the community: It became not just a forum, social support and repository for documentation of open language, but it also started to have new sections and features that were more business-oriented. From the geographical point of view, the importance of opening and expanding in order to meet other market areas has increased significantly: Thus, French and Latam communities have been introduced, the latter born in April 2013 for the countries of Latin America (Figs. A.8.5 and A.8.6).

New community sections such as the "professional network" and the "app gallery" supported the integration process within the platform, progressively increasing the appeal of the community and, consequently, the number of its members: Currently, a total number of 14,700 subscribers has been reached (February 2015). "Professional network" is a showcase for everyone in the community who wants to promote himself, his knowledge and experience about integration and software development in order to manage a home automation system. Reserved for people that develop integration solutions for My Home there is a section named "app gallery" where they can share their applications built for every device and every operating system.

8.7.1. *The evolutionary phases of the community*

We could identify some community stages to summarize the evolution and history of the community (taking into account that it is useful to interpret periodized steps focused on MyOpen and not periods in absolute):

- 2006–2008 — MyOpen is configured as a non-structured and a bit anarchist "experiment" for sharing of information and support to information on OpenWebNet language. It is a collaborative environment to download technical information and receive peer-to-peer support from members of the community.
- 2008–2010 — gradually, along with this kind of support and information tool, the community begins also to integrate the functionality of technical support starting a virtuous circle between its members that not only share information, but also create networks and small business ecosystems (installers–developers–configurators).

- 2010–2014 — with the new platform, MyOpen is redesigned to encourage the development of business by responding to the needs of the community that calls for new support services such as professional network and application gallery. This feature was introduced with the porting to the new platform in October 2013 and it consists in sharing on social networks and downloading by community applications for different devices (desktop, tablet, mobile web-based, also applications for remote control, third party devices, third party integration). In addition to that, registered users can evaluate (with social score) the various applications available which they have downloaded.
- 2015 — new innovative projects for MyOpen are still considered to further expand the purpose, nature and dynamics of the community. Nowadays, it is more and more the asset that allows the group Legrand to communicate to the business ecosystem the readiness, as the infrastructure is open to the technological partnerships with brands (Elica, Hitachi, Mitsubishi, Indesit) interested in a home automation, increasingly oriented towards the paradigms of the internet of things and towards open innovation model.

The objectives of the community are increasing and changing, and also its importance is increasing in the strategies of the Legrand Group. The opening of the language and the community not only led to the creation of a networking among installers and system integrators (see the next section on community targets), but also to the creation of partnerships and emerging collaborations thanks to the new technological revolution of the internet of things. In 2010, the change came with the revolution of the app and the application gallery, today a plus for the home systems, is represented by the possibility of a dialogue between the objects themselves and, therefore, the winning strategy is represented by the possibility to be open (also in line with the increasing trend of open innovation) and be within consortia which promotes the interconnection.

Since 2005, Bticino with MyOpen and open language has been a pioneer in the approaches to interoperability, but today there are more and more new players which are able to expose themselves with greater visibility (e.g., Google with the thermostat Nest or Apple with Homekit). But contrary of this media visibility, Bticino has instead an open infrastructure (as well as a data modeling) enabling it to offer compatibility operators and brands interested in a dialogue between the objects. The technology of Legrand/Bticino is ready to interconnect objects and there are thousands of people who, thanks to the community, know and can already use an open infrastructure. Also, the Legrand Group achieved full awareness, because it understood that, through the opening of the language and the innovative drive of the community, it was possible to substantially decouple the development of the internal product (R&D Legrand/Bticino) with the development time of the app and the software, which can connect products and services in the market.

From this point of view, this is not giving up the internal product development by Bticino, but it is an acceleration of the innovation processes relying on the capabilities of application and software development of third parties. In addition, the prospect of open innovation of Legrand/Bticino has also led to the emergence of new professions and new companies based on the development, implementation and marketing of products born through the open language and infrastructure. The challenge in the coming years will be to develop this open infrastructure, an eco-system service, in a way to support other manufacturers, brands, and companies seeking to connect their devices and household appliances. We need to remember that Legrand is a manufacturing company (produces physical objects and will continue to do so in the future), and it is not a company that sells services (although in the future it could, but it would change the DNA of the company directing it to service-based ecosystem logic). In fact, having an open infrastructure allows Legrand/Bticino to make it available, with specific agreements, to third parties (for example, to an insurance company or service and personal care companies, or even to building management companies).

The competitors do not have such an open structure that can be interfaced in a rapid and simple way. The last aspect of the evolution of the community is linked to its governance. Following a deep reorganization of the Legrand Group in 2014, the community MyOpen that before the reorganization referred to the business unit that cured residential products and services, from 2015 is managed by the Innovation and Systems team, which aims to further expand the scope of the community by opening, with appropriate modality and timing, to other markets. In this perspective, the trajectory of open innovation is pushed even further: In this sense, a series of evaluations on more fruitful models to extend the open approaches in other areas is being made. In fact, in May 2012, with the objective to stimulate the development of apps, a pilot contest has been launched,"Energy Management", which is the first free contest launched by MyOpen in order to encourage the development of applications focused on home automation in energy management. The focus was: Development of apps for Android OS that upgrade the OpenWebNet integration with other systems. Bticino received relevant ideas from Italy, Belgium, France, Greece, and Poland.

8.7.2. *The active targets of the community*

The evolution of the community was accompanied by an evolution (and by a clearer and focused understanding) of targets and actors active in MyOpen.

At the beginning, in fact, as we now know, the target was represented by small companies and software houses that required customization of home automation systems and home automation and which were invited to join the community in order to find information and support. Over time and with the growth of the objectives of the community, the targets have been better identified, known, profiled, and managed.

System integrators represent the main target of the community. Typically, they are installation, design, and electrical systems arrangement companies that work with integration of systems and technologies for the automation of the residence. For example, they integrate the sound engineering since the opening of the system I sat IP level, there is a need to develop appropriate software like supervising software or app for iPad for hotels or nursing homes.

A second target is represented by installers, technical professionals called operationally to install home automation devices. It was important for MyOpen to develop and promote a virtuous circle in which installers and system integrators could communicate profitably. MyOpen must, in fact, bring together the two targets. In this way, if the installer has problems (or is seeking solutions for the end customer before saying "it is not possible"), he can find a suitable system integrators. Thus, this triangulation expresses all its potential: the end customer is happy, the installer is able to satisfy him and the system integrator has provided the requested solution.

Other targets (less significant in terms of current business, but still important in terms of positioning and communication) are represented by: (a) universities with students and researchers interested in home automation; (b) home automation enthusiasts, who love this subject and have fun by writing on the forum and providing suggestions and ideas that can sometimes become new products.

For social communities, a major component of community challenge is to identify and encourage potential members who have the characteristics, skills, and competencies to join and to contribute to the community. Also, established online communities must attract a stream of new professional members to replace others who have, for example, left. In addition to that, users commitment is relevant. Commitment represents members' feelings of attachment or connection to the group, organization or community. Commitment underlies members' willingness to stay in the community and contribute to it. To be successful, online communities need people who actively participate in them by contributing to the resources on which the group's existence is based. Another key point is the level of engagement of the community with the different stakeholders who are present and active in their business network and ecosystem. The capability of the community to interact and co-create value with a large numbers of actors is a key factor to maintain its health and success over time. In this perspective, community analytics and intelligence is a crucial activity in the Bticino effort to cultivate and support the MyOpen community.

8.7.3. *MyOpen — Community and analytics intelligence*

A key role in the evolution of MyOpen has been the capacity of building commu- nity analytics and social business intelligence to support business decisions and ensure that the guidelines were prosecuted and that it was possible to find responses in the activities of community members. A significant point was the strategic analytics and community intelligence. The practice of advanced analytics and intelligence insights of communities become important as they become rele- vant corporate assets in business development and innovation process. Although measurement and management methods may be intuitive and *ad hoc* in the early stages of a community-based initiative knowledge, they become more rigorous over time as investments increase, gaining influence and garnering control over resources in the organization. Even in the early phases, Bticino found that meas- ures, analytics and insights reinforce the support of executive sponsors and accel- erate the legitimacy of communities in the eyes of teams, business units and managements. In light of this, more pressing than before, there is the necessity of a deep dive and intelligence of community from the perspective of social business value creation.

At the beginning of its evolution, the community managers of MyOpen were used to measure basic metrics such as the number of members and the most popular sections of the community forums. Analytics built on the log files (php server) measured the access and the use of the platform, the con- nection activity and navigation between pages, the sections of the forum and the number of posts periodically loaded. Community measures were dis- played for different dimensions: time scale (day, month, etc.), for company's membership of the community, role and profile (if installers, system integra- tors, etc.). With the opening of MyOpen to foreign markets, it has become important to profile by country too: it was necessary to understand where the members came from.

Along with these metrics and basic KPIs, over time it started to become increasingly important for Bticino to measure and evaluate other elements: the level of participation in the life of the community started to be measured also in terms of time spent in the forum and activity type. Also, the monitoring of the topics most discussed became a crucial factor. The discussion was defi- nitely an open window on the market, but the company wished to monitor that MyOpen did not turn into something far from the community objectives, in particular, a community for customer care of Bticino products. Therefore, it was essential to verify that the issues were not too unbalanced in this sense; a fair share 50% or 60% of the discussions had to be on the open language (a lower figure meant that the communication activities and community management were not very successful), because the community was not seen as a channel for technical assistance.

In 2010, when the community had produced larger volumes and was recognized as a business tool, Bticino had the need to understand in detail who were the members of the community and profile them in-depth in order to better understand the target of the community and, according to that, create a tailor-made communication and interaction.

So, gradually, the metrics have been extended to analyze and understand the needs of the cluster of active members in the community. With the new platform, the community managers have also started to evaluate and quantify the sentiment of the community and, therefore, not only who, what, how much and where members discuss on the various forums, but also with what sentiment they are communicating (if the solutions, services and products satisfy them or if, conversely, there were critical issues related to the provided information or to the resolution of technical problems or support).

It is important to remember that the assessment and the measurement affect not only the members of the community, their activities and interactions, but also the operational efficiency of the community management of Bticino and Legrand people, responsible for the care and efficiency of MyOpen. In this case, for example, the response time of the community, together with the community manager to requests from members, is being measured in order to assess the responsiveness and readiness to support and manage the needs of the community. Using the new analytical features, community managers also started to segment and profile the members according to their social behavior and "social footprint" (connectors, originators, askers, and so on, Fig. A.8.8).

Along with these quantitative metrics that are available in the analytics section of Telligent (Figs. A.8.7–A.8.11), also integrated with a more traditional system of web analytics such as Google Analytics also, more recently a qualitative survey has been launched (a questionnaire provided to community members) in order to better understand the usability of the platform. Having in mind the enlargement scope of the community, Bticino believes it is necessary to update the layout and usability of the platform (the layout was designed in 2010) as well as, more generally, to examine the response of the platform to the new activities in program in terms of creativity and innovation (not only with challenges and sporadic contests, as done in the past, but also in a structured engagement vision).

8.8. Results

MyOpen community is considered as very successful project. These are the results:

Total number of registered users: 14,759 with a monthly average of 140 new registered users in 2014.

Roles: The majority of the user population consists of system integrators and installers. In 2014, a significant number of end users, searching for support, were also registered.

Engagement and innovation: The community is particularly active. The contribution of users is at 70%, the community acts as base for social support and business interaction for its members.

In July 2014, it was decided to make the community visible to these non-members without the possibility to interact, who were not registered. Though, in order to interact it is mandatory to register and become a member of the community. In line with the strategic objectives of the project, there is a relevant amount of posts with suggestions for new solutions and products. With regards to download analysis, technical guides and OpenWebNet language are of major interest, followed by the app gallery and tutorials.

Satisfaction: A survey of usability and user satisfaction done in 2014 found that the majority of members appreciate the organization and functioning of the community platform.

Appendix

Fig. A.1.1.   The homepage of Legrand Group website.

Fig. A.8.2.   The homepage of BTicino website.

Fig. A.8.3.   The homepage of MyHome website.

Fig. A.8.4.   The homepage of MyOpen website.

Fig. A.8.5.   The homepage of MyOpen community website.

Fig. A.8.6.   The threads of MyOpen Community website.

Fig. A.8.7.   Data dashboard of MyOpen community.

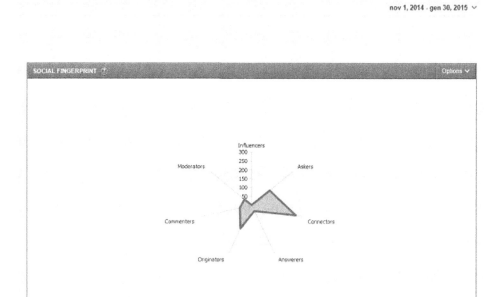

Fig. A.8.8. Data dashboard of MyOpen community.

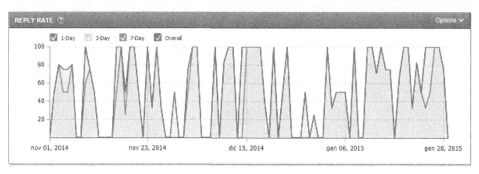

Fig. A.8.9. Data dashboard of MyOpen community.

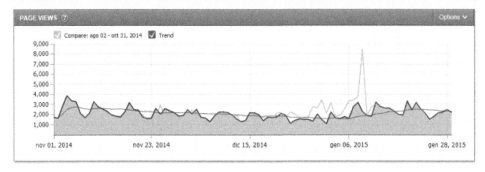

Fig. A.8.10.　Data dashboard of MyOpen community.

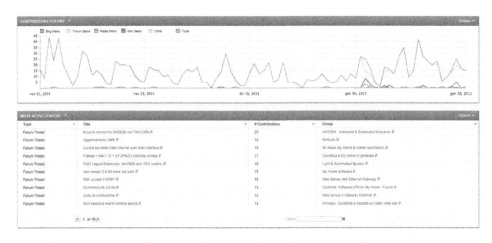

Fig. A.8.11.　Data dashboard of MyOpen community.

About the Authors

Cosimo Accoto

Cosimo Accoto is Partner & VP Innovation at OpenKnowledge, a leading international consulting firm focused on social and digital business transformation. He supports organizations and marketers to envision and enable their digital and social business transformation (Philips, Luxottica, Eni, A2A, Vodafone, Autogrill, Ermenegildo Zegna, Bticino/Legrand Group). He lectured in Digital Analytics & Big Data at IE University (Madrid), and collaborates with "Digital Markets" research (IMCA, University of Italian Switzerland) and "BIT" (Business Information Technology) at SDA Bocconi. He has published four books and several business articles: "La grande sfida della digital business disruption" (Harvard Business Review, June 2015); "Social Mobile Marketing" (SDA Bocconi Egea, 2014 2e); "Social Business Toolkit" (Harvard Business Review, 2013); "Marca e Metriche nei Social Media" (USI, 2010); "Misurare le audience in internet" (FrancoAngeli, 2007). Working at international data and software firms (15+ years), Cosimo has a solid experience in digital analytics and data intelligence. Formerly, he was Commercial Director (Confirmit & Kantar networks), Business Development Director (Jupiter MMXI, now Comscore), Service Account Lead (Agb, now Nielsen Audience Measurement).

Enrico Valtolina

Enrico Valtolina has a degree in Computer Engineering. He worked in software development at Bticino SpA in the Home Automation Open Solution / Technologies. Since 2010, he is at Legrand Group as "Partnership and Community Manager". In 2013, he joined the Innovation & System Department of Legrand Group to manage inter-SBU project mainly related with IoT, Cloud, BigData, interoperability topics. He is responsible for the worldwide web community MyOpen (www.myopen-legrandgroup.com). He promotes, within Legrand, social networks to get opportunities from the paradigms of open innovation, social support, social marketing.

Andreina Mandelli

Andreina Mandelli obtained her PhD in Mass Communication from Indiana University, Bloomington (USA), after completing MBA from Università Bocconi. She is presently working as an SDA professor at the Faculty of Marketing & Communication since 1995. She is also adjunct professor at USI, Lugano, and IE, Madrid since 2010 and faculty at Bocconi Global Business School, MISB Bocconi in Mumbai, India from 2013. She had previously worked as Senior research fellow at 'Center for Digital Future', Annenberg School for Communication, USC, Los Angeles (USA). She has been one of the Founding partners of World Internet Project (WIP) and Business Information Technology study (BIT) international research networks, coordinated at Annenberg School for Communication, University of Southern California, e UCLA Los Angeles. Her research interests include digital innovation in communication, marketing, consumer behavior and services.

CHAPTER 9

MOBILE HEALTH TECHNOLOGIES

HEMANT K. BHARGAVA AND JULIA TANGHETTI

Abstract

Mobile health (mHealth) solutions are expanding rapidly and have become a part of the health care landscape. Over a 100,000 mobile apps exist today, and create value in very diverse ways. This chapter proposes a framework for classifying mHealth solutions on three dimensions, type of technology (form factor), level of institutional integration, and function. It examines the underlying process by which different types of mHealth applications create value, and maps the classification dimensions to potential ways in which these solutions can impact patient health, costs, and other metrics. The optimal choice and design of mHealth technology will depend on patient population characteristics or the settings in which these technologies are deployed. We apply this classification by reviewing a small number of mHealth applications which have been described in the literature. In many cases, the potential impact of such technologies may not be easy to identify, to measure, or to attribute it to the technology. Moreover, while many solutions aim to make patients better informed, this may not necessarily lead to better patient health, because there is evidence in other domains that, when given more information and control, non-experts develop over-confidence, make poorer decisions, and achieve worse outcomes.

9.1. Introduction

Today's computing devices are extremely powerful, small, lightweight, and ubiquitous. One such device is the modern smartphone, which carries more processing power than was available to NASA when it landed the first man on the moon in 1960. These tiny devices also have incredible capacity to communicate data, documents, images, and video across the world. As general purpose computers, they have unlimited capability for information processing, due to which over a million applications are available on iTunes and Google Play, the dominant repositories of smartphone apps. These applications range from what some might consider frivolous (e.g., the app "Yo" which lets users message each other with just the word "Yo"), to ones used to signal status (e.g., the app "I Am Rich" which costs $999 and does nothing), to others that hope to save the world (e.g., detecting the spread of life-threatening diseases). Smartphones have also witnessed an unprecedented penetration rate, reaching over a billion people in just a few years.

Not surprisingly, many entrepreneurs and researchers are excited about the possibility of harnessing the phenomenal power and reach of these mobile technologies. One area of particular interest is also one of the biggest sectors of a modern economy, health care. Mobile health (or, mHealth) technologies are expanding rapidly. A recent article notes that "over 100,000 health apps are available in the iTunes and Google Play stores, according to Research2Guidance, a mobile market research firm" (Krisch, 2015). These apps range from motivating users into a regular fitness regimen to tracking health metrics and even medical interpretation and advice. Concurrently, several leading health care organizations have begun making major investments in developing mobile apps and integrating them into the health care process.

A recent study of the US wireless industry by Roger Entner found that mobile devices improve worker productivity in four critical ways: Reducing unproductive travel time, improving logistics, enabling faster decision-making, and empower small businesses and improving communications. Entner projects productivity gains from wireless in the medical industry to reach $305 billion over the next 10 years (Entner, 2012). The gains from mHealth technology have the potential to extend beyond the patient to the entire health care system.

Mobile health technologies hold the potential to fundamentally change and improve health care experience and outcomes. But mHealth technologies are extremely diverse in the impact they can potentially have. It can be hard for both developers and adopters to understand the potential of a specific technology, which also makes it difficult for developers to build the solution in a way that realizes its true potential. As Damien Bennett recently noted in the BMJ, just distinguishing between the different types of health apps is critical to understanding how these technologies may affect individuals. (Bennett, 2015) This chapter aims to shed some light on this subject by classifying different categories of mobile health apps, and discussing the potential impacts of each of these categories by means of illustrative examples. We describe a framework to classify apps based on the type of technology deployed, the level of institutional integration, and the purpose of the technological intervention. We then examine a set case examples to illustrate the application of the framework, employ the framework to analyze the nature of impact, and discuss how aspects of the framework can facilitate or limit different types of impact. We also comment on additional factors needed to ensure that the intended impact is actually achieved, measurable and demonstrable.

9.2. Types of Technology Deployed in mHealth Interventions

One dimension useful in classifying mHealth solutions is the form factor (or, simply, form) of the technology. The common form factors are "app", "sensor", and "device". As explained below, these form factors differ on critical capabilities such as the ability to capture data, the ability to process data, and the ability to communicate the data.

An "app" is a software application, usually running on a smartphone or other handheld device that has an operating system and network connection. Therefore, it is capable of receiving and communicating data, some level of resident computing power, plus the ability to leverage the power of networked computers on a remote cloud. Because of these features, an mobile health app (mHealth app) could potentially be weaved into a bigger and broader solution that could encompass physicians, hospitals, pharmacies, and insurance companies. For instance, a app might employ short message service (SMS) to promote treatment or medication adherence. An app does not, however, have the capability to capture and collect data on its own, such as a patient's blood pressure, level of pain, dosage of medication consumed etc. It requires human or other intervention to capture data and to enter it into the solution environment. Many mHealth applications currently on the market are stand-alone apps. Despite their ability to leverage the power of general-purpose computing and communication, their potential impact remains constrained by the limitations of self-reporting: possibility of errors in data capture and transcription, inability to automatically collect data based on certain triggers, and failure to collect and report the data at required intervals.

A "sensor" is usually physical hardware that is capable of automatic data capture. The key advantage of sensor-based solutions is that they take the burden off patients for self-reporting their own data. A sensor is usually embedded into a communication device so that the collected data can immediately be transmitted to another piece of the overall solution. Sensors may also have integrated data storage capability, so that repeated observations of the data may be stored, and then transmitted in batch mode. With some sensor-based mHealth solutions, the physical hardware may be endowed with limited computing and communication capabilities, to extend the solution into a special-purpose "appliance". For instance, a Fitbit may link to and share data with other Fitbits in the patient's social network.

Finally, mHealth devices may combine app and sensor capabilities into a general-purpose computing environment. The most direct way to achieve this is to augment a general-purpose computing device with sensors that feed information to the device. For example, the iGBStar solution from Sanofi Aventis is a blood glucose-monitoring device for diabetes patients that connects directly into Apple phones. Blood glucose readings from the device are uploaded to a diabetes manager app that allows patients to track their condition. As biosensors become increasingly more sophisticated and discreet, researchers are also evaluating their use in conjunction with mobile applications given the ultimate aspiration for passive monitoring solutions. MHealth solutions that incorporate devices for measuring or sensors for passive monitoring take the burden off patients for self-reporting their own data. Additionally, when deployed successfully, devices and sensors give patients the ability to record and transmit their biometric data into a user interface providing an actionable and informative picture of their health that can be shared with physicians, caregivers, family members, or their social networks (Steinhub *et al.*, 2015).

9.3. Level of Institutional Integration

The development and deployment of patient-centric mHealth solutions create numerous possibilities for the participation of other institutional players involved in health care provision and regulation.

Pharmaceutical companies, physicians, hospitals, and medical researchers can potentially be involved in the development and testing of a new solution. Such testing can produce a valued seal of approval, which can be useful in marketing the product. For instance, if a solution seeks to measure a patient's cardiac activity and create alerts based on certain triggers, then suitable medical testing and certification can convince users that the product functions as certified. The developer can also try to secure FDA approval for the product, which provides a further certification of safety, or at least that "benefits of the product outweigh the risks for the intended use".

Similarly, multiple institutional players can be involved in deployment and use of the solution. For instance, mHealth solutions may communicate patient data to the patient's care provider either in real-time or batch mode, or may make it available when the patient visits the care provider. Physician participation may also be integrated into the solution more deeply, either by embedding physician-provided rules and logic into the system, or by creating mechanisms for real-time input and advice from physicians. For instance, such rules and logic might be used

Development	Deployment
• Stand-alone	• Stand-alone
• Expert-certified	• Requires physician prescription
• FDA approved	• Provides data to caregiver
• Approved by insurance provider	• Caregiver logic and rules embedded into system functioning

to compute medication dosage for the patient, or to personalize a self-managed physical therapy routine.

While over 100,000 health apps are currently available on iTunes and Google Play, a vast majority of these are "stand-alone" solutions that are used by the patient but have no institutional connectivity either in the development process or in use. Only approximately 100 apps are FDA approved (Foreman, 2013). This might be explained by the FDA's risk-based approach to regulating mobile health apps, which focuses on apps that meet the criterion for medical devices. Due to this, only apps that meet the regulatory criteria for a medical device and "are intended to be used as an accessory to a regulated medical device, or transform a mobile platform into a regulated medical device" are potentially subject to FDA approval (Mobile Medical Applications, 2014). While the FDA approval process imposes costs of both time and money on mHealth app developers, gaining approval may impart a legitimacy upon these apps that could be useful in increasing adoption in both health care providers and patients. Furthermore, as the health care system begins to answer the question of whether mHealth technology use is reimbursable, having FDA approval for mHealth apps may become critical. Given institutional knowledge of the FDA approval process, both medical device manufacturers and pharma companies may be advantaged due to their experience in this area. However, many mHealth applications do not fall under FDA purview and it may be possible for these technologies to create value without meeting the regulatory criteria for a medical device. In general, a greater degree of institutional integration creates greater barriers to entry and deployment, but also enhances the potential impact of an mHealth solution.

9.4. Functions of mHealth Technologies

The form factor of mHealth technologies — app, device, and sensor — works in service of the underlying functionality of these technologies. While mHealth technologies may have a variety of stated aims, such as improving medication adherence or helping patients gain control of chronic conditions, these aims do not capture the underlying function by which these technologies enable behavior changes. In examining how mHealth technologies enable behavior change, there are several broad functions that may drive these solutions regardless of the problem they are trying to solve or condition they treat. Viewed broadly, mHealth technologies may have any of the following functions or they may combine them to achieve the desired result.

Examining the various functions of mHealth technologies helps illuminate the potential impact of these technologies. An app may inform users by educating them on their disease state or medications they take. These technologies also may

Functions of mHealth Technologies
• Inform
• Advise
• Communicate
• Measure
• Monitor
• Motivate

advise patients if their symptoms or readings necessitate the need for a visit to the doctor or a change in their medication. The mHealth technology can also enable communication with a patient's health care team. Through either self-reported outcomes or data captured through devices or sensors, patients can measure their disease biometrics. Through integrating these same patient-reported outcomes or results of passive data collection mHealth technologies may provide data visualization allowing both patients and physicians can monitor a patient's condition and track progress over time. Finally, many mHealth technologies fundamentally seek to motivate patients to make better health decisions. This may come in the form of motivational messages that reach patients at the right time, such as when they need to take their medication.

While mHealth technologies can combine these functions to enable better health outcomes, they also may employ these purposes to varying degree. For example, looking at the function of communication, an app may provide for communication with a patient's care team through the ability to email a patient's physician the data from the app. Alternatively, an app may also automatically push data to the physician or automatically integrate it into the patient's EMR. Thus, along this dimension of communication, mHealth solutions may vary in the degree to which this function is implemented. This classification of function and degree of function is important in steering the discussion of mHealth technologies towards the potential impact these solutions can have on the health care system.

9.5. Case Study Examples

9.5.1. *Ovia pregnancy tracker and baby calendar*

Ovia, the pregnancy tracking app from Ovuline, allows women to track the progress of their pregnancy and provides personalized feedback to users from conception to birth. Ovia has over 1 million active users, which speaks to the fact that many women have found the app to be of some value during their pregnancies (Pai, 2015). As of May 2015, Ovia was number eight in the App Store for free medical apps. Through both user reported data and data which can be uploaded from fitness and sleep trackers, the app allows users to measure their progress and monitor changes over time through analyzing users' data and visually charting it, allowing users to see their data mirrored back to them. Based on the stage of pregnancy or symptoms a woman is experiencing and reporting, the app curates personalized articles to educate and inform. Ovia allows women to communicate their progress, as the data from the app can be exported via text, email, or uploaded to social media. Presumably women could share this information with their physician as well, however, the app does not allow users to send this data to their physicians using a physician's portal or using EMR integration, so this communication function is limited. The app suggests goals for weight based on pre-pregnancy BMI (body mass index), sleep, nutrition and exercise, helping and motivating expectant mothers towards healthy behaviors. The app also provides an advisory function if a user enters symptoms that may indicate a health risk, the app also alerts them to contact their physician.

While the Ovia pregnancy app combines many of the functions of mHealth applications, the app is not well integrated into the formal health care system. The app does not enable efficient contact with user' health care providers, but it seems to have the potential to succeed in making pregnant women more informed and empowered patients. Recently Ovuline announced the launch of Ovia Benefits, which allows women to choose their health insurer in the app and then receive health plan specific information (Pai, 2015). While over 250 health plans have signed up to participate in the program, their levels of partnership with Ovuline vary. Blue Cross Blue Shield of Massachusetts launched a pilot program with Ovuline in February of 2015 which allows users of the app on that health plan to receive location specific information and information about health care services the plan offers, such as gestational diabetes screening (Bartlett, 2015). This move reflects the broader push in the health care system towards empowering and engaging patients. Additionally, it suggests that without integration into the formal health care system, these apps reach a limit in the value they can provide.

9.5.2. *Mango health*

Mango health provides an app for users to manage their medications. The app utilizes both gamification and rewards to promote medication adherence. Users enter their medication and dosing schedule, then the app provides reminders to users to take their medications. The app can also educate users about drug interactions and side effects. Users earn points every time they report they have taken their medication correctly and these points accrue, giving users the chance of winning rewards like gift cards. With the data from the app, Mango Health reports that users show an increased adherence to anti-hypertensives to 89%, versus 59% average for the general population, adherence to diabetes medication at 85%, versus 51% average, and adherence to statins to 84%, versus 52% average (Comstock, 2014). However, it is not clear if this data is self-reported from patients. As such, its accuracy is questionable.

While Mango health started as a consumer-focused technology, the company is seeking greater integration with the health care system. Mango health's CEO Jason Oberfest has noted that the company is partnering with "one of the top three integrated care delivery systems in the country, one of the top three pharmacy benefit managers, and one of the top five largest US health plans" (Comstock, 2014). Mango health's statistics show that users average 17.1 sessions per week and 77% of active users open the app every day (Cutler, 2015). While these are impressive statistics for any type of mobile application, Mango health's move towards a greater health system integration may be indicative of the limits in impact this app faced as a primarily direct-to-consumer product. While an app encouraging medication adherence is valuable, without connecting this potential for behavior change to the health care ecosystem, its impact may be blunted.

9.5.3. *Ginger.io*

Some mHealth technologies are starting to embrace the idea that the way patients interact with all types of technology in their lives, including smartphones and social media, may be indicative of the health of the individual. Dr. Sachin Jain of CareMore recently proposed the idea of a "digital phenotype", which holds that a patient's digital footprint contains information that is clinically valuable to physicians (Jain *et al.*, 2015). Ginger.io's platform of a mobile application, behavioral analytics engine and physician dashboard builds upon this insight in their solutions for depression and behavioral health. Combining short daily surveys with passive data collection from smartphones, Ginger.io can detect warning signals in a patient's behavior that might be problems and alert the patient's care team, who can then intervene. For example, if the application detects that a patient has not left their house in three days or is unresponsive to texts and calls from friends, this may presage a slip into a depressive episode. This can help physicians detect symptomatic episodes in between regularly scheduled visits and allow them to help their patients at the right time. Ginger.io also purports to help drive down health care costs for these conditions by a more efficient use of resources, reduced admissions into high-cost care settings such as the emergency room, and extended health care capacity. While a small pilot study of the platform conducted in conjunction with Verizon and The Centerstone Research Institute showed a decrease in hospitalizations and readmissions in the 10 patient group of Medicare "super users" in the study, more research is required to determine if these results can be replicated on a larger scale (Solving Healthcare's Superutilizer Challenge, 2015).

Ginger.io mobile and web platform creates value on all levels of the proposed framework. The app provides convenience to patients given that much of their data is captured passively. The behavioral analytics engine gives patients, physicians, and caregivers the ability to understand how this data is reflective of the health of the individual. Finally, this platform also enables the ability to reach patients when they need help most, thus meeting requirements for the high-value impacts that are possible with mHealth technologies.

9.5.4. *AliveCor*

The AliveECG app and complimentary Heart Monitor device enable patients to capture their ECG (electrocardiogram) and heart rate. The FDA approved app alerts patients if their ECG is normal and it can also detect possible atrial fibrillation. Patients can either send this data to their physician for review or patient in the US can also pay a fee to have their ECG read by either a cardiologist or cardiac technician. The technology could be used for various patient types. Patients who may suspect a heart arrhythmia but are asymptomatic during doctor's visits could use this device when they experience the symptoms, thus helping physicians accurately diagnose the condition. Alternatively, this device could be used for patients that have been diagnosed with atrial fibrillation to track the efficacy of other care interventions such as medication. By monitoring patients over time, the device could help providers determine if their prescribed therapy is working. While no clinical studies have been published tying this device to health outcomes, a feasibility study for the device, monitoring patients after an atrial fibrillation ablation procedure, showed that patients preferred this device to a traditional transtelephonic monitor (TTM) and found it easy to use (Tarakji *et al.*, 2015).

This device and app provides patients with an easy solution to measure their ECG's and heart rate and monitor their condition over time. It also gives health care providers the ability to monitor their patients' progress in between regular office visits through either emailed reports, a physician dashboard or integration with one EMR provider. However, users of the app must have the ability to properly understand and react to the information captured and reported by the device. For example, AliveCor has had to emphasize in the past that this device is not intended to diagnose heart attacks (Dolan, 2014). Additionally, if a patient detects a possible atrial fibrillation with the device and is not properly educated on what response to take, this may result in an escalation such as an unnecessary office visit or ER trip. This problem raises the question of how much data is actually beneficial to patients. Additionally, without educational content and clear and understandable data visualization, these type of apps may not be effective tools to help patients monitor their condition.

9.5.5. *BlueStar by WellDoc*

The BlueStar app by WellDoc is the first FDA approved mHealth application available only by prescription, which fully integrates this solution into the traditional health care system and thus provides a mechanism for health plan reimbursement. The BlueStar app and accompanying physician portal have shown success in treating patient with Type 2 diabetes. In a cluster randomized trial involving 26 practices and 163 patients in Maryland, patients using the app had a 1.9% decrease in glycated hemoglobin levels over one year, compared with a 0.7% decline in the standard of care group (Quinn *et al.*, 2011). The app provides patients with a way to keep a digital journal of their condition through self-reported data tracking glucose readings, medications, food, and exercise. Based on the information patients enter, BlueStar can provide motivational messages, educational tips, or suggest action. Because the app recommends treatments for the disease, it falls under the purview of FDA regulations. For example, if a patient using the app enters a low blood glucose reading, the app might provide specific instructions to eat a certain amount of fast-acting carbohydrates to help regulate levels. Alternatively, the app may alert the patient when they need to take a specified amount of insulin. Though the physician portal, a patient's care team can track how they are managing their condition between visits.

While this app combines many functions of mHealth technologies, in that it provides a mechanism for communication, motivation, advice, measuring, and monitoring, the self-reported nature of the patient data provided poses problems for both patients and health care providers. For patients, entering all the data on every blood glucose reading, medication taken or food eaten certainly seems to present a rather onerous burden. Additionally, if a patient is only entering measures for blood glucose readings but fails to enter their medication or diet choices, the question of whether the app can provide appropriate advice is unclear. Similarly, if the patient is not entering all the relevant data, the clinical value to health care providers is unclear.

9.5.6. *Mayo cardiac surgery patient recovery study with Fitbits*

While the case studies already discussed involved technology deployed primarily for patient use, mHealth technologies may also be utilized primarily for the use of physicians and patient care teams (Table 9.1). The Mayo Clinic recently published a study that examined the length of stay in hospital for post-operative cardiac

Table 9.1. Classification of examples.

mHealth Technology	Type of Technology	Level of Institutional Integration	Function
Ovia Pregnancy Tracker	App	Low	Inform Advise Measure Monitor Motivate
Mango Health	App	Low	Inform Measure Motivate
Ginger.io	App and Sensor	High	Advise Communicate Measure Monitor
AliveCor	App and Device	Medium	Communicate Measure Monitor
BlueStar by WellDoc	App	High	Inform Advise Communicate Measure Monitor Motivate
Mayo Clinic Fitbit Recovery Study	Sensor	Medium	Measure Monitor

surgery patients and incorporated Fitbits to track patients' levels of activity in recovery (Cook *et al.*, 2013). This study followed elderly patients (age 50 and above) and patients were equipped with a Fitbit attached to their ankle. The data from the Fitbits was transmitted to a physician dashboard. The study showed a significant relationship between the number of steps taken in the early days of recovery and the length of stay in hospital and dismissal disposition.

While much of the literature on mHealth touts the potential for patient behavior change, this study is interesting because it shows a practical use for these technologies in a physician-focused way. The study notes that patient mobility data is generally captured twice or thrice daily by the nursing staff, if at all, but these notes are not part of the workflow of the surgical team. The Fitbit sensors enabled the continuous capture of objective data that is easily accessible to the care team and can facilitate in the decision of when to discharge patients. While the study had a narrow focus of measuring steps and monitoring patients, the use of such technologies has the potential to impact both patient outcomes and hospital resource utilization (Cook *et al.*, 2013). Additionally, while this study only followed patients during their stay in hospital, this technology could also be utilized to follow patient recovery once they have left hospital and returned home or transferred to a skilled nursing facility. Mayo is also studying patient-focused apps post-surgery. The integration of a patient and physician platform would seem to hold even greater potential to affect patients' post-surgical outcomes and potentially reduce length of stay and hospital readmissions.

9.6. How do mHealth Technologies Deliver Value?

Motivated by the underlying question of "how do mHealth solutions create value", the preceding discussion has offered a framework for classifying mHealth solutions along three dimensions, "type of technology", "level of institutional integration", and "function". We described several real-world examples of mHealth solutions to illuminate how the position of a solution along these three dimensions can create possibilities and impose limitations on the potential value created by the solution. The case studies also illustrate that mHealth solutions can provide several levels of value.

- Behavioral change.
- Medication adherence.
- Change in health system utilization.
- Quicker diagnosis.
- Patient health outcome.
- Patient satisfaction ("feel good").

Some mHealth solutions may induce a positive behavioral change in the patient (e.g., better fitness regime or better diet, or more timely visits to a medical clinic). Commonly used techniques are motivational tools, better information and data-tracking, gamification, and social competition. In a similar way, mHealth solutions, such as Mango Health or BlueStar, can also improve medication adherence and more generally, adherence to a treatment protocol. Further, mHealth solutions, such as Ginger.io, might cause a change in the degree to which patients employ the health system, such as a decline in emergency visits or utilization of expensive procedures.

The collection of mobile health technologies available today is extremely diverse, hence there is also huge diversity in the nature of their impact, what sort of value they create, and who they create value for. Many of these technologies have the power of general-purpose computers, even though they may look nothing like a standard computer. Examining these mHealth technologies through a framework that technologists have often used to understand the value of computer-based technologies, we see that such systems are developed for purposes of Convenience, Computation, and Chestnuts (Kimbrough *et al.*, 1990).

The first purpose, Convenience, represents the most rudimentary use of computer-based technology. Computers can greatly simplify, or significantly lower the cost of data-related activities, including data capture, measurement, and storage. Hence, they can vastly increase the frequency of these activities. For instance, many mHealth apps and devices seek to measure and maintain data about some health-related metrics such as glucose level, blood pressure, or temperature. They may be viewed as electronic versions of notebooks that a patient may otherwise keep, with periodic notations about these metrics. However, compared with traditional notebooks and data capture, the app or device delivers such extreme convenience that it can make these activities incredibly granular. The vast majority of such apps are patient-centric, and deployed by private developers who transact directly with the patient. Hence, their benefit tends to remain limited to giving patients better information, or motivating and inspiring them to make behavioral changes in response to observed data.

The second purpose, Computation, begins to truly leverage the power of these computer-like technologies. These applications create value through computation, which may cover mathematical processing, data visualization, storage and retrieval, and communication of the data. For instance, an app that captures a patient's blood pressure may communicate its readings to the patient's health care provider, whereupon the chart could be displayed to an attending physician on the patient's next visit. Such solutions usually require integration into the patient's health care system. It creates the potential for higher value because the information now becomes available to those who can best interpret and leverage it. Such applications also have the potential to benefit multiple stakeholders besides just the patient.

The third purpose, Chestnuts, reflects truly high-value mHealth solutions which leverage the power of today's technologies to deliver transformational results. These solutions not only deliver information to the right person in the right format, but do so at the right time. This is especially relevant for time-critical medical events. For instance, consider a device like AliveCor that monitors cardio-related metrics and, upon sensing a potential anomaly, instantly conveys relevant data (e.g., an ECG) to multiple cardiologists (who may be located anywhere and have signaled availability to immediately review the data). Within minutes, the app receives opinions from multiple experts, then makes a determination whether the patient needs immediate and expert care, picks a health care facility and physician for the patient, and communicates all relevant data to the physician. While this device does not currently allow for such a level of functionality, it is certainly possible. In such time-critical health care events, this ability to make a timely determination and arrange for care can be life-saving. It would simply not be possible without the kind of mobile technologies that are available today.

Even when a solution has some "intended" purpose, there are several notes of caution regarding the evaluation of this purpose. The solution may be unable to realize the intended purpose (e.g., because of unfavorable conditions in deployment, or incorrect usage by patient), there might not be clear and quantifiable metrics to determine the extent to which the purpose was realized, and moreover there might not be demonstrable attribution of outcomes to the solution itself. Another note of caution is regarding accuracy of data. While many mHealth solutions purport to either capture raw data or to compute various derivative measures, their users and other stakeholders should be cautious of over-reliance and over-confidence on the accuracy of these measures. For instance, sensors that measure a patient's blood pressure or collect an EKG reading may have inherent limitations in accuracy, and moreover may not be well-calibrated to the characteristics of the patient, weather, altitude, or other factors in the measurement environment. Similarly, apps that compute the level of calories burned by a patient, or devices that measure a user's body mass index and bone density may suffer from similar limitations.

To understand the value mHealth technologies provide, the intended impacts must be compared to the actual impacts of these solutions. Some of the case study examples discussed above contain data from clinical trials that point to ease of use and efficacy of such technologies. However, the vast majority of health apps currently available have no clinical data tying the mHealth intervention to better health outcomes. Additionally, developers of mHealth technologies must be aware of how the different configurations of type of technology, level of institutional integration, and function affect these stated aims. For example, if main purpose of the Ovia Pregnancy Tracker app is simply to provide women a way to follow the progress of their pregnancy, the app seems to provide the necessary tools to achieve this aim. However, if this app aims to change health care utilization by pregnant women, further institutional integration above and beyond their pilot programs involving health insurers may be necessary. Similarly, if the Mayo Clinic's use of Fitbit trackers is solely to provide a better way for physicians to monitor patients' ambulatory patterns post-surgery, then the technology provides an efficient means to reach these aims. If rather the Mayo Clinic hopes to reduce the length of hospital stay for cardiac surgery recovery patients, utilizing the Fitbit trackers with a patient-focused app may prove useful. This is not to suggest that mHealth technologies must incorporate all aspects of the classification framework at a high level to create value and drive impact. Rather, to reach the desired impact, the appropriate configuration must be determined.

A clarity of intended impact is also required given that the capabilities of these technologies may be immense, but the question of the right patient type for these solutions and the appropriate utilization for these technologies may be unclear. For example, the AliveCor ECG device and app may be used for patients who may suspect a heart arrhythmia but are asymptomatic when they visit the physician. It could also be used for patients with atrial fibrillation to track the effect of different medications or treatments on their condition. However, it is unclear what the main impact the makers of this technology desire. Additionally, although this technology gives patients the ability to capture their ECG, there is still the question of what they should do with this data. A physician review of the device noted that while anyone could easily use this device, "we did not have a good sense of when (or whether) they should" (Misra and Husain, 2013). As such, it is difficult to measure what the actual impact of the AliveCor device may be given that the makers of the device do not have a clear positioning for their product.

9.7. Conclusion

It is evident that mHealth technologies create value in very diverse ways. Given this range of different types of potential impact, and after studying numerous examples and articles, we have proposed a more detailed framework, specifically for classifying mHealth technologies by type of technology, level of institutional integration, and function. Moreover, in many cases, the potential impact of such technologies may not be easy to identify, to measure, or to attribute it to the technology. Hence, the framework ties into the underlying process by which different types of mHealth applications create value. We then applied this classification by reviewing a small number of mHealth applications, which have been described in the literature.

The optimal choice and design of mHealth technology will depend on patient population characteristics or the settings in which these technologies are deployed. In resource-limited environments where patients may not have regular access to health care, mobile phone access may nonetheless be prevalent. For example, recent randomized controlled trials in Kenya have shown SMS messaging to be effective in promoting treatment adherence to antiretroviral therapy in patients with HIV. (Horvath *et al.*, 2012) Certain patient populations may exhibit a lower degree of technological friendliness. As such, in certain cases simple text messages interventions may prove more effective than utilizing a smartphone application. Alternatively, patients with access to smartphones who are also relatively tech savvy may respond better to more complex mHealth solutions that agree with their technological temperament. Given the heterogeneity of patient populations and the varying settings in which they reside, health care entities must tailor their mHealth approach to the group they are serving.

Though the proper configuration of type of technology, institutional integration, and function may enable high-value impact from mHealth technologies, there may be barriers to adoption that could also blunt their potential. While platforms, such as Ginger.io, hold the possibility the help patients when they need it most, though passive data collection and behavioral analytics, patients must also be willing to adopt these solutions. Apps such as Ginger.io passively track users' movements, sleep patterns, and interaction with technology. While many smartphone owners may already have apps on their phones that collect some of this data and sends it back to app developers, the explicit acknowledgment that this data is being used for medical purposes may make some patients uneasy. However, if users experience enough benefit from these technologies, such as better care or better control of their conditions, this may overcome such barriers to adoption.

With a clarity of intended impact, mHealth technologies, such as Mango Health and BlueStar, hold the potential to create value through adherence to a treatment protocol. Mango Health's platform has increased medication adherence for patients using their app and the BlueStar app has been shown to decrease glycated hemoglobin levels, a key measure of how well diabetes is controlled, in patients using the technology. Given that the BlueStar app is available by prescription only, this also introduces the question of whether these technologies act in similar ways to other prescription therapies, such as medication. For example, do patients who use mHealth technologies exhibit a dose-response to these technologies? That is to say, do patients who use mHealth apps consistently experience better outcomes than those that use them only intermittently? Posed differently, is there a minimum level of user engagement with mHealth technologies required for behavior change? While this question is still unresolved, if this is the case, then tactics employed by apps like Mango Health, such as gamification, may provide a way to increase patient engagement with these technologies and thus better affect health outcomes.

Underlying this suggestion of a positive dose-response to mHealth technologies is the assumption that the more informed a patient is, the better the outcome. However, there may be a level of information at which patients start experiencing diminishing returns from such technologies. If too much information is presented to a patient, they may become lost in the data and also lose the ability to make appropriate health-related decisions. More perniciously, this information may also lead to bad decisions due to overconfidence bias. Looking at data from the financial markets, we find that overconfidence leads individual investors towards high trading levels and a resulting poor performance. (Barber and Odean, 2000) Why would we expect patients to make better decisions about their health than their wealth? Recent work on energy efficiency labeling also addresses a similar issue. The literature on better consumer choices through such labeling shows that consumers are "rationally inattentive". Given this characteristic, the role of information provision is elevated and "it matters what information is provided and how it is provided". (Davis and Metcalf, 2014) If consumers of health care are similarly rationally inattentive, the way information is provided through mHealth technologies will prove critical to their potential to create value for patients, physicians, and the entire health care ecosystem.

Bibliography

1. Barber, BM and T Odean (2000). Trading is hazardous to your wealth: The common stock investment performance of individual investors. *The Journal of Finance*, 55(2), 773–806.
2. Bartlett, Jessica. (2015). Blue Cross Partners with Ovuline to Personalize Insurance for Members. *Boston Business Journal*, April 9. Available on: http://www.bizjournals.com/boston/blog/health-care/2015/04/blue-cross-partners-with-ovuline-to-personalize.html.
3. Bennett Damien B (2015). Importance of Distinguishing between Different Types of Health App. *BMJ* 2015, 350(5), h2334.
4. Comstock, J (2014). Mango health gets $5.25m to focus on provider business, *MobiHealthNews*.
5. Cook, DJ, JE Thompson, SK Prinsen, JA Dearani and C Deschamps (2013). Functional recovery in the elderly after major surgery: Assessment of mobility recovery using wireless technology. *The Annals of Thoracic Surgery*, 96(3), 1057–1061.
6. Cutler, KM (2015). Mango health's drug prescription, health apps eye the ideal spot on the apple watch. *TechCrunch*, March 16. http://social.techcrunch.com/2015/03/16/mango-health-smartwatch-app/.
7. Davis Lucas and Gilbert Metcalf (2014). Does Better Information Lead to Better Choices? Evidence from Energy-Efficiency Labels. Cambridge, MA: National Bureau of Economic Research. doi:10.3386/w20720.
8. Dolan Brian (2014). AliveCor Launches Smartphone-Enabled Heart Monitor, Analysis Services Direct-to-Consumer | Mobihealthnews, February 11. Available on: http://mobihealthnews.com/29801/alivecor-launches-smartphone-enabled-heart-monitor-analysis-services-direct-to-consumer/.
9. Entner, R (2012). The wireless industry: The essential engine of us economic growth. *Recon Analytics*, 30–33.
10. Foreman, C (2013). Keeping up with mobile app innovations. FDA Voice. March 21. http://blogs.fda.gov/fdavoice/index.php/2013/03/keeping-up-with-mobile-app-innovations.
11. Tara Horvath, Hana Azman, Gail E. Kennedy, and George W. Rutherford (2012). Mobile Phone Text Messaging for Promoting Adherence to Antiretroviral Therapy in Patients with HIV Infection. *Cochrane Database of Systematic Reviews* 3 (March), CD009756.
12. Jain, SH, BW Powers, JB Hawkins and JS Brownstein (2015). The Digital Phenotype. *Nature Biotechnology*, 33(5), 462–463.
13. Kimbrough Steven O, Clark W Pritchett, Michael P Bieber and Hemant K Bhargava (1990). The Coast Guard's KSS Project. *Interfaces*, 20(6), 5–16.
14. Krisch, JA (2015). Questioning the value of health apps. *The New York Times*, March 16. http://well.blogs.nytimes.com/2015/03/16/health-apps-provide-pictures-if-not-proof-of-health/.

15. Misra, S and I Husain (2013). Physician review of the iPhone AliveCor ECG heart monitor, the clinical reality of the device. *iMedicalApps*, March 12. http://www. imedicalapps.com/2013/03/physician-review-iphone-alivecor-ecg-heart-monitor/.

16. Mobile Medical Applications (2014). *FDA.GOV.*, Center for Devices and Radiological Health. April 4. http://www.fda.gov/MedicalDevices/ProductsandMedicalProcedures/ ConnectedHealth/MobileMedicalApplications/default.htm.

17. Pai Aditi (2015). Ovuline's Average Pregnancy App User Is 27, Happy, Employed and Working until Due Date | Mobihealthnews. *MobiHealthNews*, April 28. Available on: http://mobihealthnews.com/42958/ovulines-average-pregnancy-app-user-is-27- happy-employed-and-working-until-due-date/#more-42958.

18. Quinn, CC, MD Shardell, ML Terrin, EA Barr, SH Ballew and AL Gruber-Baldini (2011). Cluster-randomized trial of a mobile phone personalized behavioral intervention for blood glucose control. *Diabetes Care*, 34(9), 1934–1942.

19. Solving Healthcare's Superutilizer Challenge (2015). *Centerstone Research Institute*. Accessed May 13. http://centerstoneresearch.org/centerstone-research-institute- ginger-io-verizon-partner-solve-healthcares-superutilizer-challenge/.

20. Steinhubl, SR, ED Muse and EJ Topol (2015). The emerging field of mobile health. *Science Translational Medicine*, 7(283), 283rv3.

21. Tarakji, KG, OM Wazni, T Callahan, M Kanj, AH Hakim, K Wolski, BL Wilkoff, W Saliba and BD Lindsay (2015). Using a novel wireless system for monitoring patients after the atrial fibrillation ablation procedure: The iTransmit study. *Heart Rhythm: The Official Journal of the Heart Rhythm Society*, 12(3), 554–559.

About the Authors

Hemant K. Bhargava

Professor Hemant K. Bhargava Lee holds a PhD is the Jerome and Elsie Suran Chair Professor in Technology Management at the University of California Davis, Graduate School of Management. He received a PhD in Decision Sciences from The Wharton School, University of Pennsylvania. Dr. Bhargava studies business strategy and competition for technology products with network effects and platform characteristics. He also studies the use of IT in clinical health care, and has previously worked on data-driven and analytical decision making in organizations.

Julia Tanghetti

Ms. Tanghetti holds MBA in Marketing and Strategy from the UC Davis Graduate School of Management. Currently, she is the Director of Corporate Relations and IMPACT Projects and runs the MBA Consulting Center at the UC Davis Graduate School of Management. Ms. Tanghetti's research focuses on digital health technologies.

CHAPTER 10

TOWARDS A TYPOLOGY
OF SOCIAL MEDIA STRATEGIES

MORANA FUDURIC

Abstract

Despite the growing popularity of social media, there is no agreement among the researchers regarding the appropriate definition of types of social media strategies. In this chapter, we conduct a critical review of existing contributions and analyze them with respect to the five criteria used to assess typologies. By developing a better understanding of existing contributions in terms of their scope and identified categorization attributes or variables, we set the base for a more rigorous classification scheme. Such a scheme could be beneficial not only to academic researchers but also to practitioners by enhancing their understanding of the various types of social media strategies that could be valuable to their businesses.

10.1. Introduction

Social media are acquiring an increasing importance among brands' marketing strategies. The memberships of various online communities have expanded so much that they can no longer be ignored and the amount of time that consumers spend on different platforms is progressively increasing. Also, the variety of activities that are taking place in online communities represent an important opportunity for the brands to relate to consumers in different ways and on the other hand, a threat, if they decide to ignore consumers' opinions, requests or comments, as that alienates them and creates a gap between the brand's projected image and consumers' expectations.

However, despite the increasing use of social media and its managerial implications, little research has addressed social media strategies or examined the factors that determine the success of such strategies. For the most part, empirical research that has examined social media strategies has focused on providing "how to" advice and explaining the planning process (see, for example, Kaplan and Haenlein, 2010), rather than developing and evaluating specific strategy types.

The main purpose of the paper is to present a review of the literature with a focus on social media strategies as the basis for the development of a social media strategy typology. Developing such a typology can benefit researchers from various disciplinary perspectives such that the classification system might be used as a foundation for theory construction or empirical evaluation of various strategy types and their impact on performance. We first present a general framework of social media, its definition, specificities and use. Next, we present an overview of existing social media strategies as the basis for the identification of domains that are crucial for the development of a typology of social media strategies. Finally, we discuss the implications and future research directions.

10.2. Social Media

There is no doubt that the emergence of social media, combined with the sharp penetration of the internet based on the increased usage of mobile devices to access online content has changed the way organizations not only approach their customers, but the way they approach their marketing activities in general. Social media, using the so-called "Web 2.0" technologies and services, has created room for social interaction and collaboration between brands and their customers (Mandelli and Vianello, 2009; Berthon *et al.* 2012). The growing interest in the field has also been confirmed by the Marketing Science Institute, that has almost continuously incorporated digital marketing, interactive marketing and social media in their research priorities since 1996 (see the MSI Research priorities 2012–2014).

Kaplan and Haenlein (2010) define social media as "... a group of internet-based applications that build on the ideological and technological foundations of Web 2.0 and that allow the creation and exchange of User Generated Content" (p. 61). The early beginnings of social media date back to the appearance of blogs and forums, while a real surge in the popularity is contributed to the Web 2.0 technologies and the development of global social networking sites such as MySpace, LinkedIn, Twitter and of course Facebook. Even though there have been some attempts to classify the numerous social media platforms, it is only recently that we see systematic classifications that identify key dimensions or continuums

Table 10.1.   Classification of social media.

Self-presentation/ Self-disclosure	Social Presence/Media Richness		
	Low	Medium	High
High	Blogs	Social network sites (e.g., Facebook)	Virtual social worlds (e.g., Second life)
Low	Collaborative projects (e.g., Wikipedia)	Content communities (e.g., YouTube)	Virtual game worlds (e.g., World of Warcraft)

Source: Kaplan and Haenlein (2010).

along which we can categorize almost every (existing or emerging) social media type. One such classifications is that of Kaplan and Haenlein (2010) who classified social media based on media and social processes theories. This resulted in a classification based on two key dimensions: (1) social presence/media richness and (2) self-presentation/self-disclosure (see Table 10.1).

To clarify the classification, blogs — special websites that display posts in reverse chronological order (Scott, 2009) — tend to be low on social presence and media richness as they tend to focus mostly on text while on the other side of the spectrum we find virtual worlds that are typically very rich as they essentially replicate face-to-face interactions in a virtual world, and enable virtually all activities a person may have in the real world (Kaplan and Haenlein, 2010). In terms of the second dimension, virtual game worlds have a lower self-presentation than virtual social worlds, as they are guided by strict regulations and guidelines when it comes to behavior and disclosure (Kaplan and Haenlein, 2010). Similarly, blogs score higher when compared to collaborative projects such as Wikipedia, as wikis tend to focus more on specific topics (Tapscott and Williams, 2006).

Aside from blogs and wikis, one of the most widely recognized social media platforms are social networks (Boyd and Ellison, 2007) defined as "web-based services that allow individuals to (1) construct a public or semi-public profile within a bounded system, (2) articulate a list of other users with whom they share a connection, and (3) view and traverse their list of connections and those made by others within the system". By listing these characteristics of social networks, we can easily explain their position in the classification of social media platforms. Social networks are high on self-presentation and self-disclosure due to the fact that they are based on a profile a user is supposed to develop, disclosing certain personal information and agreeing to certain terms of use. This is also the main difference between social network sites and content communities such as YouTube where a lot less is being disclosed.

To sum up, even though social media cannot be considered as absolutely new and groundbreaking, combined with Web 2.0 technologies and UGC, it has brought forth important changes in the industry and the way companies approach consumers. Even though the three terms have often been used interchangeably, we argue in favor of distinguishing them based on social versus technical and content versus creation dimensions (Berthon *et al.*, 2012). Even though blogs and forums were the original form of social media, the former has been experiencing exponential growth after the emergence of Web 2.0 technologies and the appearance of global social network sites. Therefore, we conclude that an observed rise in the importance and impact of social media is based on technological advances, as well as economic, cultural and social changes. In that context, Berthon *et al.* (2012) identified three key effects that, as a result, call for a paradigm shift in marketing. These are: (1) activity shift from the desktop to the web; (2) power shift from the company to the collective, and (3) shift of value production from the company to the consumer. These changes are forcing companies to rethink the way they approach customers in social media, and develop new marketing strategies to support their presence.

10.3. Social Media Strategies

As mentioned earlier, the changes in the locus of power, activity and value production due to the appearance of Web 2.0 and social media, brought a radical change to marketing as it profoundly transformed the way companies communicate with consumers (Berthon *et al.*, 2012; Michaelidou *et al.*, 2011; Scott, 2009) and how consumers respond to brands' marketing and advertising (Campbell *et al.*, 2011). Before the Web 2.0 era, a company had the ability and power to control the majority of the content being published; it was the producer and distributor of content. Today, as the power shifts toward the consumers of content, the companies are losing their power, as more and more consumers actively engage in creating, commenting, and distributing content related to the company or brand. Whether it is something a company does online or offline for that matter, it is highly likely a consumer will express his or her opinion, share the experience or produce own content (such as videos, reviews, blogs, etc.) with friends and acquaintances via social media, for all interested to see.

The traditional hierarchical approach was replaced by open conversations between brands and consumers. Additionally, the traditional division of roles of marketers and their audience was replaced by a dynamic, flexible, and constantly changing marketing process. In short, in the new social media marketing, the company must act as the consumer's partner or ally, rather than attempting to "run the show". That being said, several researchers suggest marketers can utilize online communities and their conversations as part of the process of value co-creation, to foster dialogue (Rybalko and Seltzer, 2010), spur innovation (Tapscott and Williams, 2006), build social presence (Kozinets *et al.*, 2010) and create linking value with other customers (Cova, 1997).

However, it is also suggested that marketers have yet to develop proper strategies on how to interact with empowered consumers (Day, 2011), cope with data deluge coming from online sites (Day, 2011) and seize the possibilities for collaboration with consumers (Day, 2011; Prahalad and Ramaswamy, 2004). Although authoritative practitioners' literature covers many different social media strategies for companies (see for example, Barlow and Thomas, 2010; Qualman, 2010; Scott, 2009), the academic literature was rather slow in picking up the pace and exploring various strategies companies may use in social media. Current contributions mostly focus on "how to" strategies, namely — determining the right steps in developing a social media strategy (Berthon *et al.*, 2012; Kaplan and Haenlein, 2010) rather than on identifying different types of strategies companies may use.

More recently, several authors acknowledged the need for the development of a social media strategy typology. For example, Wilson *et al.* (2011) analyzed strategies of over 1,000 companies and identified four social media strategies based on two main criteria: a company's tolerance for uncertainty and the level of results sought. The four strategies were labeled as follows: (1) the "predictive practitioner" (2) the "creative experimenter", (3) the "social media champion", and (4) the "social media transformer". According to the authors, each company has a strategy that is generally oriented towards one of the four identified types. For example, a company that limits the use of social media to one specific area (e.g., customer service) and is mostly project-based but without any or very little cross-functional coordination between projects is using the "predictive practitioner" social media strategy. Typically, such companies are risk-averse and use existing metrics assess the results. The "creative experimenters" are companies that tend to embrace the uncertainty by conducting small-scale social media experiments and use the findings to improve their practices. Such companies aim at enabling engagement and facilitating conversations in order to learn from their social media projects. As a result, they are more concerned with learning an understanding the social media conversations and experiments they conduct, rather than focusing on a set of predefined outcomes. "Social media champions" are those companies that undertake large initiatives designed for predictable results (Wilson *et al.*, 2011). Such companies have a centralized group of leaders that are dedicated to the management and coordination of various social media projects across departments and functions. Social media champions also pay close attention to the development and implementation of social media policies and guidelines, which are particularly important given the fact that such companies tend to enlist a large number of brand evangelists both within and outside the company. Finally, the "Social media transformer" can be described as the pioneer in terms of their social media activities and to a degree reflects a social media enterprise. Such companies engage in large-scale social media projects and interactions and embrace the uncertainties social media may bring. Their projects regularly include internal and external stakeholders such as customers and business partners and span across different functions and departments. Additionally, social media are embedded in all aspects of the business in a way they tend to influence the company's business strategy and corporate culture by identifying and reporting on market changes and trends.

Wilson *et al.* (2011) suggest the identified strategies are temporal: that is, most organizations will start off as "creative experimenters" or "predictive practitioners" (usually depending on the available resources) but should gradually progress towards the more elaborate, complex strategies of "social media champions" or "social media transformers" in order to fully exploit the benefits social media have to offer. As the authors point out, "both the predictive practitioner and creative experimenter strategies can quickly create significant results and learning and serve as a training ground for larger efforts" (Wilson *et al.*, 2011, p. 25).

This approach shares a lot of common ground with the Altimeter Group Network Report (2013) in which they identify and present six stages of social business transformation. Essentially, the six stages — planning, presence, engagement, formalized, strategic, and converged — represent the degree to which a company approaches social media in terms of its integration with the business as a whole (Table 10.2). Here, the planning stage mainly reflects listening and monitoring as a necessary condition for any social media engagement. It is important to note that the stages are intertwined and the earlier stages are in a way embedded in the ones that follow. For example, even if the company finds itself in one of the more mature stages of social media strategy development, it only means that, in addition to the basic goals and incentives, the company is now using more elaborate research methods, metrics, and incentives. In short, it is an ongoing process that becomes more elaborate, complex, and coherent as the company moves to the mature stage of social media strategy development. Furthermore, the authors of the report identify several key issues regarding the company's social media strategy, namely: unaligned executives, uncoordinated efforts, incremental funding, and limited training. These findings suggest that companies suffer from the inability to develop coherent social media strategies that are often in contrast to the general business objectives of the organization.

Table 10.2. Stages of social media strategy development.

	Planning	Presence	Engagement	Formalized	Strategic	Converged
	Listen to learn	Stake our claim	Dialog deepens relationship	Organic for scale	Become a social business	Business is social
GOAL	Understand how customers use social channels Prioritize strategic goals where social can have the most impact	Amplify existing marketing efforts Encourage sharing	Drive considerations to purchase Provide direct support Internal employee engagement	Set governance for social Create discipline & process Strategic business goals	Scale across business units Moves into hr, sales, finance, supply chain C-level involvement	Social drives transformation Integrates social philosophy into all aspects of the enterprise
METRICS	Mentions Sentiment	Share of voice Fans, followers, shares Brand metrics Traffic	Path to purchase Lower support costs Customer satisfaction	Process efficiency Link to department Business goals & ROI	Enterprise metrics like net promoter score, itv	Deep analytics tied to functions and lines of business (lobs) Insights lead to adaptive and predictive strategies
INITIATIVES	Listening / monitoring Internal audits Pilot	Social content Risk management Training	Campaigns long term programs Social support Communities	Create center of excellence Enter Social Network	SMMs to scale employees Social part of planning process	Redefine processes Enter prosewide training One strategy process managed through disparate but complementary teams and efforts
ORGANIZATION & RESOURCES	Monitoring platform Part-time headcount Agency support	Dedicated Manager Content Management	Social Strategist Small, dedicated teams SMMS	Staffing up CoE Tech Investment	CoE Coordinates Hubs Dedicated Spoke Headcount	Social is everyone's responsibility

Source: Altimeter: The evolution of Social Business — Six stages of Social Business Transformation, March 2013.

Kozinets *et al.* (2010) used a different approach to social media strategy and focused exclusively on the communication aspect of social media. In their research of WOMM in online communities, they analyzed 83 blogs during six months and discovered that such a network of communications can identify four social media communication strategies — evaluation, embracing, endorsement, and explanation. They also found that each strategy is influenced by character narrative, communications forum, communal norms, and the nature of the marketing promotion. It is important to note here is that Kozinets *et al.* (2010) have identified such strategies based on a WOMM campaign incorporated into the character narratives of bloggers. The underlying reasoning they adopt is that WOMM is based on the assumption that marketers can take advantage of the credibility and bonds that develop in C2C interactions by balancing between the established communal norms and commercial objectives. In that sense, the marketers must pay close attention in balancing the communal-commercial tensions in a manner that does not undermine the communal norms. Additionally, the blogger as the communicator now takes on two roles — on the one hand as a community member and on the other as the marketer. To tackle this hybrid role, Kozinets *et al.* (2010) found that bloggers tend to modify the marketing messages so that they fit the community norms and culture. More specifically, the blogger performs three key services for the marketer: (1) communication of the marketing message, (2) staking the bloggers' reputation and trust relationships on the marketing message, and (3) modification of the marketing message — its tone, language or substance — to conform to the norms and expectations of the community (Kozinets *et al.*, 2010).

As a result, the four strategies reflect the bloggers behavior in two dimensions (see Table 10.3 for details) — the interpersonal orientation of communications (communal versus individualistic) and the commercial-cultural tension (implicit versus explicit).

The authors also incorporated the community members' response to each of the strategies identified, showing that the explicit acknowledgment of the commercial-cultural tension, and a communal orientation of the "explanation strategy" (top right in Table 10.3) result in the most favorable outcome for the marketers. This finding is consistent with the social media literature and research that stresses the importance of open and transparent communication with community members. It also stresses the notion that the messages that the marketers one to get through to community members have to be altered to fit the communal norms, otherwise the message may be perceived as negative and intrusive, and destroy the credibility of certain community members. As mentioned earlier, this typology has been developed for blogging communities that have a central member — the blogger — which has to be considered when applying to other types of communities and

Table 10.3.   Narrative strategies.

	Evaluation (e.g., Alicia, Joseph, Jasper)	Explanation (e.g., Frank, Sammy, Randy)
Communal	**Communication Strategies** •*Concealment*: minimizes or avoids mention of WOMM campaign and their participation. •*Product focus*: focus on product itself, rather than WOMM campaign. •*Communal acknowledgment*: proactively asserts communal orientation. •*Leadership*: asserts or affirms membership in the community while positioning as safe or preferred information source. **Community Reaction** •*Negative* regarding WOMM campaign, due to avoidance of campaign's moral issues, dependent on forum and communal norms. •*Hostility toward opinion leader role*, dependent on congruity with communicator narrative, forum and norms.	**Communication Strategies** •*Disclosure*: explicitly reveals WOMM campaign and their participation. •*Awareness of cultural tension*: explicitly signals awareness of cultural tension between WOM marketing goals and community orientation. •*Communal acknowledgment*: proactively asserts communal orientation. •*Leadership*: asserts or affirms membership in the community while positioning as safe or preferred information source. **Community Reaction** •*Supportive or neutral* regarding WOMM campaign. •*Acceptance of opinion leader role*, dependent on forum and communal norms.
	Embracing (e.g., Carrie, Franklin, Svetlana)	Endorsement (e.g., Judith, Troy, Shane)
Individualistic	**Communication Strategies** •*Acceptance*: consumer–marketer dual role enthusiastically adopted. •*Justification*: personal needs emphasized over community needs, in terms of privilege or equity. •*Professionalization*: promotional marketing language and terms used; additional marketing opportunities requested. **Community Reaction** •*Mixed, polarized responses*. •*Negative* regarding WOMM campaign if not related to prior forum content and communicator narrative. •*Positive* if communal norms, forum, and communicator narrative are congruent with WOMM campaign. •*Resistance to opinion leader role*, dependent on congruity.	**Communication Strategies** •*Disclosure*: explicitly reveals WOMM campaign and their participation. •*Awareness of cultural tension*: explicitly signals awareness of cultural tension between WOM marketing goals and community orientation. •*Justification*: personal needs emphasized over community needs, in terms of privilege or equity. •*Professionalization*: promotional marketing language and terms used; additional marketing opportunities requested. **Community Reaction** •*Tempered negative* regarding WOMM campaign. •*Support for opinion leader role*, dependent on whether narrative is deemed "deserving," if narrative integrates WOMM campaign, and if communal norms are supported.

Interpersonal Orientation of Communications: Communal ↑ ↓ Individualistic

Commercial-Cultural Tension: Implicit ◄─────── ─────────► Explicit

Source: Kozinets *et al.* (2010).

platforms such as consumption or brand communities that develop in platforms such as Twitter or Facebook characterized by different type of narrative.

Additionally, Etter (2014) identified three CSR communication strategies companies can use based on communication symmetry. More specifically, when companies simply disseminate information and do not respond to questions or engage in any sort of dialogue, they pursue a broadcasting strategy. According to Etter (2014), such a strategy that relies on one-way communication will not see a relevant increase in relational outcomes. On the other hand, if a company uses the reactive strategy then it replies to questions but does not proactively approach other members. With such a strategy, the organization embraces the possibilities of symmetric communication and relationship management to a certain degree. However, such a strategy does not imply any sort of direct action towards any of the stakeholders, which may lead to the perception of the company as purely reactive and without any own incentives or initiatives (Etter, 2014). Finally, when companies react to questions and remarks but also approach the stakeholders directly, they apply an engagement strategy. By using such a strategy, the company can fully utilize the benefits of perfectly symmetrical communication and interaction, as well as expect an increase in relational outcomes (Etter, 2014). These strategies can be understood as ideal types with different contributions to symmetrical communication and relationship management.

Finally, from a relational perspective, two types of strategies have received special attention, especially in the communication literature: the communicated commitment and conversational human voice strategies (Kelleher, 2009; Smith, 2010). It has been argued that by adopting the communicated commitment strategy, organizations communicate legitimacy and openness (Kelleher and Miller, 2006), while the conversational human voice strategy allows the organizations to connect personally with publics (Kelleher, 2009). These strategies are dominantly based on different communication efforts that aim at establishing or maintaining relationships with different publics. More specifically, the "communicated relational commitment" examines the degree to which an organization demonstrates their commitment to the relationship, communicates desire to build a relationship, stresses commitment, implies the relationship has a future, emphasizes the quality of the relationship, and directly discusses the nature of the organization (Kelleher, 2009). On the other hand, the "conversational human voice" strategy represents an "engaging and natural style of organizational communication as perceived by organization's publics based on interactions between individuals in the organization and individuals in publics" (Kelleher, 2009, p. 177).

10.4. Discussion

In general, a strategic typology is a useful tool for categorizing as well as understanding the types of strategies to be followed by an organization (McDaniel and Kolari, 1987). In the context of social media, Wilson *et al.* (2011) emphasize that an understanding of different types of social media strategies and their evolution is not only of use to scholars, but can also help guide practitioners in their endeavors to participate and adapt to the wide array of social media platforms, some of which have yet to be developed in the years to come.

One of the key steps in developing a typology is the identification and definition of key attributes or domains. Every typology is based on an attribute space which results from the combination of the selected attributes and their dimensions

(Kluge, 2000). This attribute space can be represented with multidimensional tables that help generate an overview of all possible combinations which are theoretically conceivable. Based on the review of the literature in social media and an overview of social media strategies, we can identify several attributes that need to be considered as the base for a typology of social media strategies. Such attributes may include the degree of social media maturity, social media embeddedness within the organization, objectives/results rigidity, risk/uncertainty aversion, communication symmetry, the interpersonal orientation of communications (communal versus individualistic) and the commercial-cultural tension (implicit versus explicit).

Current research offers a number of contributions on social media strategies from three different perspectives: marketing, communicational, and relational perspective. However, existing typologies do not meet the necessary requirements. According to Hunt (1991), there are five criteria that should be used to assess a typology: (1) Is the phenomenon to be classified adequately specified? (2) Is the classification characteristic adequately specified? (3) Are the categories mutually exclusive? (4) Is the typology collectively exhaustive? (5) Is the typology useful? While the usefulness of a social media strategy typology is clear, both in terms of research and practice, there are several issues that still require more attention. Looking back at the strategy typologies presented in the paper, we can conclude that the observed contributions exhibit issues in terms of the remaining four criteria. For example, the specification of the phenomenon to be classified — in this case — social media strategies — should encompass strategies for all social media platforms. However, in most cases, the strategies presented earlier mostly reflect only one social media platform such as Twitter (Etter, 2014) or blogs (Kozinets *et al.*, 2010). As Wilson *et al.* (2011) pointed out: "It's worth remembering that despite their ubiquity, Twitter and Facebook are only five and seven years old, respectively. Who knows what new technologies lie ahead? Understanding how company strategies are evolving to use existing social media not only will be of use today but also should guide managers as they adapt to platforms developed in the years to come." Therefore, an adequate and comprehensive view of strategies in all social media platforms is required.

The second issue refers to the specification of classification characteristics. Earlier in the paper while examining various strategies, we identified some of the key attributes or characteristics that served as the basis for the identification of key dimensions of the typology. The question is — are these attributes adequately specified and defined, and can they be used consistently throughout the typology. In some cases, the key criteria for the typology is rather vague and ill defined. For example, in their attempt to develop a social media strategy typology, Wilson *et al.* (2011) use the following two criteria for classification: (1) company's tolerance for uncertainty and (2) level of results sought. However, the authors do not adequately describe or define these two variables, making it difficult to follow their line of reasoning when examining the four identified types of strategies.

The two previously described issues, if not handled appropriately, can lead to problems in terms of categories' mutual exclusiveness or the degree to which a typology is collectively exhaustive. That is, the assessment of whether the categories in the typology are mutually exclusive is based on whether categorization variables support the distinct types of social media strategies. If the categorization variables are not specified adequately, there is the risk of overlapping of categories (i.e. the categories are not mutually exclusive). Similarly, a social media strategy typology implies that every social media strategy should fall in only one identified category or type. Looking back at the literature review, none of the existing typologies meet these criteria. For example, while the typology presented by Wilson *et al.* (2010) is focused on social media as a whole, because the categorization variables are not adequately defined, the typology exhibits problems in terms of the categories' mutual exclusiveness making it difficult to determine a clear distinction between the categories, and as a result, social media strategies. On the other hand, other typologies that meet this criteria focus only on specific social media platforms (e.g., blogs or Twitter) which does not make the typology collectively exhaustive. However, the final test of whether a typology has a set of categories that is collectively exhaustive can only occur over time, and following empirical evidence.

10.5. Concluding Remarks

In this chapter, we set out to provide a critical review of the literature with special focus on different types of social media strategies. Even though the literature offers a number of contributions and perspectives on social media strategies, we can conclude that none of them fully complies with the five criteria used to evaluate a typology (see Hunt, 1991). More specifically, the analyzed typologies do not adequately specify the concept of social media strategy; define the associated attributes or categories; present categories that are not mutually exclusive or are not collectively exhaustive. Still, these contributions provide relevant insights regarding the potential categorization variables, and do set the base for a more rigorous classification scheme. Such a scheme could be the first step toward developing strong theory to help develop a better and deeper understanding of social media strategies (Corley and Gioia, 2011). Second, a typology with broad acceptance would support the accumulation of scientific knowledge about social media strategies by facilitating research agendas. Finally, a comprehensive and useful typology would benefit not only academic researchers, but also practitioners by enhancing their understanding of the various types of social media strategies that could be valuable to their businesses.

Bibliography

1. Altimeter Group Network Report (2013). *The State of Social Business 2013: The Maturing of Social Media into Social Business* (Business & Mgmt). http://www. slideshare.net/Altimeter/report-the-state-of-social-business-2013-the-maturing-of-social-media-into-social-business.
2. Barlow, M and DB Thomas (2010). *The Executive's Guide to Enterprise Social Media Strategy: How Social Networks Are Radically Transforming Your Business*. Hoboken, New Jersey: John Wiley & Sons.
3. Berthon, PR, LF Pitt, K Plangger and D Shapiro (2012). Marketing meets Web 2.0, social media, and creative consumers: Implications for international marketing strategy. *Business Horizons*, 55(3), 261–271. doi:10.1016/j.bushor.2012.01.007.
4. Boyd, DM and NB Ellison (2007). Social network sites: Definition, history, and scholarship. *Journal of Computer-Mediated Communication*, 13(1), 210–230. doi: 10.1111/j.1083-6101.2007.00393.x.
5. Campbell, C, LF Pitt, M Parent and PR Berthon (2011). Understanding consumer conversations around ads in a Web 2.0 World. *Journal of Advertising*, 40(1), 87–102. doi: 10.2753/JOA0091-3367400106.
6. Corley, KG and DA Gioia (2011). Building theory about theory building: What constitutes a theoretical contribution? *Academy of Management Review*, 36(1), 12–32.
7. Cova, B (1997). Community and consumption: Towards a definition of the "linking value" of product or services. *European Journal of Marketing*, 31(3/4), 297–316. doi: 10.1108/03090569710162380.
8. Day, GS (2011). Closing the marketing capabilities gap. *Journal of Marketing*, 75(4), 183–195. doi: 10.2307/41228619.
9. Etter, M (2014). Broadcasting, reacting, engaging — three strategies for CSR communication in Twitter. *Journal of Communication Management*, 18(4), 322–342.
10. Hunt, SD (1991). *Modern Marketing Theory: Critical Issues in the Philosophy of Marketing Science*. Cincinnati, OH: South-Western Publishing Co.
11. Kaplan, AM and M Haenlein (2010). Users of the world, unite! The challenges and opportunities of Social Media. *Business Horizons*, 53(1), 59–68. doi: 10.1016/j.bushor.2009.09.003.
12. Kelleher, T (2009). Conversational voice, communicated commitment, and public relations outcomes in interactive online communication. *Journal of Communication*, 59(1), 172–188. doi:10.1111/j.1460-2466.2008.01410.x.
13. Kelleher, T and BM Miller (2006). Organizational blogs and the human voice: Relational strategies and relational outcomes. *Journal of Computer-Mediated Communication*, 11(2), 395–414. doi: 10.1111/j.1083-6101.2006.00019.x.
14. Kluge, S (2000). Empirically grounded construction of types and typologies in qualitative social research. *Forum Qualitative Sozialforschung/Forum: Qualitative Social Research*, 1(1). http://www.qualitative-research.net/index.php/fqs/article/view/1124.

15. Kozinets, RV, K de Valck, AC Wojnicki and SJ Wilner (2010). Networked narratives: Understanding word-of-mouth marketing in online communities. *Journal of Marketing*, 74(2), 71–89. doi:10.1509/jmkg.74.2.71.

16. Mandelli, A., and S Vianello (2009). Beyond Knowledge and Branding: the Impact of Online Communities on Buying Behavior. *Finanza, marketing e produzione*, 27(2), 83–115.

17. McDaniel, SW and JW Kolari (1987). Marketing strategy implications of the miles and snow strategic typology. *Journal of Marketing*, 51(4), 19–30. doi: 10.2307/1251245.

18. Michaelidou, N, NT Siamagka and G Christodoulides (2011). Usage, barriers and measurement of social media marketing: An exploratory investigation of small and medium B2B brands. *Industrial Marketing Management*, 40(7), 1153–1159. doi: 10.1016/j.indmarman.2011.09.009.

19. Prahalad, CK and V Ramaswamy (2004). Co-creation experiences: The next practice in value creation. *Journal of Interactive Marketing*, 18(3), 5–14. doi: 10.1002/dir.20015.

20. Qualman, E (2010). *Socialnomics: How Social Media Transforms the Way We Live and Do Business*. Hoboken, New Jersey: John Wiley & Sons.

21. Rybalko, S and T Seltzer (2010). Dialogic communication in 140 characters or less: How Fortune 500 companies engage stakeholders using Twitter. *Public Relations Review*, 36(4), 336–341. doi: 10.1016/j.pubrev.2010.08.004.

22. Scott, DM (2009). *The New Rules of Marketing and PR: How to Use Social Media, Blogs, News Releases, Online Video, and Viral Marketing to Reach Buyers Directly*. John Wiley & Sons. Hoboken, New Jersey

23. Smith, BG (2010). Socially distributing public relations: Twitter, Haiti, and interactivity in social media. *Public Relations Review*, 36(4), 329–335. doi: 10.1016/j.pubrev. 2010.08.005.

24. Tapscott, D and AD Williams (2006). *Wikinomics: How Mass Collaboration Changes Everything*. New York Portfolio Hardcover.

25. Wilson, JH, P Guinan, S Parise and BD Weinberg (2011). What's your social media strategy? *Harvard Business Review*, 89(7/8), 23–25.

About the Author

Morana Fuduric

Morana Fudurić is a postdoctoral researcher and lecturer at the Faculty of Economics & Business (FEB) — University of Zagreb. She received her PhD at the Universita della Svizzera italiana on the topic of social media and relationship marketing. She teaches several marketing courses at FEB Zagreb including Marketing, Advertising, Marketing for non-profit and Marketing Strategy. She is also a visiting faculty member at the Faculty of Architecture, School of Design (Zagreb, Croatia) and lectured at SDA Bocconi (Milan, Italy). Her primary research interests include digital marketing, social media and marketing strategy. She is actively involved in several research projects and collaborates with researchers from SDA Bocconi, Universita della Svizzera italiana.

INDEX

Printed in the United States
By Bookmasters